Sin City North

Sin City North

SEX, DRUGS, AND CITIZENSHIP IN THE
DETROIT-WINDSOR BORDERLAND

Holly M. Karibo

The University of North Carolina Press / Chapel Hill

Set in Miller by Westchester Publishing Services

Manufactured in the United States of America

The paper in this book meets the guidelines for permanence and durability
of the Committee on Production Guidelines for Book Longevity of the Council on
Library Resources. The University of North Carolina Press has been a member
of the Green Press Initiative since 2003.

This book is derived, in part, from the following articles by the author:
"Detroit's Border Brothel: Sex Tourism in Windsor, Ontario, 1945–1960,"
American Review of Canadian Studies 40, no. 30 (2010): 362–78, http://www.tandfonline
.com/10.1080/02722011.2010.496905; "Mainlining along the Line: Consuming Heroin
in the Great Lakes Border Region, 1945–1960," *49th Parallel* 30 (Autumn 2012): 1–32,
http://fortyninthparalleljournal.files.wordpress.com/2014/07/2-karibo-mainlining-along
-the-line.pdf; "Swashbuckling Criminals and Border Bandits: Fighting Vice in North
America's Borderlands, 1945–1960," *Histoire sociale / Social History* 48, no. 95 (November
2014): 705–28, http://www.tandfonline.com/10.1080/02722011.2010.496905.

Cover images: Woman with drink and cigarette (Courtesy
of The Tony Spina Collection: Walter P. Reuther Library, Archives of Labor and
Urban Affairs, Wayne State University); Detroit skyline (Courtesy of Library of Congress,
Prints and Photographs Division, LC-DIG-ppmsca-15308)

Library of Congress Cataloging-in-Publication Data

Karibo, Holly M.

Sin city north : sex, drugs, and citizenship in the Detroit-Windsor borderland /
Holly M. Karibo.

pages cm. — (The David J. Weber series in the new borderlands history)

Includes bibliographical references and index.

ISBN 978-1-4696-2520-1 (pbk : alk. paper) — ISBN 978-1-4696-2521-8 (ebook)

1. Detroit (Mich.) — Moral conditions — History — 20th century.   2. Windsor (Ont.) —
Moral conditions — History — 20th century.   3. Vice control — Michigan — Detroit —
History — 20th century.   4. Vice control — Ontario — Windsor — History — 20th century.
5. Borderlands — United States — History — 20th century.   6. Borderlands — Canada —
History — 20th century.   I. Title.

HN80.D6K37 2015

306.09713'32 — dc23   2015006178

Contents

Illustrations

Acknowledgments

This book was inspired by my own experience of crossing borders. What I thought would be a temporary move from Michigan to Ontario turned into a decade-long adventure, one that shaped my life in unexpected ways. Settling in southern Ontario—relatively close to home yet at times seemingly worlds apart—I became intrigued by the borderlands relationship and the long and complicated history of migration in the Great Lakes region. This project has since brought me to the border states of Arizona and Texas, and in each new place I have been reinspired by the complex and contested meanings of borderlands. If in the following pages the "border" is never static, it is this very ever-shifting meaning of borderlands that has sustained my personal and intellectual interest over the span of this project.

The foundation of this project came together during my time as a graduate student at the University of Toronto. First and foremost, I'd like to thank Dan Bender for his unyielding support. He encouraged me to push the boundaries of my research and to think beyond borders—national, disciplinary, and methodological. Over the past eight years, his mentorship and advice have enabled me to grow both professionally and personally. While countless scholars provided intellectual and emotional support during the many stages of this project, I would especially like to thank Elspeth Brown, Steve Penfold, Franca Iacovetta, and Victoria Wolcott. At the University of Guelph, Norman Smith and Catherine Carstairs provided some of the earliest mentorship and inspiration that helped me get this project off the ground. My new colleagues in the Department of Social Sciences at Tarleton State University have likewise provided encouragement and intellectual engagement in the final months of the review and publication process.

I would like to thank the Social Science and Humanities Research Council of Canada, the Canadian Embassy in Washington, D.C., the Bentley Historical Library, the Centre for the Study of the United States, and the Department of History and School of Graduate Studies at the University of Toronto for their generous financial support. Similarly, the help of many archivists made my hunt for the "illicit" much more manageable and ultimately very fruitful. I'd like to thank the archivists and staff at the

Archives of Ontario, the Bentley Historical Library, the Windsor Municipal Archives, the Michigan State Archives, and the Washington, D.C., and Chicago branches of the National Archives and Records Administration. When I came to them in search of drugs, prostitution, and other vices, so to speak, their insight and knowledge helped me find creative ways to comb through their many collections.

I am also deeply grateful to have had the opportunity to serve as a Postdoctoral Fellow in Comparative Border Studies and the School of Historical, Philosophical, and Religious Studies at Arizona State University. My tenure there deepened my understandings of borders and borderlands, and the rich intellectual community enabled me to hone my arguments in the final stages of this book project. I would especially like to thank Matt and Desiree Garcia for their friendship, guidance, and generosity. My many discussions—and diversions—with Megan Carney, Laia Soto Bermant, and Elizabeth Cantú similarly made my time in Phoenix inspiring and one that I will never forget.

I would sincerely like to thank my editors at the University of North Carolina Press. Andrew Graybill, Ben Johnson, and Chuck Grench showed their enthusiasm from the beginning and provided extremely helpful feedback throughout the review process. I am honored to be part of the David J. Weber Series and to have my work published alongside new and exciting scholarship in the field of borderlands history. The feedback I received from the anonymous reviewers enabled me to transform this project in important ways, and I am indebted to them for their detailed, insightful, and thoughtful feedback. Finally, I would like to thank Iza Wojciechowska for helping to streamline the publication process and for answering my many questions along the way.

The labor of researching and writing, as any scholar knows, would not be possible without the love and support of friends and family. No matter how far apart we were, I had many amazing people provide a timely phone call, a conversation over a glass of wine, or a much-needed diversion. This goes especially to Lara Tobin, Jodi Giesbrecht, Erika Hughes, Nagheme Thomas, and Camille Bégin. To my brothers and sisters—Collin Karibo and Holly Lutsenko, Rory and Lauren Karibo, April and Jeff Meganck, Kali Karibo and Jamie Schaller, and Matt and Vicki Drohan—your love and support made this long journey possible. Thank you to my mother, Kathryne Karibo, for providing an important role model as a strong and determined woman, and to my father, David Karibo, whose encouragement remained constant throughout this process. To Grant and Wendy Drohan, thank you for your love, for your kind and encouraging words, and for always believing in my abilities. A paragraph is woefully insufficient to express my deep gratitude and love for each and every one of you.

Last, and certainly not least, to my partner in crime and in life, Chris Drohan. There are not enough words to describe what your love and support have meant to me over the past twelve years. You have read version after version of this book—from its first inception as a conference paper to the final draft. We have talked about borders, sin, and vice more than any two people probably should. Your critical feedback and your intellectual insight have been most appreciated. More important, you encourage me to take a break when needed, to be adventurous, and to not take life too seriously. For these and many other reasons, this one's for you.

Sin City North

INTRODUCTION

In March of 1950, Essex County Magistrate J. Arthur Hanrahan sentenced local bootlegger Joseph Assef to six months in jail and "plunged the city of Windsor [Ontario] into two weeks of explosive investigations of vice-related activities in what has long been Canada's best publicized 'wide-open town.'" During the course of the eight-week-long trial, the Crown presented evidence that Assef had received more than 5,400 illegal liquor deliveries, sometimes as many as sixty a day. While sentencing Assef to the maximum penalty, the judge blasted the Windsor Police Department for its wanton disregard for vice-related crimes. Confirming Hanrahan's growing conviction that there was something "seriously wrong" in Windsor, Assef's sentence was meant to call attention to what the judge believed was a growing problem in the city: the expansion and tacit acceptance of vice economies across the Detroit-Windsor borderland.[1]

The public flogging of the Windsor police, which ultimately resulted in a provincial inquiry and the forced retirement of the chief of police, placed an international spotlight on the Canadian border city. Local and international publications began to run stories about the rampant prostitution, gambling, liquor smuggling, and illegal drugs available in Windsor.[2] In seedy establishments like the Blue Water and Ambassador hotels, the articles explained, men and women could mingle virtually unhampered by provincial or municipal laws. Anyone who listened closely could hear jazz music, or the sound of loudspeakers calling out illegal bets, pouring out of local establishments. Inside, Americans and Canadians—often strangers to one another—sang, danced, and consumed too much alcohol.

Illegal drugs were sometimes sold, and sexual favors were often bought as easily as glasses of beer. Although charges of moral laxity were not new to the Detroit-Windsor region, these accusations took on new salience in the 1950s, a time when many viewed their city as clean and safe, a shining example of postwar prosperity. Was it possible that Windsor was falling victim to urban problems common in American cities, where crime and violence seemed to be running rampant? Had postwar social dislocation indeed had a serious impact on the border cities? Could upstanding citizens help stamp out these unwanted elements without hampering the social and economic ties that linked residents of the Canadian border city to their American neighbors? Many local residents grappled with these questions in the immediate aftermath of the public scandal.

Debates over the meaning of vice in the Detroit-Windsor region reflected a profound tension many North Americans felt as World War II came to an end. On the one hand, breaking free from economic depression and war, cities like Detroit and Windsor seemed uniquely poised to ascend to great prominence. Industrial growth, expanding expendable incomes, and increased mobility seemed to climax in a period of extreme economic optimism. City boosters boasted that Windsor was the most important up-and-coming city in Canada, poised to become the largest and most powerful city in the nation. Detroit similarly retained its position as a vibrant industrial city, with bustling nightlife and safe suburbs, where one could buy a home, make a living, and raise a family. At the same time, though, there were underlying fears over the changing nature of life in a world that had just witnessed the unimaginable horrors of a world war. Along with unprecedented growth came mounting racial tension, white flight, the deterioration of urban centers, and Cold War paranoia. With the rise of these competing issues, Detroit and Windsor began to look more and more like other urban centers across North America. If residents were not attentive to these serious issues, they, too, could face an environment where lax moral attitudes, racial antagonism, and economic decline would stunt the growth and potential of the local communities. Within this context, vice became one distinct lens through which local residents expressed their competing optimisms and fears in the postwar period.

By examining the rise of illicit economies in the Detroit-Windsor border region during the 1940s and 1950s, *Sin City North* places these seemingly contradictory narratives of hopefulness and despair, of booming economic growth and industrial stagnation, at the forefront. Focusing on cross-border prostitution and heroin economies, this book traces the social history of these illegal industries, as well as the broader cultural meaning they came to embody in the urban borderland. I tell the story of "vice" from multiple perspectives: from the women and men who worked in the illegal trades, from the customers who kept their businesses booming, and from middle-class residents, moral reformers, and legal authorities who attempted to eliminate what they considered to be unwanted and dangerous activities spreading across the national line. Placing illegal and informal interactions at the forefront, this study provides new insight into the cultural meaning of the U.S.-Canada border in the mid-twentieth century and the ways in which race, gender, labor, and citizenship were defined through illicit interactions between local residents living on the margins of their respective nations.

Borders and Borderlands in the North American Context

When newspapers proclaimed that rampant vice threatened to make Windsor a "border brothel" for Detroit, they were articulating fears that the Canadian city was particularly vulnerable to corrupting influences because of its position along the national line. Situated on the banks of the Detroit River, which connected the region to the broader Great Lakes basin, the cities had long been shaped by debates over the meaning of the national divide and the nature of the relationship between Canadians and Americans who resided along it. At a time when the American and Canadian governments were promoting the relationship between their nations as one of mutual trust, benefit, and friendship, and when more Americans and Canadians were crossing the border for leisure purposes than ever before, the emergence of cross-border crime and vice after World War II laid bare the contradictory nature of the border itself: the national line was supposed to make travel and trade between residents on the other side easier and more efficient, while also filtering out those goods and people deemed illegal or unwanted. This book makes clear that not only were these dual objectives impossible to achieve but also they were often at odds with the desires of local residents who crossed the border for work, travel, and entertainment on a daily basis.

Studies of borderlands in North American history have traditionally focused on the region surrounding the American Southwest and the Mexican North. Over the last two decades, inspired by this rich and nuanced literature, scholars have begun to push for more detailed analyses of the economic, political, and national interests that intersected along the "49th parallel." Historians have provided insight into how the U.S.-Canada border was created and how immigration and formal economic policies developed

The Detroit-Windsor skyline, ca. 1929, as seen from downtown Windsor. (Courtesy of the Library of Congress, LC-DIG-ppmsca-15308)

across the northern border regions.[3] Yet we still know very little about the informal, short-term, and extralegal travel that brought women and men across the border during the twentieth century. This book examines the borderlands relationship that developed as women and men engaged in informal, illegal, and temporary exchanges across the national divide. It is less about the border itself—the legal line separating the United States from Canada—than an examination of the borderland that emerged around it, the *social spaces* in which people grapple with the national boundary on a daily basis.[4]

National borders work as regulatory tools that enact a wide array of state objectives and are meant to produce or reinforce the power of the nation-state and the disciplinary role of its government. In response to the imposition of state control and regulation, informal social and economic networks, or "borderlands," are created by men and women who live in the local communities.[5] Borderlanders tailor their engagement with the national border to fit their needs, desires, and personal perceptions of the local community. Engaging in alternative cross-border interactions is one way borderlanders challenge the ability of the state to dictate the terms of the border relationships. Lying to border guards, hiding goods to evade customs duties, staying longer than allowed, and forging documents are some examples of the ways that men and women push back against state powers on a regular basis. Borders, then, are not only created by the state; they are also defined, produced, and undermined by the women and men who engage with them on a daily basis.

As the busiest crossing point between the two countries, the Detroit-Windsor region provides a fruitful opportunity to explore how informal and illegal exchanges shaped the social spaces of the northern borderland. Our story begins at the turn of the century, when the rise of industrialization, and especially the automobile industry, brought unprecedented growth to the region. People moved to Detroit and Windsor from across North America and the world, seeking to make a new life in the booming border cities. At the same time that people and goods began flowing across the Detroit-Windsor border in unprecedented numbers, the American federal government passed the National Prohibition Act of 1919, setting the stage for the birth of a new industry in the border cities: illegal liquor smuggling. As Americans flocked to Canada to quench their thirst, and as Canadian booze poured into the United States, this exchange profoundly shaped the borderlands relationship. By the late 1920s, Detroiters had dubbed the neighboring Canadian bordertown "Wicked Windsor," and local residents began referring to the Detroit-Windsor Tunnel that connected the two cities as the "Detroit-Windsor Funnel," a euphemism that acknowledged the fact that the illegal liquor trade had emerged as the second most lucrative industry in the region. Prostitution, gambling, and illegal drugs went hand in hand with the illegal liquor trade, and by the end of the Prohibition experiment in 1933, local residents had established intricate cross-border networks uniting Detroit and Windsor residents in unseemly forms of leisure and moneymaking. Contrary to the small body of literature that examines illegal trade across the U.S.-Canada border, this book does not end with the repeal of Prohibition.[6] Instead, it demonstrates that this wild and tumultuous period in the region's history laid the foundations for the booming illegal economies that continued to shape life in the border cities for decades to come.

In moving our focus beyond the Prohibition years into the 1940s and 1950s, *Sin City North* provides an additional intervention into the field of borderlands studies, which tends to treat the borderlands relationship as the primary factor shaping life for residents living along a national line. North American borderland studies often focus on border spaces as "contact zones," as highly contested spaces where multiple cultures collide, compete, and overlap.[7] These conceptions of borderland spaces, though, do not fit as easily within the U.S.-Canada border context because, as several scholars have noted, similarities across the border are often as influential on northern borderlanders as are differences between them. As one 1943 *Windsor Daily Star* editorial satirically explained this relationship: "You see, [Windsor] is so much closer to Detroit than Michigan is."[8] Rather than shy away from a borderlands framework, I argue that scholars can effectively take up these projects by carefully determining when and how the northern border matters. Detroit and Windsor were bordertowns, but they were also urban centers that shared many features common across large North American cities. Segregation, mounting racial tensions, a widening suburban-urban divide, and a push toward narrow definitions of normative gender and sexual roles shaped life in the border region, but they were not unique to it. In other words, the border cities were also embedded in larger structural processes shaping the region, processes that developed in relation to, in response to, and sometimes despite national boundary lines. In weaving together the analytic frameworks of "borderlands" and "vice," I am careful to allow the evidence to determine when and how each of these frameworks matters in order to more fully understand when the border was a pervasive force in the lives of local residents and when its presence was overshadowed by other social, cultural, and economic developments.

Vice and the Postwar City

The meaning of vice has a long genealogy in North American history and has most often been associated with the underbelly of society—with the polluting and corrupting activities that nonetheless attracted countless participants. Although vice has often been used as a code word for prostitution, it is also a blanket term that covers a wide range of activities such as gambling, drinking, and drug use. I employ the term in this broader sense and use it to identify the multiple and interrelated activities that violated normative moral codes while often—though not necessarily—breaking the law. As Itty Abraham and Willem van Schendel argue, ideas of "licit" and "illicit" at the heart of vice denote meanings beyond the actual letter of the law. They are instead ways of defining the social perception of activities that become defined as criminal.[9] Terms like "vice," "prostitution," and "drug addict" were not descriptive titles for static categories—they were constantly being defined and reinterpreted by the men and women who invoked them. In this way, this study is less concerned with the legal status of illicit activities than with contested social meanings they came to signify.

In tracing the fluid lines separating licit and illicit activities in the border cities, I focus on prostitution and heroin economies for several reasons. Their regulation followed similar paths in North American history, with the first burst of sustained political attention toward both prostitution and drug use in the late-nineteenth and early-twentieth centuries.[10] Progressive reformers waged large-scale campaigns against these activities and viewed prostitution and drug use as the literal manifestations of the most dangerous elements of modernity.[11] Their close association during the Progressive Era continued over the following decades, and by the mid-twentieth century, commercial sex and recreational drug use were perceived and stigmatized in similar ways. Prostitution and heroin alike invited "a slew of gender and racial fascinations, notions of the domesticated and the alien, . . . and elaborate fantasies about human loss of control—or, inversely, fantasies about the state's possible 'control'" over them.[12] By the postwar years, sex and drug economies aroused a wide range of social and cultural anxieties, and reformers regularly invoked the image of the drug-addicted prostitute as the quintessential example of the degrading nature of vice. As one member of the Royal Canadian Mounted Police unabashedly asserted in 1955, women who sold their bodies for drugs were "a dreary lot of parasites" feeding on the nations' cities. They were, "in truth, the dregs of society."[13]

The focus on vice in the Progressive Era has left the study of illicit economies in the period between 1945 and 1960 woefully underexplored.[14] Indeed, we know very little about the social functions illicit economies served in postwar cities or the ideologies that led some contemporaries to believe that sex workers and drug users were parasites sucking the moral lifeblood out of urban communities. I argue that attention to illicit economies sheds new light on the effects of the major social and economic changes that reshaped urban centers after the war and the competing ways that city residents grappled with those changes on a daily basis. Beginning in the mid-1940s, many industrial cities' centers entered a period of economic decline. Residents across Canada and the United States witnessed the deterioration of many older, once vibrant, working-class communities, as suburban growth wrested tax money and power from city centers and refocused it on the surrounding middle-class neighborhoods.[15]

At the same time, the influx of African American migrants from the rural South reshaped race relations in northern American cities, and informal and institutionalized racism transformed urban landscapes into contested spaces marked by segregation, inequality, and, at times, interracial violence.[16] Detroit's race riot of 1943, which began on the beaches of Belle Isle and left thirty-four people dead in its wake, was a clear omen of the challenges to come.

Though much of the postwar literature focuses on flight and movement out of urban neighborhoods during these decades, illicit economies provide one way to explore the lives of those who continued to live and work downtown and who grappled with these rapid social and economic transformations on a daily basis.[17] Selling sex and drugs took increasingly visible roles in many downtown neighborhoods left behind in the shifting postwar economy, and many men and women came to rely on illicit activities as a source of entertainment and income in increasingly depressed urban centers. Across Detroit and Windsor, bars, brothels, jazz joints, and gambling houses provided spaces in which men and women could gather, socialize, and make money to supplement the limited incomes they earned in blue-collar and service occupations. Sex workers and heroin users and sellers alike relied on large social networks—which included bartenders, hotel owners, cab drivers, bellhops, and others—whose cooperation made their illegal transactions possible. In this way, sex and drug economies were more than simply fringe activities taking place on the margins of urban communities; they were, in fact, interwoven into the lives of many downtown residents and became part of the cultural life of the working-class neighborhoods in which they emerged.[18]

Participating in sex and drug economies had broader cultural and political implications, at times serving as a way for marginal men and women to assert their place as productive citizens and valuable community members. The concept of citizenship in the postwar context has most often been explored through the lens of normative cultural values based around suburbanization, consumption, and the rise of the middle class. Historians have largely focused on the process of "domestic containment," in which the suburban, heterosexual family (headed by the white-collar male breadwinner) came to be regarded as a social ideal.[19] *Sin City North* joins the growing body of scholarship that challenges the characterization of the 1950s as a period of cultural conformity, economic prosperity, and the dominance of middle-class values.[20] Rather than framing illicit economies as an anomaly in an era of social, cultural, and political consensus, I examine the ways in which participants in illegal economies drew on dominant cultural tropes of consumption and mobility, reformulating them to fit their own socioeconomic and cultural realities. Sex workers capitalized on the large number of tourists and travelers crossing through the border region, creating an unofficial tourist economy centered on the commodification of illicit sexual pleasure. By marketing nonnormative forms of sexual interactions, which included sex across racial and ethnic lines, participants challenged the belief that the heterosexual, monogamous marriage was the only legitimate form of sexual expression in the postwar years. Similarly, the heroin subcultures that emerged by the late 1940s were based on the consumption of pleasurable substances, and users created expansive cultural networks with their own styles of dress, slang, and social hierarchies. Rather than rejecting consumerism itself, the heroin subcultures retooled their consumption in a way that allowed even the most marginal community member to participate. Vice, in other words, was not an aberration in the cultural life of the 1950s—it was deeply embedded within it. By engaging in illicit forms of consumption, leisure, and moneymaking, participants built alternative forms of community in the cities' downtown neighborhoods, ones that were a far cry from the sanitized image of the suburban family city boosters tried to present.

If selling sex and drugs offered alternative forms of leisure and money-making in the Detroit-Windsor region, as well as a chance to claim membership in an alternative urban community, it did so in uneven ways and with varying consequences for the women and men involved. The very fact that vice was embedded in local working-class neighborhoods meant that these illicit activities often came to reflect many of the structural inequalities that shaped the formal economy. Take the heroin trade as an example. Though selling the drug provided some local residents with the additional income needed to pay for their basic living expenses and their drug habits, the heroin market also functioned with an internal logic of inequality that relegated poor, African American sellers to the lowest, least profitable levels of the trade. In contrast to white ethnic men who tended to dominate the lucrative business of large-scale importation, local pushers—the ones most likely to be arrested for their activities—also made the least amount of money. Thus, the racial stratification present in many formal economic sectors also became entrenched in vice industries. Though it is easy to slip into a celebratory narrative that views men's and women's work in illicit economies as transgressive attempts to counter their social and economic marginalization, a closer look demonstrates that participation in illicit economies often failed to solve their problems and instead sometimes compounded them. While we need to take into account people's decisions to participate in these economies, the social and physical dangers of sex work and heroin use remind us that they were often temporary solutions that were unable to address the broader structural changes taking place in the urban environment.

Race, Space, and Regulation in the Urban Borderland

The structural inequalities that emerged in the illicit economy were, in part, the result of attempts to regulate and suppress them. In the Detroit-Windsor region, antivice activism took place in formal and informal ways and reached far beyond law enforcement officials enforcing particular laws. Countless local residents also worked to ensure that their neighborhoods would be safe and free from the corrupting influence of vice. While their approaches differed in important ways, Canadian and American reformers were united by a drive to define who did or did not count as desirable members of postwar urban communities. These various attempts to eliminate cross-border vice at the local, state, provincial, and national levels, then, also worked to define conceptions of proper citizenship across North America—efforts that took on particular salience in cities that were literally on the edge of their respective nations.

Across the border cities, seemingly disparate groups—such as the Detroit Urban League, the Women's Local Council of Windsor, the mayors' offices, and local reporters—actively campaigned against the rise of vice. Efforts ranged from informal letter-writing campaigns designed to pressure elected officials to conduct vice cleanups to formal public inquiries like the one that occurred after the 1950 police scandal.[21] In the early 1940s, antivice efforts were focused more narrowly on defending the health of soldiers and civilians within a wartime context. This changed by the late 1940s, when reformers began to incorporate the language of freedom, democracy, and citizenship defined through the ideological lens of the Cold War. Antivice rhetoric drew on the binaries of good versus evil, insiders versus outsiders, and healthy versus diseased, which worked to reinforce the belief that there were desirable and undesirable types of citizens. These perceptions took on a spatial dimension, as antivice activists began articulating fears that illicit economies were both symptoms and causes of an emerging "urban problem." Within this context, moral reformers blamed illicit economies for a wide range of social ills—from transience, to deteriorating neighborhoods, to juvenile delinquency. In short, prostitution and drug economies were easy targets for politicians, law enforcement officials, community groups, and middle-class residents who needed something or someone to blame for the complex issues affecting urban neighborhoods by the 1950s.

The so-called urban problem was also laden with racialized perceptions that blamed vice on African American residents living in the border region. As the Second Great Migration brought thousands of southern blacks to the city of Detroit, debates over the place of nonwhite citizens intensified in local communities.[22] White Detroiters and Windsorites alike expressed fears that African Americans brought lawlessness, vice, and crime into communities, and debates over illicit leisure often emphasized the problem of race mixing that took place in these contexts. Contemporary antivice advocates were particularly concerned with the growing number of African American women working as prostitutes in Detroit and the fact that it was largely white male customers who kept the industry afloat. These fears were expressed by both black and white reformers, the former primarily concerned with the deterioration of black neighborhoods and the latter worried that black vice districts would spill over into white communities. At the same time, Windsor functioned as a segregated city where white Detroiters—intimidated by the racial antagonism that characterized many neighborhoods in the city's core—could escape for a weekend of illicit fun and pleasure. In fact, Windsor's sex industry catered almost exclusively to white clients despite the fact that Detroit's African American population more than tripled in the postwar period.[23] Canadians tended to frame the "race problem" as an American issue during the postwar years, but a detailed examination of vice regulation in the borderland shows that this was far from the case. With the shifting racial dynamics in the city of Detroit, white residents on both sides of the border were united in their fears that the influx of black southerners would have a negative impact on their communities. This sense of cross-border "whiteness" helped transform nation-building projects on both sides of the border into racialized projects, and, by the late 1950s, the line between productive citizen and unwanted outsider was increasingly determined by the color line.

Finally, though local antivice activism emerged in particular ways due to the social geography of the Detroit-Windsor region, it was also shaped by larger national debates over the dangers of porous borders. During the postwar years, North American newspapers, magazines, television shows, and films began portraying bordertowns as vice towns and as sites of danger where lawful citizens were at the mercy of dope smugglers and other figures of ill repute. According to these narratives, Chinese Communists and organized crime syndicates were using bordertowns as launching points for their expansive drug networks, which were penetrating the heart of the nations' largest cities. As the public rhetoric about porous borders intensified, and as concerns over the global spread of Communism placed new urgency on the need to secure the nations' borders, the federal governments undertook detailed studies of the problems of vice. An analysis of these investigations reveals that Canadian and American authorities shared similar prohibitionist agendas, ones that defined drug users and prostitutes as dangerous and immoral and federal enforcement officers as heroes fighting their corrupting influences.

If American and Canadian reformers adopted similar language to present a unified front against vice on the northern borderline, there were important limits to the cooperation. Indeed, tendencies to blame vice on outsiders often led to tensions between community members on each side of the national line. This grew, in part, out of the asymmetrical relationship between Detroit and Windsor, which often left residents of the small Canadian city feeling as though they were sitting in the shadows of their larger American neighbor.[24] If Windsorites courted American tourists and dollars, they also regularly complained that American officials were not doing enough to stop undesirable Americans from crossing into their seemingly quiet community. As one Canadian magazine put it, "Like every Canadian city, Windsor has its quota of sinners." But it also had the misfortune of having to deal with "the legions of afterdark [*sic*] that come from Detroit" on a nightly basis.[25] Just as Detroiters blamed their vice problems on the influx of southern migrants, Windsor residents saw their local crime problem as, in part, the result of lax attitudes on the part of Detroit authorities. Ultimately, antivice rhetoric embodied the multiple tensions inherent in trying to build a cross-border community while filtering out unwanted elements. Borderlands, as it turns out, were difficult to control, and perceived shared values across the national line often fell apart as residents struggled to eliminate what they saw as dangerous and polluting economies infecting their communities.

ON THE SURFACE, the Windsor police scandal of 1950 seems like a common, albeit colorful, story about authorities turning a blind eye to tacitly accepted vice activities. Upon closer examination, it becomes clear that this brief incident embodied some of the key cultural and economic struggles developing in the urban borderlands in the mid-twentieth century. The chapters that follow analyze both the political economy of the Detroit-Windsor region and the larger symbolic meaning vice economies came to represent in the postwar borderlands.[26] Chapter 1 begins by tracing the roots of the local border culture in the late-nineteenth and early-twentieth centuries. While industrial growth, the building of a bridge and tunnel across the river, and relatively relaxed border policies facilitated close community ties that transcended the national line, the border community was also profoundly affected by the rise of cross-border smuggling during the Prohibition years. I therefore trace the conflicting impact this industry had on Detroit and Windsor residents, as some welcomed the illicit trade and others fought vehemently to end it. While the repeal of the Eighteenth Amendment and the combined effects of the Great Depression and war stunted illicit trades in the border cities, the memory of the Prohibition years—and the wide-open nature of the border cities during its heyday—would not be forgotten by local residents.

As trade routes opened up after the war and as leisure travel began to increase across the U.S.-Canada border, illicit economies once again flourished in the border cities. Chapters 2 and 3 chart the rise of prostitution and heroin economies in the late 1940s and 1950s, exploring the ways in which they functioned as forms of both entertainment and labor in the cities' downtown cores. I examine the experiences of sex workers, heroin users and sellers, and their customers and the intricate ways that race, gender, class, and sexual lines shaped the nature of their illicit interactions. At times participating in vice economies offered a way to escape normative social codes and to engage in alternative communities and subcultures. In Detroit, for example, interracial commercial sex challenged the belief that sexual pleasure should be confined to the marriage bed, as well as segregation policies that worked to keep black and white residents separate, particularly in intimate forms of entertainment and leisure. Yet the transgressive nature of illicit economies was limited by race and class hierarchies that often determined who could participate in these illicit exchanges and in what capacity. In this way, chapters 2 and 3 detail when the sex and heroin economies were transgressive and when they worked to reinforce larger structural inequalities shaping the border region.

In the final two chapters, I turn to the issue of moral regulation and the way that a wide range of social actors, with varying degrees of political power, attempted to eliminate illicit economies along the national line. Chapter 4 focuses on the local Detroit-Windsor context and examines how perceptions of transience and urban decay shaped public debates over prostitution and heroin economies. Fears over moral disorder—particularly in the form of juvenile delinquency, urban blight, and racial violence—were at the heart of antivice activism in the early postwar years. In Detroit and Windsor, the national line heightened local fears that these problems were caused by outsiders, by people who did not belong in the border cities. Thus, though these debates resonated in many North American cities, the border cities provide unique insight into the ways in which ideological constructions of citizenship and community belonging were defined through illicit interactions. In chapter 5, I situate local efforts to fight cross-border vice within larger national debates about bordertowns and border enforcement. I examine the way border cities along the northern border were portrayed in the media and popular culture, arguing that they were framed as spaces inherently open to corruption and vice. These public perceptions were bolstered by the Canadian and American federal governments, who blamed much of the drug problem on the porousness of the national line and the unscrupulous nature of transnational criminals. While prohibition policies reigned supreme through the end of the 1950s, federal officials were less successful at enacting border policies that could effectively filter out illegal activities across the national line. The very success of vice economies highlights both the limits to state power and the ways in which uneven power relations between American and Canadian authorities could undermine their abilities to present a united front.

This book is about multiple borders. It is about the national border that connected two industrial cities during the first half of the twentieth century. But it is also about the borders of race, class, and gender that developed across industrial North America at mid-century. By refocusing our attention on the men and women who participated in illicit forms of leisure and labor, we gain new insight into the lives of those most affected by economic downturns, urban decline, and the Cold War moral politics that were at the heart of the era known as the 1950s. An attention to vice economies also allows us to trace the competing ways in which men and women engaged with the concept of citizenship on a daily basis. While states attempted to define this in terms of legal categories, this book traces how ordinary people worked to determine who counted as welcomed and legitimate members of their communities. Ultimately, the Detroit-Windsor border region became a microcosm of larger social debates over the future of the North American city and the meaning of citizenship across the Canadian and American nations.

BUILDING THE
"DETROIT-WINDSOR FUNNEL"
Tourism, Prohibition, and Border Politics
before World War II

On November 11, 1929, hundreds of thousands of Detroit and Windsor residents celebrated the opening of the Ambassador Bridge that connected the two cities over the Detroit River. Planned to coincide with Armistice Day celebrations, thousands of onlookers from both sides of the river stormed to the center of the 7,500-foot bridge to watch the ribbon-cutting ceremony. According to a *New York Times* reporter on the scene, "the throngs sensed the spirit of this gesture of friendliness, and burst into tremendous cheering. Canadian bands were on the American terminal playing 'America' the anthem while American bands were at the Sandwich end playing 'Oh, Canada.' Outstanding citizens of both communities looked on with bared heads. The miracle that was dreamed of fifty-five years ago had come to pass." As part of the celebration, Michigan Governor Fred Green gave a speech in a radio broadcast explaining that this was "a physical connection between the highways of our own State and those of a friendly people who live across a national boundary from us. It is a spiritual bond of steel between the territories of two nations, each striving to achieve the best purposes of their own citizens and for the citizenship of the world." Similarly, Charles McRae, Minister of Mines of Ontario, spoke for the Dominion: "The Ambassador Bridge opens today as another link in the friendship chain of the peoples of the United States and Canada."[1]

There was no shortage of flowery language and hyperbole in the news reports that covered this event.[2] For many, the opening of the bridge became an important symbolic moment representing the close relationship between Americans and Canadians and the modern methods of building and production that allowed this dream "of fifty-five years" to come to fruition. In the first decades of the twentieth century, the Detroit-Windsor border developed into the central crossing point between the two countries, with millions of tourists, commuters, and immigrants traveling across it. Between 1900 and 1939, people came to the region from across North America and the world, hoping to take part in growing industrial centers and the cross-border fluidity that allowed men and women to travel between the two countries with relative ease. They participated in industries, travel, and trade that crossed the national line and subsequently emboldened the transnational nature of the region. The opening of the Ambassador Bridge was both the result of this increased traffic and a symbol of the hopes of future prosperity, freedom of movement, and cross-border community building between Michigan and Ontario.

These jovial festivities, though, overshadowed an important paradox that developed in the borderland during the first decades of the twentieth century. While this period brought an increase in trade and travel across the national line, it also ushered in a range of legislative changes that curtailed the fluidity of the border in important ways. Sparked in part by growing fears over an influx of so-called new immigrants coming from Asia and Eastern and Southern Europe, Canadian and American federal officials began strengthening inspection procedures that would enable them to filter out "undesirables." Consequently, between the 1890s and the 1930s, both countries passed increasingly stringent border control mechanisms that formalized the crossing process and changed the nature of the relationship between residents. The opening of the Ambassador Bridge itself was deeply embedded in this process. By providing expansive "modern" inspection booths and a highly structured crossing process, the bridge—while celebrated as a sign of friendship and freedom across the national divide—also reflected the growing incursions of the federal state in the lives of borderlanders who crossed for work and entertainment on a regular basis.

The tension between building a vibrant cross-border culture while tightly patrolling the national line that separated one side from the other became increasingly apparent with the rise of illicit economies in the border region. Though vice activities were deeply rooted in the fluid nature of working cultures in the border cities, which had long drawn large numbers of single men across the border for both labor and leisure, they emerged in full force when the United States outlawed the sale of alcohol in 1919. Capitalizing on disparate liquor laws in Michigan and Ontario, local residents built thriving smuggling networks to bring Canadian liquor into the United States. They subsequently gained reputations as wide-open towns where illegal economies were rampant and criminal gangs controlled much of the business. This increasingly unpopular legislative move also brought average citizens into contact with the law, and crossing the line to purchase alcohol or drinking illegal Canadian liquor on the Detroit side of the border became embedded in the social life of the borderlands community. By the 1930s, borderlanders were demonstrating the limits to strict border enforcement on a daily basis, helping to turn these boomtowns into vice towns where one could enjoy a range of illegal forms of entertainment, right under the noses of local and federal officials.

Ultimately, the first decades of the twentieth century brought profound changes to the border cities that would shape the Detroit-Windsor region for years to come. In the working-class cities, men and women crossed the border for labor and entertainment, helping to build a transnational region in which the lives of many Canadians and Americans became intimately intertwined. In turn, these transnational connections raised important questions about the nature of the national boundary and who should be allowed to cross. The Ambassador Bridge ceremony provided a positive narrative of cross-border friendship and cooperation, but a closer look at developments in the Detroit-Windsor region demonstrates the conflicting and often contradictory ways in which the national line shaped life in the urban borderland in the early-twentieth century. On the border, morality could be difficult to enforce, money difficult to trace, and the movement of people difficult to control.

Borders and Borderlands in the First Decades of the Twentieth Century

The histories of Detroit and Windsor were from their very start complex ones, weaving together native power brokering, colonial aspirations, and the troubled process of nation building. Ranging from peaceful and co-operative to violent and contested, the area that now forms the dividing line had been the site of renegotiation since at least the seventeenth century.[3] What we might recognize as the modern borderland emerged in the last decades of the nineteenth century, as industrial growth, migration, and cross-border travel reshaped the Detroit-Windsor region in profound ways. As the quickly emerging automotive capital, Detroit in particular came to symbolize ideals of hope, prosperity, and modern manufacturing in the national imagination. While it did not invent the automobile, its contribution was in the organization of methods of production and distribution, "transforming what had been little more than a toy, into a universal and indispensable mass product whose impact upon cities has been equaled only by that of the steam engine and electricity."[4] Local industries built on businesses that had developed in the nineteenth century, converting them over the first decades of the twentieth century into massive production plants structured by the principles of Taylorism. By the 1940s, automotive and related industries made up more than 60 percent of the manufacturing in the region, with industries like furniture building, brewing, stove making, oil refineries, salt mines, steel mills, and food-processing plants also expanding in size and scope.[5]

Similarly, Windsor's growth was due to several related factors that came together in the first decade of the twentieth century. The extensive rise of branch plants, in which American companies opened factories in Ontario to avoid international tariffs, meant that the city became increasingly intertwined with American corporate and economic interests.[6] This began on a large scale in 1904, when the Ford Motor Company moved its Detroit-based operations across the river and into the surrounding Canadian cities of Windsor, East Windsor (later Ford City), Walkerville, and Sandwich (known collectively as the Border Cities). With the industrialization sparked by World War I, Ford became the predominant industry in the region, and in the early 1930s, the Border Cities merged politically into a single community with a population of more than 100,000.[7] By then, more than 100 companies in Windsor had American affiliations, some among the largest industries in the country.[8] These various car producers required plants that would manufacture automobile parts and accessories, and by 1935, thirty such plants were located in the city.[9] By 1939, 65 percent of those employed in the newly amalgamated city worked in the thriving auto industry.[10]

Over the first decades of the twentieth century, men and women flocked to the border region in search of work, quickly turning the Detroit-Windsor corridor into one of the largest cosmopolitan centers in the Great Lakes region. This was especially true during World War I, when rapid industrialization for the war effort attracted men and women from across North America and the world. In 1910, foreign-born migrants from Canada, Russia, Austria, England, Hungary, Poland, Italy, Ireland, Scotland, and Belgium made up roughly a quarter of Detroit's population.[11] African American migrants from the rural South also moved to the northern city to work in the wartime industries, and the black population grew from a mere 1 percent of the population in 1910 to more than 7 percent of the population in 1930.[12] By the end of the 1920s, Detroit boasted more than 1.7 million residents.[13] At the same time, smooth connections between steamships, Great Lakes steamers, and railroads brought thousands of workers to Windsor.[14] The first major influx of migrants occurred in the 1910s and was mainly members of the so-called New Migration.[15] Ukrainians, Poles, Russians, Yugoslavians, Hungarians, Germans, Finns, Scandinavians, Italians, Greeks, and Syrians were chief among the newcomers, and the city's population increased dramatically from 15,198 in 1901 to 55,935 in 1921.[16]

The hopes of high-paying jobs that drew men and women to the border cities also brought them across the national line, and in the first decades of the twentieth century, the region developed a strong transnational commuter culture. Because many lived on one side of the border but worked on the other, for thousands of local residents, crossing the border became engrained in their daily lives. In the morning and evening rush hours, one could stand on either side of the Detroit-Windsor Ferry docks and watch thousands of citizens returning home from jobs on the other side of the river.[17] While this "reciprocity of citizens" worked in both directions, the booming metropolis of Detroit brought more Canadians across than the other way around.[18] In 1913, almost 30,000 people crossed between the cities on a daily basis, including a sizable number of men working in Windsor who, due to a shortage of housing on the Canadian side of the border, chose to live in Detroit.[19] By 1927, 15,000 of 25,334 employed residents of the Canadian Border Cities worked in Michigan, a situation unparalleled in any other large Canadian city.[20]

Prior to the opening of the bridge and tunnel in 1929 and 1930, the Detroit-Windsor Ferry provided the chief mode of travel across the river. The ferries carried passengers and automobiles in this two-way trade, dropping them in the heart of the cities' business districts on Woodward and Ouellette Avenues. Canadians and Americans built on this convenient method of travel (when running smoothly, the ferries took between five and ten minutes), crossing the national line for everything from necessary services like doctor visits and cheap groceries to leisure activities and social outings.[21] Sporting events, horse racing, amusement parks, and holiday celebrations became transnational events that brought Canadians and Americans together. Local businesses and civic leaders encouraged these cross-border excursions, seeing them as ways both to bring much-needed capital into the region and to build diplomatic ties between the two countries. As the Border Cities Chamber of Commerce promised Americans who came to visit, "in the Border Cities and District you will spend no dull moment. Excursion Steamers ply throughout the seasons to famous picnic parks and upon daylight and moonlight excursions. There are over 100 miles of beautiful driveways along the Lakes and River where sails the waterborne commerce of two nations. Bathing beaches, playgrounds, picnic parks, casinos, dance pavilions, lakeside hotels, public and private tourists' camps, and summer homes abound."[22] The importance of attracting American visitors—and by extension American money—led the Chamber of Commerce to establish the annual "Good Will Tour" in the late 1920s. On these trips, representatives of the Border Cities headed to "distant section[s]" of the United States (as far as Brownsville, Texas, and Miami, Florida) to inform Americans about the excitement that awaited them in the booming border region.[23] By 1920, the growing popularity of cross-border travel enabled Detroit-Windsor to surpass Welland County (despite its two bridges at Fort Erie and Niagara Falls) as the most popular crossing point between the United States and Canada.[24] Dining, dancing, drinking, and cheering for sports teams in the neighboring city helped to maintain the permeability of the borderland and create cultural spaces in which Americans, Canadians, and recent newcomers could mingle on both sides of the national line.

Although the unprecedented number of men and women crossing the border contributed to the cultural life of the Detroit-Windsor region in important ways, it also sparked heated debates about who was crossing and for what purpose. Federal officials on both sides of the national line began to worry that this extensive flow of travelers would enable illegal immigrants, criminals, and other undesirables to pass between the two nations undetected. In part, these fears reflected growing national concerns over the rise of new immigrants coming from Asia and Southern and Eastern Europe. Across both countries, as early as the 1850s, the need for cheap immigrant labor was tempered with fears over job competition, racial degeneration, and labor radicalism supposedly caused by these immigrant groups.[25] Headlines about illegal smuggling rings bringing Chinese workers across the Detroit-Windsor border or the massive "invasion of unwanted aliens" from "European farms" sneaking by border guards fueled local debates.[26] In Canada and the United States, anti-immigration laws like the Page Act of 1875, the Chinese Exclusion Act of 1882, the Chinese Immigration Act of 1885, the 1917 Immigration Act, and the 1924 National Origins Act (Johnson-Reed Act) ultimately had the effect of cutting off immigration from the targeted countries. Immigrants could be detained for months at inspection stations like Angel and Ellis Islands and were often ultimately turned away if determined to be inadmissible according to ever-shifting immigration policies.[27] These restrictive policies, which delineated between proper citizens and outsiders along racial, ethnic, and national lines, significantly changed the experience of immigration and cross-border movement at all entry points.[28]

The new restrictions and quota systems had a profound effect on the U.S.-Canada border, forcing immigrants in banned classes to migrate to Canadian bordertowns, where they hoped to eventually cross into the United States.[29] Federal officials therefore turned their attention to building stronger border control mechanisms along the U.S.-Canada border, putting in place a series of legislative changes that affected short-term travelers and immigrants alike. In 1893, the two nations entered into the Canadian Agreement, which held Canadian transportation companies to U.S. immigration laws and allowed American customs inspectors to be stationed at Canadian ports of entry. Over the following decades, this agreement was expanded to include streetcar companies, bus lines, the Detroit and Windsor Tunnel, and eventually airlines.[30] The Immigration Act of 1917 gave American authorities further power to inspect all aliens, including Canadians, who were required to prove "clearly and beyond a doubt" that they were entitled to enter the country.[31] In 1924, the same year that Congress passed the Johnson-Reed Act, they also established the U.S. Border Patrol, which was tasked with monitoring the movement of people at and between border crossing points.[32]

By the 1920s, the growing volume of traffic across the Detroit-Windsor border, combined with the increasingly stringent inspection requirements, began to make the process of border crossing frustrating for immigration officials and local residents alike. For officers tasked with policing the national boundary, the chaos that ensued at the ferry dock landings made it very difficult to implement the strict inspection guidelines. In an attempt to control the crowds, immigration officers tried different schemes, such as shuffling travelers through inspection points in two-by-two formations, but these met with little success.[33] In 1917, Border Crossing Cards were introduced for frequent travelers in the hopes this would leave immigration officers free to focus on long-term immigrants and questionable characters, but they, too, did little to quell the problem.[34] For travelers, having to wait in these long lines just to face enforcement officers they often found to be rude and unfriendly made cross-border trips increasingly unpleasant.[35] Local Detroit artist Percy Cromwell portrayed this frustration in a cartoon depicting a "clumsy" border patrol agent, who in his attempts to catch an illegal smuggler inadvertently blocked otherwise good citizens and tourists from crossing the national line freely.[36] Such experiences encouraged the author of a *Border Cities Star* article to declare: "Never before

This Percy Cromwell cartoon, titled "Clumsy!," demonstrates the frustration many local residents felt with the intensified policing of the national line that began in the 1920s. Even law-abiding citizens saw their mobility limited by these new policies. (Percy W. Cromwell cartoons, ca. 1918–ca. 1932; Box 2; Folder 23. Courtesy of the Bentley Historical Library, University of Michigan)

was the need for more adequate ferry service or better still, an international traffic bridge, more in evidence."[37]

Plans to build the Ambassador Bridge and the Detroit-Windsor Tunnel thus emerged at precisely the right time. Supporters built on public frustrations, claiming these massive infrastructure projects would solve the problems of both travelers and immigration officials. The major players behind the bridge company, Treasurer James Austin and Vice President Joseph A. Bower of the New York Trust Company, put forth a proposal for a private international bridge to be funded by a combination of public and private funds.[38] When Bower asked for support by the Essex County public, he argued that it was fitting that the Canadian public and government cover the cost of the project, since they had much to gain from the bridge project. He predicted that it would increase tax revenues and property values, produce a rise in local tourism, boost real estate development in Essex County, and bring American dollars into the border region.[39] It appears that Windsor residents agreed with this logic, because by January 1925 elections were complete, and the bridge plebiscite won a majority of votes.[40] While labor leaders and real estate developers in Detroit fought the bridge project, arguing that it would open the floodgates for cheap Canadian labor and destroy the beauty of the riverfront, the Detroit public was unmoved by these arguments. On June 28, the bridge plan passed with a margin of eight to one, and a record 75,557 Detroit voters made their voices heard.[41] It appears that despite several recessions in the 1920s, Detroit and Windsor residents continued to see their cities as intimately intertwined and welcomed the opportunities for trade and tourism that bridging the two communities would open up.

With the support of the public, the bridge project was underway. The McClintic-Marshall Company assumed the primary role of designing and building the massive structure, which they promoted as both a modern engineering feat and a step forward in the diplomatic relations between Americans and Canadians. According to a publication produced by McClintic-Marshall, "'Ambassador' is the name appropriately given to the vehicular bridge opened on November 15, 1929, spanning the Detroit River and connecting the City of Detroit with the 'Border Cities' grouped about Windsor, Ontario. Long inadequately served by ferries at this important point of interchange," the company claimed, "the two great countries will henceforth be impressively linked by this new servant of the two friendly peoples."[42] The bridge, which was "carefully designed in striking, modernistic form," was intended to facilitate quick and efficient crossing for travelers. On each side of the bridge, the customs terminals would (at least theoretically) allow customs officers to inspect border crossers with minimal delay, at a rate of as many as 4,000 cars per hour.[43] Covering a full city block on each side, they were imposing structures that clearly signaled one was entering a new country. Prospective crossers who arrived at these new terminals would choose one of twenty-six lines, where they were expected to patiently wait for the impending interrogation by customs officials. The bridge also included an additional area where suspicious cars would be parked for further inspection and interrogation by border officials. The massive size of the new infrastructure, combined with the large staff of Customs and Immigration officials needed to run it, created an

The Ambassador Bridge, which promoters billed as a great engineering feat and a modern architectural structure, became a visible connecting point linking the Canadian and American sides of the border. (Courtesy of the Southwestern Ontario Digital Archives, University of Windsor)

increasingly formal process for men and women looking to cross into the neighboring city.[44] No longer would border crossers have to fight the chaotic scenes that ensued at the overwhelmed ferry docks; they now had a quick, efficient, and orderly place to cross the national line.

When thousands of Americans and Canadians came out to celebrate the unveiling of the Ambassador Bridge on the sunny November afternoon in 1929, they were witnessing much more than an important engineering feat. They were standing on a structure that embodied some of the pivotal changes that shaped the Detroit-Windsor region in the first decades of the twentieth century. Sparked by the need to move an unprecedented number of people and goods across the national line, the bridge was partly a response to growing economic and social ties linking the border communities. Borderlanders who crossed between the two cities for both work and leisure welcomed the new infrastructure as something that would make their lives easier and their commutes shorter. At the same time, the expansive customs lanes and inspection booths built into the structure itself signaled an important shift in the meaning of the national line, which over the first decades of the twentieth century went from a relatively un-

Two border guards speak with a man as he tries to enter Canada at the Detroit-Windsor Tunnel. (Courtesy of the Walter P. Reuther Library, Wayne State University)

monitored space to a highly regulated and formalized crossing point. The modern borderland had become one in which federal authorities regularly inspected both long-term immigrants and local border city residents, making sure that those deemed undesirable, be they criminals or ethnic others, would not pass through the border undetected. Gone were the days of the anonymous border crossing. As one commentator noted, "anyone who thinks of the border as an imaginary line will get a rude shock."[45] Auto license cards, Border Crossing Cards, and immigration inspections had become commonplace for Americans and Canadians who crossed the border for both work and entertainment. In this way, the very paradox of this era in border history was built into the bridge and tunnel structures, which functioned at once as both barriers and connecting points. Local residents might be able cross in a shorter amount of time, but they now also had to submit to the authority of the federal government as they passed across the world's "longest undefended border," a phrase becoming increasingly questionable by the 1930s.

"Hordes of Lawbreakers along the Border":
Prohibition and the Expansion of Vice

While the intensified regulation of the border signaled a new level of government oversight in the lives of borderlanders who crossed the national line for both work and leisure, these modern border mechanisms were not able to eliminate illegal cross-border interactions. Alongside the expansion of the legal traffic in goods and people came illegal enterprises that benefited from the boomtown conditions in the industrial borderland. In many ways, the male-dominated, working-class character of the region helped to bolster economies based on drinking, gambling, and prostitution, and illicit cross-border connections brought Americans and Canadians across the national line. The massive expansion of these industries during the countries' experiments with prohibition, the very time when the federal governments were attempting to exact tighter controls on cross-border activities, demonstrates the limits to border enforcement. As more and more citizens engaged in economies stemming from illegal liquor smuggling, they openly challenged the lines separating licit and illicit activities and helped to shape public perceptions of the border communities for decades to come.

Local vice economies developed as early as the seventeenth century, when the French established a military post along the Detroit River. In his 1890 analysis of Detroit's early years, Silas Farmer argued that the fluid nature of male populations, cross-cultural trade between the French and the Natives, and the "semi-military character" helped grow local vice activities. According to Farmer, "there were men continually hovering about, occasionally for a length of time, whose presence made impossible the prevention of disorder."[46] The high number of single, unattached males and the complex networks of trade that developed around illicit goods and services like alcohol and commercial sex were in fact similar to that found in many frontier settlements.[47] The dynamics in the region changed with the imposition of colonial, and later national, jurisdictions and jurisprudence, and vice economies shifted to reflect the needs and desires of the community. As the towns and cities grew along the border region, so, too, did more organized forms of illicit industries, including saloons and brothels. Though these establishments came under periodic attack throughout the eighteenth and nineteenth centuries (in 1857, for example, Detroit residents set fire to the brothels in the city's tenth ward), many continued to operate relatively unhampered until the establishment of the first metropolitan police department in the city in 1865.[48]

Illicit economies rapidly expanded alongside the region's industrial growth, with cheap hotels, boarding houses, and saloons emerging to cater to the transient male population.[49] The gendered segregation of labor (which relegated immigrant and African American women to the lowest-paying jobs in the border cities) facilitated women's move into illicit forms of work, and many migrant women found employment in the hotels, saloons, and brothels that attracted the cities' working men.[50] In Detroit, vice districts developed on the Lower East side between the Detroit River and Gratiot Street, as many legitimate businesses expanded northward, leaving dilapidated structures in which illegal enterprises could flourish. This became known as the Potomac Quarter, "where one could allegedly find 'the worst species of outlaws'" or where "the vilest thieves, pimps, and cutthroats" operated. The city's vice districts were also explicitly racialized by the late-nineteenth century, with the development of "Niggertown" around Fort and Beaubien streets on the East Side.[51]

In the first two decades of the twentieth century, the wide-open nature of the border cities attracted vocal outcries from moral reformers who viewed vice as the unwanted byproduct of rapid industrial and urban growth. These antivice campaigns, which emerged as part of the Progressive Era obsession with solving the nation's urban problems through a combination of government intervention and public engagement, were successful at pushing for new laws that placed vice firmly within the jurisdiction of legal regimes.[52] While prostitution itself was never officially outlawed in Canada, the 1891 Criminal Code made it a crime to operate a bawdy house and to solicit sex in public places. Amendments in 1913 and 1915 widened these offenses to include living off the avails of prostitution (pimping) and other similar charges.[53] In the United States, prostitution was regulated by states and municipalities, though the federal government enacted the Page Act in 1875 and the Mann Act in 1910, which gave the federal government the power to regulate prostitution when it crossed state and national lines, and the Chamberlain-Kahn Act in 1917, which allowed the government to force suspected prostitutes to undergo medical exams.[54] Similarly, the Canadian and American federal governments outlawed narcotic drugs in 1911 and 1914, respectively, targeting users and traffickers in a series of laws designed to combat the evils of drug addiction.[55] In city after city, Progressive Era reforms tightened the laws governing vice activities, pushing participants into the realm of the criminal.

Ironically, it was the Progressive Era's signature campaign—the prohibition of alcohol—that led to a massive expansion of illicit activities in the border cities. Across the United States and Canada, temperance campaigns had followed similar trajectories in the first decades of the twentieth century, using the growing reform impulse to successfully push for bans on alcohol in local jurisdictions. By the teens, the growing power of the "dry" lobby had pushed many states and provinces to ban the sale, importation, and consumption of liquor. Ontario enacted prohibition at the provincial level in 1916. Soon after, in 1918 the Canadian federal government passed national prohibition, purportedly as part of the country's efforts at wartime resource conservation. Unlike the prohibition amendment to the American constitution, national prohibition in Canada was intended as a temporary measure and only in effect until "one year after the cessation of hostilities."[56] Ontario's prohibition laws remained on the books after the war but did not include a ban on producing and exporting liquor. As a result, by "1921, 'dry' Ontario had forty-four breweries, a dozen native wine plants, and nine distilleries. . . . Liquor exports continued, and during the 1920s, alcohol excise and taxes formed an important percentage of federal and provincial revenues."[57] As public opinion shifted over the course of the 1920s, so, too, did provincial policy. By 1927, the Liquor Control Act (LCA) overturned the Ontario Temperance Act and set up a system of government-controlled liquor distribution. The LCA established the Liquor Control Board of Ontario (LCBO), which was tasked with monitoring liquor stores; posting inspectors at distilleries, breweries, and wineries; and investigating businesses licensed to sell light beer.[58] This move would not only restructure the liquor trade in Ontario but also have a profound effect on neighboring American states.

Michigan, too, banned alcohol at the state level in 1916. Yet, as if to foreshadow the national experiment, there were clear troubles from the start. During the first month after the passage of the legislation, over 1,000 citizens had been arrested for trafficking in liquor. Much to the chagrin of local authorities, men and women intent on attaining alcohol for private consumption or to sell on the emerging black market had merely to travel to the neighboring state of Ohio, which remained a "wet" state. Even before the passage of nationwide prohibition, Michigan residents were entering the criminal justice system in large numbers, enforcement officers were overwhelmed with the new policing requirements, and illicit markets were rapidly expanding.[59]

With the official enactment of the Eighteenth Amendment in January 1919, the national border became a key player in the smuggling trade. Since Ontario could legally produce alcohol for export sales, shipping liquor out of the city of Windsor was protected by Ontario law. Boats bound for

"Cuba" regularly ended up docking on the American side of the Detroit River, where bootleggers unloaded the illegal commodity. With its close proximity to the large concentration of distilleries in southern Ontario and Midwestern cities like Detroit and Chicago, the Detroit-Windsor region became a primary site of smuggling between Canada and the United States. Some estimates suggest that four-fifths of the illegal liquor trade was conducted across the "Detroit-Windsor Funnel."[60] By 1929, smuggling, manufacturing, and distributing liquor had become a major industry in Detroit, second only to the automobile industry. The trade in illegal booze employed at least 50,000 people and grossed more than $300 million a year.[61] The number of blind pigs (illegal drinking establishments) increased rapidly throughout the mid-1920s, from about 7,000 in 1923 to about 15,000 in 1925. By 1928, that number stood at about 25,000, making Detroit "the wettest city in the United States."[62]

The growth of the illegal liquor trade shaped the relationship between borderland residents in contradictory ways. In the eyes of many Americans, Windsor gained a reputation either as a den of sin and debauchery or as a place of reprieve where people could quench their thirst unhampered by the long arm of the law. Reformers dubbed the Canadian border city "Windsor the Wicked" and the "Tia Juana [sic] of the North," the latter a reference to the perceived lawlessness growing in towns along the U.S.-Mexico border.[63] Reformers became increasingly vocal in their condemnations of Canada when Ontario passed the Liquor Control Act, a move that politicians, clergy, and reformers impugned as a "curse" on the Dominion and on their neighbors to the south.[64] Some went so far as to claim that the act, which required Ontarians to drink the legally purchased liquor in their own homes or hotel rooms, was promoting violence against women and children by hiding the evils of drinking away from the public eye.[65] Increasingly, Windsor took the blame for the booze-soaked streets of Detroit and the correlating moral degeneration that supposedly resulted. Percy Cromwell produced several sketches that depicted Windsor as the boozy devil on Detroit's shoulder. One drawing, "Here's Lookin' Atcha," pictures the "The Thirsty One" standing on the Detroit side of the river trying to refuse the larger-than-life beer being offered to him by his Canadian neighbor in Windsor.[66] The supposed lax moral attitudes of the Canadians across the river were thus framed as at best a thorn in the side of reformers intent on stamping out the liquor trade, and at worst the beginning of the downfall of otherwise temperate Americans who could not resist the wiles of the Canadian bootleggers and government-sponsored liquor dispensaries.

This Percy Cromwell cartoon, titled "Here's Lookin' Atcha," shows a more sinister Canadian man offering the temperate Detroiter a larger-than-life beer. (Percy W. Cromwell cartoons, ca. 1918–ca. 1932; Box 2; Folder 23. Courtesy of the Bentley Historical Library, University of Michigan)

The "wild tales of the northern border" that filled newspapers across North America did in fact attract countless Americans across the national line who wanted to enjoy Ontario's relatively lax liquor laws.[67] This was especially true after the passage of the Liquor Control Act. Beginning in the spring of 1927, Detroit became the "rendezvous of motorists northward bound," and resorts and hotels that stretched across the 300 miles separating Windsor and Niagara Falls were virtually sold out due to the influx of American customers. As one *New York Times* reporter observed, "Detroit streets are full of the dusty mud-spattered cars bearing license plates from the four points of the compass. States as far away as Kansas and Oklahoma have sent delegations. Apparently every tourist within a thousand miles turned toward the border by common consent during the last few days, just to open one more bottle without an apprehensive glance over the shoulder."[68] This excitement temporarily turned to disappointment when the Ontario government announced that it did not have enough permits to accommodate the massive crowds and would therefore have to delay opening the stores. One man from Salinas, Kansas, summed up his frustration: "Gosh," he told one reporter, "here I have been driving a week on the worst roads I ever saw, dodging the Mississippi flood and taking my vacation early so as to be on hand for this party, and they are not even ready. How can I wait around here? My crops need tending now and I've got to get back home. Guess I'll have to look up a bootlegger and hold my party anyway."[69] For many Americans near and far, the Detroit-Windsor region became a space where they envisioned they could evade the restrictive federal laws and enjoy a cold drink without risk of arrest. While the Salinas man returned home without experiencing the wide-open party he thought awaited him, within a couple of weeks the liquor stores were up and running, and Americans were regularly traveling to the region to purchase the newly legal spirits on the Canadian side of the border. During the Fourth of July holiday that summer, cars were backed up at the Windsor ferry docks for ten miles, and local police were busy directing Americans through the docks into the early hours of the morning. The prospect of legally purchasing and consuming liquor no doubt contributed to this massive holiday traffic jam.[70]

Canadian borderlanders were also split on the implications of the illicit industry. On the one hand, it was good business and brought an influx of capital into the growing region. A 1929 news report explained that the extremely lucrative trade could not be ignored by Windsor residents just because of a pesky constitutional amendment in the neighboring country: "Each Canadian town near Detroit is in the boom and boost stage and cannot afford to be reticent about an important industry merely out of respect" for the neighbor's laws. With "ferries running between Detroit and Windsor carry[ing] 20,000,000 passengers a year and approximately 1,000,000 motor cars," and a "great deal" of the passengers being American citizens from Detroit and elsewhere who traveled to Windsor to attend to their own bootlegging, there was little economic incentive among local Canadians to curb the trade.[71] Canadian government officials regularly

This postcard of Windsor's Ouellette Avenue was sent from an American woman to her children in Milwaukee, Wisconsin, in 1920. The back of the card reads, "Dear kids, I just came over here to get some beer and wish you were both [with me]." (Courtesy of the Southwestern Ontario Digital Archives, University of Windsor)

denied U.S. claims that they were the cause of the American Prohibition problem, arguing instead that it was their economic and legal right to continue selling spirits according to their own laws. As one Canadian newspaper proclaimed, "American prohibition is none of our affair. Liquor exportation is a business with us and we cannot be responsible for the failure or success of Uncle Sam's dry law. Our transactions are strictly legal and under the very close supervision of dominion and provincial police."[72]

Many local businesses went beyond simply defending their right to sell liquor—they openly courted America tourists in an effort to draw them across the national line. Newly built subdivisions across the border from Detroit and Buffalo put up billboards with slogans reading "Come to Canada and Enjoy Life!" Real estate values grew substantially on the Canadian side of the border, and the price of summer cottages skyrocketed.[73] New "super hotels" emerged, adopting slogans like "an electric refrigerator in every room" to attract Americans looking for comfortable places to enjoy their legally purchased drinks.[74] Building on the new business brought by the sales of alcohol, Windsor hotel owners, restaurateurs, and shop owners worked hard to promote Ontario as a "tourist Oasis" to pad their own yearly earnings.[75]

Not everyone, though, was thrilled about these new drinking tourists. Indeed, many Ontario residents also feared that the influx of Americans would bring an increase in crime and tarnish their reputation as a place of "peace, order, and good government." As one Ottawa paper lamented, "most Americans believe that all these rum-runners are Canadians. They see in this situation a band of armed 'Canadians' defying the American government. . . . The Dominion is gaining a reputation as the home and refuge of rum-runners and as a country that prefers the cash benefits of this traffic to co-operating in the one way deemed essential with the United States government."[76] Similarly, a *Montreal Gazette* article explained that, "because of its geographical position, Windsor is a difficult city to keep clear of offenders against the law, especially as regards gambling and illicit liquor-selling. Its nearest American neighbor, Detroit, is also having trouble with criminals, there having been a hundred murders there within a comparatively short time." According to the article, the close relationship between Detroit and Windsor facilitated this problem: "When the police there make war on thugs, some of the latter go over the border to Windsor in the hopes of making a living there by crime, so the authorities in the Ontario city have to contend with the outsiders as well as any Canadians there may be of the same brand."[77] Much to the chagrin of Canadian authorities, who tried to present their bordertowns as cities governed by law and order rather than vice syndicates, it was hard to counter the sensational stories about bootleggers, smugglers, and speakeasies circulating in communities across North America. While local business owners were able to profit off Windsor's wide-open reputation, many residents continued to worry that American bootleggers, gamblers, and mobsters would also invade their towns.

Whether one viewed the cities' positions along the national line as a benefit or a curse, by the late 1920s, it was impossible to deny the effects Prohibition was having on the bordertowns. While Windsor's illicit trade centered largely on alcohol and gambling, in Detroit the businesses of commercial sex, narcotics, and gambling developed hand in hand. Speakeasies, often accompanied by gambling and prostitution, operated in the basements of residences, garages, alleys, commercial buildings, and the back rooms of party stores and ice cream parlors across the city. The businesses built around blind pigs ranged from small-scale family affairs to profitable ventures run by organized criminals like the infamous Purple, Hallissey, Rubenstein, and O'Riordan gangs.[78] Across the city, Prohibition enabled the growth of what one *New York Times* article described as the "gray zone" of criminals—"the genial bootlegger, the prostitute, the professional gambler, the racketeer, the blackmailer, the extortioner, and, with them, the political grafter, the 'fixer,' the suave operator of bucket-shops, the smuggler, and the rest." These businesses operated somewhere in between the dangerous criminals that made up the organized syndicates and law-abiding citizens. Prohibition widened this gray zone by bringing even law-abiding citizens into contact with businesses run off the profits of illegal liquor sales.[79] In effect, Prohibition was blurring the line between licit and illicit activities in the border region and earned Detroit the dual image as both a thriving industrial center and a wide-open city of hustlers, gamblers, and prostitutes.[80]

The money flowing from the importation of Canadian liquor had a particularly profound effect on Detroit's African American community, and vice became increasingly intertwined with the economic and social lives of many of the city's black residents. Across Paradise Valley, a neighborhood that grew in conjunction with the Great Migration that brought southern migrants to the city, businesses were thriving from the influx of cash stemming from the illegal liquor trade. In his autobiography, Coleman Young (who would become the first African American mayor of Detroit in 1974) recalled the Prohibition Era as a time of "enthusiastic debauchery in which nothing on the street was what it seemed."[81] Young's family had moved to Detroit from Alabama in the early 1920s to escape the "social order of the Deep South." Like many black southerners who envisioned Detroit as the "land of opportunity," though, Young's family soon discovered that segregation, employment discrimination, and racial violence also shaped life in the northern city. Since the war, tensions between new migrant groups staking claims for housing, social status, and jobs in the city led to growing racial tensions. In fact, the very summer the Young family moved to Detroit, the Ku Klux Klan burned crosses in front of city hall—an event that seemed to have a formative effect on the five-year-old.[82]

Young's family had settled in the Black Bottom neighborhood, which was in the process of shifting from a neighborhood of predominantly European immigrants to a largely black neighborhood. In those early years, Young came to understand the important role that underground economies played in the segregated black community. He characterized the neighborhood as a "haven for hustlers of every stripe," due largely to the influx of cash and illicit activities sparked by Prohibition. His father held a series of formal jobs in the city, but he supplemented his fluctuating income through a range of illicit enterprises, including bootlegging and gambling. As Young explained, "With all of the little [informal] enterprises we had going on, our family was never indigent. We did particularly well during Prohibition, which can be said for all of the Black Bottom and Paradise Valley. I never saw such prosperity in the black community—hell, in the city—as there was then. The money was practically jumping from pocket to pocket in those days. If you weren't making any," he explained, "you either weren't trying or were inhibited by an unusual code of lawfulness."[83]

For men and women like Young, participating in illicit economies was about more than just making money. It also provided an avenue of social mobility wherein even the most marginal members of the community could work to attain social status and some level of respect. Following in his father's footsteps, Young himself began playing poker and selling bootlegged Canadian liquor to local blind pigs. "I basically had two role models in those days," he explained, "the hustlers, with their flashy clothes and money clips, and the Ford Mules . . . straggling home from work all dirty and sweaty and beat."[84] Here Young draws a stark contrast between the choice of realities he perceived open to him as a young black man growing up in the Black Bottom. He observed with great fascination and awe the earning abilities and consumerism enabled through participation in illicit markets. These individuals demonstrated both literal and cultural capital, with their incomes subsidizing and enabling their coolness, exemplified by their "flashy clothes." This is in clear opposition to his perception of men who held traditional blue-collar jobs, the "Ford Mules," who seemed to work endlessly for none of the cultural or financial payoffs afforded to the neighborhood hustler. Their clothes were dirty, and their bodies worn out as they "straggled" home from the factories, creating a rather unglamorous image. By participating in the illegal liquor trade and related enterprises, those who came to escape poverty and unemployment in the South might in fact find some solace.[85]

Many working-class women also participated in the illicit economy, engaging in prostitution and related activities as a way to counter their marginal status in the formal labor market. Though black and white prostitutes tended to work in different neighborhoods (the former in the Black Bottom and Paradise Valley, and the latter in four square blocks west of Woodward Avenue between the business district and Grand Boulevard), interracial prostitution became increasingly common during the Prohibition Era. Indeed, many black prostitutes serviced white clients as a way to make more money, since they could charge more for sex that crossed the color line in the highly segregated city.[86] In the city's downtown core, open solicitation became so common that everyone seemed know what was going on. As one former sex worker recalled, "Even the little brats ten and eleven years old know what we're doing and yell at us 'Hi, Babe! How much are you making today?'"[87] In her 1964 autobiography, Helen McGowan, a former prostitute and madam, similarly recalled the Prohibition years as the heyday of illicit economies in Detroit, where transactions took place out in the open and where women could make a living wage. As she explained, "A very popular girl then could earn with tips over two hundred dollars in a twelve hour period. . . . The prostitute [of the early 1960s] now makes far less than her older sister of the roaring twenties." Though McGowan acknowledged that some of this money had to go to madams, pimps, or to pay off the police, many women still retained enough to make a comfortable living.[88]

While recollections like those of McGowan and Young were likely influenced to some degree by nostalgia for a bygone era—and especially by the "roaring twenties" mythology that continues to shape North American popular culture—their accounts do affirm the extent to which illicit smuggling reshaped the economic and cultural lives of border city residents. The visible nature of vice on the cities' streets and the large amount of illicit capital flowing through even the poorest neighborhoods meant that for many men and women alike, illegal forms of moneymaking became a part of their daily lives. This was especially true for recent migrants from the South—black and white—who made their way to the booming region. In speakeasies, hotels, apartments, and other spaces throughout the cities' centers, the money from the illegal liquor trade enabled the growth of extensive vice industries in the region, earning the cities reputations as "the American Mecca of prostitutes," bootleggers, and gamblers and the "Tia Juana of the North."[89]

Hard Times: Repeal, Depression, and the Decline of Vice in the Borderland

The conditions that helped the Detroit-Windsor region earn the reputation as the "blackest hole of crime and vice in the United States" began to change in the 1930s, and the booming illicit economy tapered off because of several interrelated developments.[90] Perhaps the most direct factor was the repeal of American prohibition on December 5, 1933. Throughout the 1920s and early 1930s, the wet and dry lobbies had engaged in vocal debates over the efficacies of the Eighteenth Amendment and the Volstead Act (which provided mechanisms necessary to enforce Prohibition laws).

Ultimately, the dries could not stave off the realities that Prohibition had created a series of unintended effects, developments that soured even some of the policy's most ardent supporters. The growth of organized crime, corruption among public officials, an overwhelmed court system, increasing enforcement costs, and the willingness of persons from all backgrounds and classes to break the law all contributed to the growing power of the repeal lobby. Across the country, women, having recently won the vote, played a vocal role in the repeal effort. Many had in fact "come to the painful conclusion that the destructiveness of alcohol was embodied in Prohibition itself" and formed powerful groups like the Women's Organization for National Prohibition Reform.[91] Across the nation, by the early 1930s, efforts to fight the restrictive policy were drowning out the power of the dry lobby.

To many, the Detroit-Windsor region exemplified the worst elements of the Prohibition experiment. Residents on both sides of the border were particularly concerned with the rise of organized crime and the violence that accompanied it. By the 1930s, syndicates were not only running gambling, narcotics, and prostitution rings but also exerting pressure on legitimate businesses. Local business owners were subject to intimidation by racketeers who threatened physical violence or burned down the stores of those who would not cooperate. In 1925, Detroit business owners formed the Citizens Committee of Detroit, Inc. in an attempt to fight this intimidation, but their power was no match for the organized gangs.[92] Newspapers regularly reported on crime waves hitting the city, like in 1930, when in a two-week period "two taxi drivers were robbed and killed, two banks were held up, and two guards killed in a gunfight when a gang of bandits held up a Western Union."[93] Later that year, in the first two weeks of July, ten men were gunned down by gang members. On July 22, a popular radio host, Jerry Buckley, was slain in a hotel lobby off Woodward Avenue and Adelaide Street. These vicious and public murders sent shock waves through the community and earned the month the unsavory title of "Bloody July."[94] By 1929, Detroit had the highest murder rate in the country, averaging 18.6 murders for every 10,000 persons.[95]

Residents' fears about the growing crime rate in the Detroit-Windsor region were exacerbated by reports about corruption among the Border Patrol agents, the very people who were supposed to protect them from the violent gangs. In 1928, the federal government began an investigation into the activities of local Border Patrol agents, alleging that rumrunners had paid them more than $2 million in graft. The investigation found that corruption was rampant throughout the force, and as a result, the government discharged 100 of the 130 border agents and indicted 50 of them.[96] Public opinion of the Border Patrol sank even lower when gun violence escalated in the region. News reports claimed that violence was intensifying between rumrunners and border agents, explaining (with considerable exaggeration) that working in the Detroit-Windsor region was more difficult than "trench warfare in France."[97] On several occasions, shooting scandals tarnished the image of local enforcement officers. In some cases, Border Patrol agents were accused of shooting into the Windsor side of the border and endangering Canadian citizens. In other instances, border guards actually killed innocent bystanders, including a young boy embarking on a fishing trip on the Detroit River and an unarmed man driving his car in Niagara Falls.[98] By the early 1930s, local anger was "running high," and citizens held meetings to discuss what they saw as the gross power and negligence of the border agents tasked with patrolling the international line.[99] President Hoover's pleas to border city residents to blame this violence on the proper culprits—on the bootleggers and gangsters—rather than on enforcement agents, seemed to move few residents.[100] It was one thing to kill gangsters and criminals; it was quite another to endanger unarmed citizens of both countries. To many local residents, their safety was too high a price to pay for the moralizing legislation, and, on both sides of the border, local residents expressed relief when the failed experiment was finally repealed.

While repeal took the wind out of the sails of organized crime, illegal economies were also hampered by the Great Depression, which had the effect of bringing the boomtown conditions to a screeching halt. Given their reliance on industrial production, the cities of Detroit and Windsor were among the first to feel the devastating effects of the economic meltdown. In 1929, Detroit had produced more than 5.3 million cars; by 1931, that number dropped to about 1.3 million. By 1932, more than 223,000 workers had lost their jobs.[101] The segregated labor market and racist hiring policies in the city's factories made the jobless rate among African Americans more than double that of whites, creating widespread poverty among black working-class residents.[102] Windsor, because of its high concentration of industrial jobs and its reliance on American branch plants, also suffered devastating losses, attaining the highest jobless rate in all of Canada.[103]

The Depression also brought hard times for illicit industries, greatly reducing both the amount of capital circulating in informal industries and the number of customers willing to purchase what were increasingly considered luxury services. In his study of sex workers in the city of Detroit,

Wayne State University researcher Glen Seymour Taylor found that the terrible economic conditions throughout Detroit were particularly devastating for women working in informal economies. On the one hand, women, especially immigrant and working-class African American women, who had relied on low-paying domestic and service work in the city found even those jobs increasingly difficult to come by. More women therefore entered informal and illegal jobs like prostitution, hoping to make up what they had lost in the formal sector. This had the effect of pushing down the rates for prostitution and stretching the dwindling client base even thinner. In effect, there were more women working as prostitutes at the same time that there were fewer customers willing or able to pay for their services, bringing increased competition and depressed wages for women working in the city's leisure districts.[104]

The economic downturn also led to a reorganization of the prostitution industry. Throughout the 1920s, many women worked in what were known as "parlor houses." These spaces, usually run by madams, afforded women some form of protection from both customers and police officers. In return for a fee, the madam of the house would provide "safety, court aid, a room and occasional board."[105] As the number of prostitutes grew disproportionately larger than the number of available customers in the early 1930s, parlor houses began to disappear.[106] By the mid-1930s, women tended to pick up customers on the streets and service them in their apartment or "call-flats" that they shared, usually with one other woman. Women also began to use various other practices to attract customers, including "automobile prostitution, referrals through agents such as taxi drivers, restaurant owners, pool room operators, pimps, etc. and solicitation in blind pigs, cheap shows, etc."[107] The decline of parlor houses and the ascendancy of streetwalking, pimps, and work in private residences left many women more vulnerable to dangerous johns and the police.[108] With speakeasies closed, police cracking down on organized crime, and the pool of customers dwindling, the bustling nightlife that had sustained illicit industries like prostitution seemed to be a distant memory.

Finally, the slowing labor demands in the mid-1920s and the Depression years that followed led to a decrease in cross-border travel. As factory jobs became hot commodities among local workers, the U.S. government pushed to tighten border restrictions and bar Canadian workers from crossing the national line. Two lobbying groups were at the heart of this push: Detroit labor unions who wanted to bar Canadian workers and real estate developers who argued that suburban Detroit home sales were tanking because it was becoming easier to "live in Canada and ferry back

Two teenage sisters working as prostitutes off Detroit's Hastings Street in the 1930s. (Courtesy of the Walter P. Reuther Library, Wayne State University)

and forth to Detroit than to live in Detroit's crowded suburbs."[109] On April 1, 1927, despite vocal protests from the Canadian government, the U.S. Department of Labor passed Order 86, a border regulation requiring foreign-born Canadians to obtain visas to commute across the border for work. This was an unprecedented change, for never before had a group of citizens whose home domicile was in a foreign country been subject to immigration laws and restrictions while undertaking temporary travel (in this case, crossing the border for work on a daily basis).[110] As the Depression deepened in the 1930s, U.S. immigration officials canceled the Border Crossing Cards of thousands of unemployed Canadians. "Once these workers lost their commuting privileges," according to historian Thomas Klug, "they could not regain them because the State Department, citing the 'likely to become a public charge' exclusion rule, was reluctant to issue new immigration visas to allow them to look for work in the United States." In one highly publicized instance, two Detroit executives—one the president and general manager of the Detroit Motor Boat Company, the other the manager of Eaton Tower, the largest office building in Detroit—had their commuter status revoked. In the case of the latter, he had been commuting regularly from Windsor to Detroit for more than fifteen years.[111] This American shift toward isolationism not only helped turn Windsor into the city with the highest unemployment rate in Canada but also fueled a "Canadian wave of anti-Americanism" that dampened the social ties built over the preceding decades.[112] At least temporarily, connections across the "world's friendliest border" were hampered by fears over the dwindling economy, and, as a result, both licit and illicit businesses would suffer through the end of the 1930s.

Conclusion

The first decades of the twentieth century brought rapid and profound changes to the Detroit-Windsor border region that shaped the experiences of men and women who engaged in cross-border travel, work, and leisure on a daily basis. On the one hand, the industrial growth that transformed the cities of Detroit and Windsor at the turn of the century helped to build stronger cross-border connections between residents on each side of the river. Emerging as the busiest crossing point between the two nations, the local border region saw millions of tourists, immigrants, and commuters cross between the river's narrow shores. This subsequently, though, raised questions about how to filter out unwanted cross-border travel without hindering economic and diplomatic ties. Ultimately, the federal governments would attempt to answer this question by strengthening regulation at border checkpoints and by tightening immigration and visa restrictions for both short-term and long-term migrants. By the time the Ambassador Bridge and Detroit-Windsor Tunnel were built in 1929 and 1930, respectively, important legislative changes had effectively formalized the process of border crossing itself and had begun to make clear distinctions between those who were welcome to cross freely between Canada and the United States and those considered undesirable or questionable characters seeking to cross the border.

The contradictions inherent in the border's role as both a barrier and a crossing point became increasingly clear as large numbers of local residents began to participate in illicit industries. While federal officials attempted to enact strict crossing policies, borderlanders continued to try to make their own rules. By capitalizing on disparate liquor laws, many local residents and businesses built a thriving illicit cross-border culture in the 1920s and 1930s. In Detroit and Windsor, if factories were booming, so, too, were illegal trades based on alcohol, sex, narcotics, and gambling. The cities' reputations became national in scope, and Detroit and Windsor became closely associated with the vice and corruption—but also the excitement and flashiness—so closely intertwined in the "roaring" Prohibition years. Across working-class neighborhoods, and in speakeasies, blind pigs, brothels, and gambling dens, men and women engaged in underground, yet often visible, economies and subsequently helped to blur the lines between acceptable and unacceptable social interactions in the border cities.

While the repeal of Prohibition and the Great Depression brought troubled times for all border city residents—including the men and women who made their money in illegal trades—the period leading up to World War II had laid important foundations for the reemergence of illegal economies after the war. As boomtown conditions once again opened up as a result of wartime industries, and as both countries eased travel bans for both work and pleasure travel as the war came to a close, the border cities were once again poised to become the center of cross-border interactions between the United States and Canada. Though the liquor trade was firmly under the purview of the state and provincial governments in the postwar years, "Windsor the Wicked" and the "Detroit-Windsor Funnel" would reemerge in new forms, attracting countless men and women who wanted to experience the seedy side of these bustling postwar cities. For many, the Detroit-Windsor region would indeed deliver.

2

BORDER BROTHELS

Sex Tourism in the Postwar Borderland

On March 14, 1950, the *Windsor Daily Star* printed an article about the rise of prostitution in the Detroit-Windsor region following World War II. With language that ranged from outright condemnation to voyeuristic intrigue, the author reported on what was happening after hours in the Ontario border city:

> The "devil himself" lacks the persistency, defiance, the outright gall of bordell[o] and bootleg operators. . . . Keepers of bordellos hawk their fare in every bar; their prostitutes hustle on their own hook, give their lush earning to procurers, who are known in the trade as pimps. In backroom sin-bins sandwiched between factories and tumble-down shops . . . the favours of a prostitute can be enjoyed at a price. In reality it is a battle of wits; prostitutes and bootleggers vying for the payroll cash made available by the automobile industry and *suckers* from Michigan and Ohio.[1]

By the end of the 1940s, local newspapers were regularly publishing stories about the growth of vice in the border region. As the *Star* report suggests, these articles highlighted the visibility of prostitutes and their clients on the cities' streets, as well as the important role that cross-border business played in the local trade. For those reading the gripping headlines, it appeared that the wide-open nature of the border region was once again on the rise. What, many residents wondered, was responsible for this seemingly meteoric surge of vice, and what impact would it have on the local border community?

While articles like the *Star* report contained more than their share of sensationalism, telling lurid stories designed to sell newspapers, they also provided some insight into why illicit economies began to expand following the close of the war. Highlighting the rising incomes of many local residents, the in-migration of men and women into the region, and the growth of cross-border tourism, local reporters convincingly argued that vice was not an anomaly in an otherwise prosperous era. The rise of illegal economies was instead directly embedded in the economic and cultural changes that took place in the border cities during the early postwar years. By examining the rise of official forms of tourism in Detroit and Windsor during the 1940s and 1950s, as well as the illicit industries that flourished in the booming postwar environment, it becomes clear that—much like earlier decades—the culture of Detroit and Windsor was forged through a combination of legal and illegal enterprises, by socially sanctioned and stigmatized activities, in the cities' downtown neighborhoods.

Detroit and Windsor emerged from World War II as boomtowns, gaining international reputations as centers of prosperity and economic growth. City officials, boosters, and local businesses all worked to capitalize on the region's reputation as an up-and-coming industrial powerhouse and began to build a thriving tourist economy. Marketing the concept of a "border spirit," they asserted that the Detroit-Windsor border provided tourists with something other destinations did not: it offered travelers the chance to exercise their democratic freedom of movement by crossing between two peaceful and prosperous nations. By presenting the border region as a decidedly modern tourist destination, boosters and city officials helped to reaffirm the place of cross-border relationships in the political economy of the Detroit-Windsor region. In an era best defined by international barriers and iron curtains, the Detroit-Windsor region also became an important symbol of the close ties that increasingly linked these two free, democratic nations.

Borderlands by definition, though, are never easy to control, a lesson city officials should have learned from the tumultuous Prohibition Era. Despite their best attempts to present a sanitized picture of cross-border travel in which shopping, dining, and family-friendly activities were center stage, the cities' entertainment districts also catered to another crowd: the men and women who wanted to explore the underbellies of the border cities. In brothels, bars, and dance halls and on city streets, Americans and Canadians came together in search of illicit forms of entertainment and income. Building on the appeal of crossing multiple boundaries—sexual, racial, and spatial boundaries—participants in the local prostitution trade provided alternative visions of the "border spirit." Rather than framing postwar years as a time best defined by affluence and the ascension of middle-class values, as local boosters hoped to do, the rise of vice suggests that alternative social networks continued to flourish in the cities and shaped the relationship between borderlanders in intricate ways.

Tourism and Travel across "The World's Friendliest Border"

It is difficult to exaggerate the optimism expressed by local residents, business owners, and city officials in the years immediately following World War II. After more than a decade of economic depression, many felt the region was uniquely poised to ascend to new economic heights. Mobilization for the war effort had transformed vacant factories and assembly lines into mass producers of military hardware, airplanes, tanks, and other war machines. While initially automotive leaders had been reluctant to participate in the war effort, fearing such a move might hamper the industry's recovery that had taken place between 1939 and 1941, as well as out of a general distrust of Roosevelt's New Deal administration, within five weeks of the Japanese attack on Pearl Harbor the auto industry fundamentally shifted its attitude in favor of war production.[2] In the United States, major manufacturers began working closely with the newly created War Production Board (WPB) and the Supply, Priorities, and Allocation Board (SPAB).[3] This government-business alliance had a transformative effect across the country, especially the Detroit-Windsor region. In the Arsenal of Democracy, as Detroit came to be known, unemployment dropped to an impressive low. Between 1940 and 1943, the number of unemployed in the city went from 135,000 to a mere 4,000, and by 1947, manufacturing employment increased by 40 percent.[4]

Under Liberal Prime Minister Mackenzie King, who had recently won reelection under a campaign theme of national unity, planning and organizing wartime production similarly became a primary concern.[5] In April 1940, the Canadian federal government established the Department of Munitions and Supply, which would control the production of munitions for Canada and its allies. Across the country, factories began to boom, and unemployment dropped precipitously. In Windsor, the Ford Motor Company began producing trucks and carriers used to transport Allied troops in Italy, France, and North Africa. Almost half of the military vehicles made in Canada during the war came from Windsor.[6] Like their American counterpart, the rise in industrial production brought a steady decline in the unemployment rate in the city, and, by 1942, 74 percent of those employed in Windsor worked in industrial labor.[7] The large number of available jobs also fueled a massive in-migration of men and women from across North America. Drawn by the prospects of industrial employment and hopes of a better life, workers—particularly those from the American South and the mining districts of Canada—poured into the cities during the early to mid-1940s. By 1950, the populations of Detroit and Windsor had blossomed to more than 1.8 million and 120,000 people, respectively, making the region by far the largest urban hub along the Michigan-Ontario border.[8]

While the large influx of newcomers signaled the region's international boomtown reputation as cities where people could benefit from the free-flowing prosperity brought by wartime industries, the experiences of men and women who moved to the region also foreshadowed some of the challenges the cities would face over the following decade. Much of the cities' infrastructure was outdated, and both were woefully unprepared for the massive influx of migrants. Indeed, if the goal of securing a job in wartime factories seemed relatively attainable, finding a decent place to live was a much more difficult task. Detroit and Windsor would eventually plan federally and municipally funded housing projects, such as the Sojourner Truth Housing Project in Detroit, to deal with the housing crisis, but these would raise tensions over who should benefit from the new infrastructure—new migrants or settled residents, black or white residents? Wartime rationing, strains on transportation and recreational facilities, poor housing, lack of child care for war workers, and concern for loved ones abroad all exacerbated the tensions growing in the region.[9] For many, the war years would prove as stressful as they were promising.

The large influx of southern migrants, particularly black southerners, to Detroit, also fueled heightened social tension in the region. Defense industries met their production needs by employing a previously underutilized pool of workers, especially white workers from the Appalachian region and the Deep South, African Americans mainly from the South, and women workers from urban and rural Michigan.[10] Although the move of these groups into industrial and other wartime work constituted important gains, they were experienced unevenly and often at great cost. While many white women secured jobs in industries previously closed to them, for example, black women were often either still barred or given the least desirable positions.[11] Attempts to integrate factories and munitions plants sparked backlash and wildcat strikes from whites (dubbed "hate strikes" by the press).[12] Whites, aided by organizations like the Seven Mile–Fenelon Improvement Association, protested when African Americans attempted to move into previously white neighborhoods, as well as federally funded housing projects. In February 1942, when the first black residents attempted to move into the newly built Sojourner Truth Housing Project, local white residents violently resisted.[13] Tensions boiled over in 1943 with the outbreak of a "race riot" in the city. Sparked by a fight that broke out at a segregated beach on Belle Isle, the fighting spread across the streets of Detroit, leaving twenty-five African Americans and nine whites dead in its wake. Thus, while the war years brought important economic and demographic shifts to the region, they likewise sparked new debates about who belonged in the border region, who should be allowed to access the best services and neighborhoods, and how the cities would adjust at the war's end.

Local residents—like North Americans more generally—celebrated the war's end in September 1945 and quickly turned to rebuilding their communities in the postwar environment. After four long years of war, Detroit and Windsor residents experienced some important advantages as a result of the prominent role the region played in the war effort. For many local residents, the wartime boom conditions brought an overall net growth in their disposable incomes. The growing power of organized labor enabled unions to push for increases in wages and stronger contracts, as workers pushed back against attempts to curtail the gains they had made during war.[14] This was seen most dramatically nine days after the close of the war, when 11,000 Ford workers walked off their jobs in Windsor. The Windsor Ford Strike, which lasted ninety-nine days, established union security among the Ford workers and helped to solidify the power of organized labor in Canada.[15] By 1950, workers in Windsor earned more than industrial workers in any other Canadian city.[16] Similarly, in Detroit, the relatively high wages paid by the auto industry allowed many workers to attain an unprecedented standard of living.[17] Local residents were bombarded with advertisements promoting the perception that the average family was able to move up the social ladder, and as wartime turned into peacetime, moving up was increasingly framed as the ability to engage in conspicuous consumption.[18] Owning your own home and car and being able to purchase modern appliances and other products formerly considered to be luxury items became central to the definition of social mobility among the city's working and middle classes.[19]

The combined effects of expanding incomes, an increasing willingness to spend that income on consumer goods, and a new emphasis on mobility made the postwar environment ripe for the rise of another industry: mass tourism. Vacations, now formally mandated in labor laws and collective agreements, became a cornerstone of the North American way of life. Across both countries, businesses and governments attempted to capitalize on this new mandate for pleasure travel. Between 1950 and 1960, governments and private companies spent more than a billion dollars developing tourism and recreational facilities on both sides of the U.S.-Canada border.[20] Highways, motels, and roadside restaurants grew across both countries, catering to travelers from a broader socioeconomic background than in previous decades.[21] Tourism bureaucracies and businesses promoted an individual's ability to travel and spend money on the pursuit of pleasure as a true expression of the democratic nature of North American society.[22]

As the busiest crossing point between the United States and Canada, the Detroit-Windsor region had a unique stake in the postwar tourist boom. With the easing of pleasure travel bans put in place during the war, the number of cross-border travelers began to increase steadily.[23] Summer and holiday weekends were especially popular and brought thousands of Americans and Canadians across the national line. On the Fourth of July and Dominion Day (July 1) weekend in 1947, 20,000 cars passed through the border region, an increase of about 5,000 from the previous year.[24] By the end of the decade, more than 5.5 million people entered Canada via Windsor in a one-year period.[25] Given Windsor's position as a medium-size Canadian city next to the teeming metropolis of Detroit, many of the local businesses came to rely on these American customers. In the summer months, the streets of Windsor were "swarming with visitors," and "the gaudy tinsel of flashy new cars and other material possessions of free-spending visitors from the United States" were visible to anyone who walked the business section of the city.[26] Restaurants, nightclubs, and shops catered specifically to their American clientele, with some (like the prestigious Elmwood Club) relying on American customers for as much as 80 percent of their earnings.[27] Canadians also traveled to Detroit to shop, dance, dine, and enjoy the amenities available in the Motor City. They attended baseball (Tigers) and hockey (Red Wings) games and sought out "better stage shows, better musicals," and lively nightclubs in the neighborhoods that bordered Woodward Avenue. A growing number of Canadians also embarked on cross-border "shopping expedition[s]," purchasing cigarettes, tobacco, gasoline, household gadgets, appliances, and other goods that carried heavy sales or excise taxes in Ontario.[28]

In the border region, though, tourism was about much more than selling goods and services. It was also about marketing an experience in which travelers could cross between two distinct, yet integrated nations. It built

Looking north on Ouellette Avenue from the intersection of Park Street, the "principal business and shopping street" in Windsor, ca. 1960. (Courtesy of the Southwestern Ontario Digital Archives, University of Windsor)

Elmwood Hotel, Windsor, Ontario, Canada.

Bars, nightclubs, and restaurants, like the prestigious Elmwood Hotel, attracted large numbers of Americans in the late 1940s and 1950s. (Courtesy of the Southwestern Ontario Digital Archives, University of Windsor)

on what one booster called the "allurement of crossing borders, of exploring foreign ports of call" and was designed to showcase the unique relationship that developed in the borderland.[29] In 1951, a *Saturday Night* article enticed its readers to come and experience the distinctive relationship that linked Detroiters and Windsorites. The region had that "indefinable thing called the 'border spirit,' which cannot be understood unless experienced." According to the authors, the connection between city residents went beyond politics, economy, or culture—it was also an affective response to perceived ties across the national line. The article warned readers against mistaking Windsor as just a "baby Detroit," encouraging them to instead understand the "atmospherically complicated" nature of both cities. It was their ability to foster peaceful and friendly relations with one another, while also remaining culturally distinctive, that made them unique.[30]

Local businesses marketed this border spirit, simultaneously promoting the convenience of traveling between the two countries and playing on the national differences that made that travel exciting. This was particularly true in Windsor, as residents, businesses, and city boosters were careful to market the cultural differences that separated them from their larger American neighbor. Residents were encouraged to make a concerted effort to show visitors the hospitality and friendliness that supposedly defined the Canadian character. As a full-page article in the *Windsor Star* explained, the farmer, laborer, and everyday taxpayer benefited from the boom in the local economy brought by tourism: "our community is known for its courtesy and co-operation, and anything that can be done to make a visitor feel and know true Canadian hospitality becomes at once a duty for each and every one of us."[31] A similar report warned Windsorites against trying to act too "American" in an attempt to attract tourists across the border. Resources Minister R. H. Winters appealed to Canadians to "resist the temptation of becoming 'mere carbon copies' of Americans and to build up a greater tourist trade by a more distinctive Canadian culture." He complained that American flags, American news, and bad attempts at reproducing American food in local restaurants actually made Americans less likely to visit their northern neighbors because they wanted to feel as though they were "away from home."[32] By displaying their patriotism and civic pride, Windsorites would not only promote the positive elements of Canadian culture but also appeal to the tourist's desire to experience something new and exciting.

Boosters emphasized that Detroit and Windsor represented the most impressive elements of a modern, transnational region, one defined by industrial power and freedom of movement. The border itself functioned as the literal and symbolic expression of this modern borderland. As a 1954 Essex County Tourist Association radio broadcast explained to its listeners, visitors would instantly be in awe of the sight of the "immense towering bridge against a line of skyscrapers . . . by day the hum of motors, supplemented at night by the flash of headlights, as motor vehicles in vast numbers cross from shore to shore far above the waters of the Detroit River."[33] A 1959 advertisement claimed that visitors to the border region would be struck by the cities' industrial might and by the democratic principles exercised through the process of crossing between them. "Just stand on either of the bordering shores between Canada and the United States," the ad begged its readers, "and you can hear it loud and clear . . . the speedy hum of buses, cars, and trucks moving from one country to the other . . . the whistle of ships passing within an arm-wave of Windsor and Detroit . . . the cordial greeting to visitors from those who stand at the doorway of the two great countries." In these moments, visitors would hear the "sound of freedom and peace" and of "progress."[34] Ultimately, boosters predicted, the border region had a bright and prosperous future, a future "in which bootleggers, smugglers . . . and other publicity-getters" would no longer be welcome.[35]

The idea that selling the borderlands experience was good business and good politics was solidified in 1959 when the cities established the International Freedom Festival. The five-day-long celebration took place over the Dominion Day (later Canada Day) and Fourth of July holidays. The festivities included a wide range of family-friendly activities, culminating in the spectacular J. L. Hudson fireworks show over the Detroit River. The "atmospherically complicated" nature of the region was at the heart of the celebrations, "which were designed to dramatize to all people the existence of the world's longest unarmed border" and the "determination of the American and Canadian people to protect this freedom they enjoy." In the words of historian Julie Longo, the Freedom Festival was based on a "transnational strategy of cultural tourism that sought to construct the international border region as a unique place where one could experience both the physical manifestations of mutual values and the distinctive local and national cultures of the border cities."[36] It was designed to celebrate and sell the border spirit.

The festival organizers' marketing strategies suggest that they believed cross-border travel and tourism had important implications well beyond the local community. It was also a way of promoting a "North American" way of life based on freedom through consumerism and mobility. As the headline of one advertisement in the official Freedom Festival booklet explained, the Detroit-Windsor region was a "gateway to another land— where the citizen's only passport is his auto registration." The ad featured a photo of cars crossing the Ambassador Bridge. Underneath this image the text read, "Strangers of the Detroit-Windsor area . . . are sometimes just a little surprised at how freely we pass between nations. The barrier at the tunnel or bridge looks like a toll-gate and the greeting is a friendly question about one's birthplace. The passage is more dramatic because it is so serene." The ad continued, "Such confidence between nations is uncommon, but then, ours is an uncommon friendship, built on the common principles of freedom-loving people."[37] That they were both freedom-loving peoples made this simplicity possible—all they needed was a driver's license to be free to experience the excitement of traveling across the peaceful border landscape.

The Freedom Festival also emphasized the larger political objectives of cross-border tourism, adopting Cold War rhetoric about iron curtains and arms races to contrast the peace and prosperity along the U.S.-Canada border with communist nations abroad. An advertisement by the Chrysler Corporation featured a sketch of the cities of Detroit and Windsor tied together by the Ambassador Bridge. Larger-than-life-size businessmen in suits stand on each side of the river, embracing in a friendly handshake across the border. Below the caption reads, "How to Bridge a Border: A Lesson to the Whole World."[38] The 1961 booklet featured the same drawing, with the caption reading, "Our Only Show of Arms."[39] The booklets were filled with similar slogans, such as "The Spirit of Freedom knows no boundaries," "Hands across the border bring better business to both sides," and "A Bridge, Not a Curtain."[40]

Thus, by the late 1950s, tourism and city boosters had solidified a transnational travel narrative in the Detroit-Windsor region that emphasized the importance of cross-border friendship within the global Cold War environment. Within this formulation, by crossing the national line and patronizing shops, hotels, restaurants, and entertainment venues in the modern border cities, Americans and Canadians were engaging in political acts that bolstered the power of these democratic, free societies. The border spirit was not about muting the cultural differences between local residents; it was about embracing and celebrating them. In their cross-border transactions, average citizens became cultural brokers, and their seemingly innocuous acts of patronizing restaurants across the national line or purchasing duty-free goods became symbols of hope and prosperity in a time of global uncertainty. In this way, the ties that bound Detroit and Windsor residents benefited not only the border communities—they had the power to positively affect all who came to experience the unique environment in the border region.

Sex and Illicit Tourism in the Border Region

While city boosters like O. Mary Hill argued that postwar prosperity would eliminate the unsavory elements that plagued the cities' histories—the "bootleggers, smugglers . . . and other publicity-getters" of the previous decades—the increasing visibility of illicit leisure and entertainment that emerged by the late 1940s made it clear that this was far from the case. Amid the booming city streets, the tourists and commuters crossing the border, and the glittering skylines of Detroit and Windsor, illicit forms of cross-border travel also flourished. Sometimes hidden behind broken buildings and abandoned factories and sometimes out in the open for all to see, vice drew men and women who wanted to discover the underbellies of the border cities. Local vice economies united a variety of interrelated enterprises, ranging from blind pigs, dance halls, and pool rooms to after-hours clubs, numbers running, and illegal drug sales. Chief among these was prostitution, an industry that expanded as the wartime boom brought people and capital into the region.

In Windsor, the majority of the women working as prostitutes during the 1940s and early 1950s had migrated to the city from across Canada. Many of the women had been working in service, domestic, and unskilled positions—as waitresses, cashiers, and low-level factory workers—before making the decision to move to the region. Hoping that they could make more money through illicit means or through a combination of legal and illegal jobs, women came to the city from as far away as Vancouver and New Brunswick, suggesting that the city's reputation was national in scope.[41] As one *Star* article explained, "Prostitutes are attracted to Windsor because they hear of it as a sort of boom town. . . . The city also, because of the fact that industrial wage earning is high . . . attracts women of loose morals." One woman who moved to Windsor from Winnipeg in 1943 put it more bluntly: she came in search of "green fields" and to make her share of the local profits.[42]

While women moved to Windsor from across Canada and occasionally from the United States and the United Kingdom, French Canadian migrants accounted for as many as a third to half of those working in the trade by the end of the 1940s.[43] This was sparked, in part, by a crackdown on vice that began in the city of Montreal in 1946. After public accusations of police corruption and laxity in the city's enforcement of moral offenses, the Montreal Police Department began raids on brothels and rooming houses. This had the effect of temporarily displacing the city's sex workers, a number of whom made their way to Windsor. As a region with a historically high French population, and one that was rumored to be teeming with men looking to spend their money, it became a desirable place for those looking to "get out of the heat."[44] Windsor was also the terminus of the Canadian National railway line that traveled through Montreal and Toronto, making it relatively accessible for working girls on the move.

During the 1940s, in-migration also shaped the sex trade on the American side of the border. The majority of women who migrated to Detroit were from the rural South and part of what historian James Gregory has termed the Southern Diaspora.[45] Like those who worked in the formal economy, white women tended to come from the Upper South, particularly Kentucky and Tennessee, and African American women were largely from the Deep South, from Mississippi, Alabama, and Georgia. In some cases, women moved in search of formal employment but found the illegal trade either more profitable or more readily available. Still others met madams and working girls in southern cities and received contacts for their entry into the trade in the North.[46] There is some evidence that Canadian women crossed the national border to work on the American side, which at 1.6 million residents in 1940 was a big metropolis compared to Windsor's 100,000, though overall women tended to remain on the side in which they held citizenship. This is due in part to the added regulation that women faced at the border, as immigration laws had long barred women suspected of prostitution from crossing the national line.[47]

If rumors of free-flowing money and an abundance of jobs initially brought women to the border region, their decisions to work in illegal trades also signaled the gender segregation of labor that developed as the war came to a close. Although Canadian and American women made some important gains during the war and were able to move into manufacturing and other jobs formerly held by men, many were laid off from their positions at the war's end to make room for returning soldiers.[48] The mayor of Windsor, in a 1946 public address, called on married women to voluntarily leave their positions so that deserving young veterans could once again fulfill their proper roles as breadwinners.[49] By the late 1940s, women's employment options on both sides of the border were once again largely limited to pink-collar, low-paying, or temporary positions. By 1950, a third of all women working in the formal sector in the Detroit area were employed in clerical positions, followed closely by service jobs and semiskilled machine operatives.[50] For African American women, the employment situation was even more dismal, and by that same year 40 percent of all black women were once again working as domestics.[51] For women struggling to make ends meet at the lower levels of the economy, prostitution became a viable option. As one Detroit woman recalled, "Many of the women, they couldn't get jobs. Rather than go to some suburban white woman's kitchen and get on her hands and knees and scrub, they found it" more profitable to make money in the city's sex trade.[52] A Canadian sex worker echoed similar sentiments. Why, she asked a journalist, when you are making a decent living as a sex worker and living in a nice apartment, would you take a job "selling stockings [in a retail shop] at $35 a week?"[53] For some, illegal ventures not only seemed to make sense financially but also provided more freedom and flexibility than scrubbing floors or working retail for minimal wages.

While migrant women in search of work fundamentally reshaped the nature of the local sex market, they were not the only ones on the move. On both sides of the border, male customers who traveled from other cities, states, and provinces made up a growing percentage of their customer base. This was particularly visible in Windsor, where, after travel bans were lifted in 1943, Americans began to make up more than half of those arrested in the city's bawdy houses.[54] Local news reports claimed that by the end of the decade there were more than forty brothels in the city and that the illegal establishments relied on American customers for as much as 95 percent of their business.[55] Perhaps not surprisingly, the majority of male patrons came from Detroit and its surrounding suburbs. Yet, men from states as far away as New York, Wisconsin, Kentucky, Pennsylvania, North Carolina, Texas, and California were among those arrested in the city's bawdy houses.[56]

Windsor's sex industry catered to its American clientele, providing convenience and affordability just a short car or bus trip across the river. Once through border inspections, American men were often met by touts waiting near the bridge or tunnel, handing out business cards, and directing them to particular brothels. In 1948, for example, two Detroiters pled guilty to being in a disorderly house, explaining to the magistrate that they "had come across to Windsor on Saturday night and had been approached by a man who took them to the [bawdy] house on Elliott Street."[57] The city did not have an official red-light district, but brothels were openly run out of houses within the downtown core. On streets like Brandt, Mercer, Pitt, and Tecumseh, seemingly quiet neighborhood homes by day turned into booming businesses at night. As one retired police detective recalled, "One of the most famous bawdy houses was right behind the arena at 359 Brandt. . . . [T]hat old gal she had business cards and maps and everything. I can remember such a line up there on weekends, they would go in and pay their money and they would have to wait out in the street with their chit, and then they would be called in." One woman, frustrated by the chaos ensuing outside the brothel in which she worked, blatantly told the cops as they passed by that they had "better shut [the brothel] down or start directing traffic!"[58] Police laxity became a common complaint among many local city residents, who were frustrated by the brazenness of these illegal businesses. One *Star* article even claimed that there was a brothel operating openly on Goyeau Street, "within half a block of the police station."[59]

Windsor brothels operated as part of an expansive vice constellation, with even legitimate businesses courting the dollars to be made off American tourists. Hotel owners, bar owners, and taxi drivers played crucial roles in connecting out-of-town clients with a range of illicit services. Working women patronized hangouts like the Oriental Café and the Border Public House, where they would mingle, flirt, and arrange transactions at nearby brothels or hotels.[60] One such establishment was the Blue Water Hotel, which served as both a watering hole and a crash pad for out-of-towners intent on a good time. Undercover agents from the Liquor License Board of Ontario (LLBO) kept detailed reports of the goings-on there, which ranged from coed mingling in the barroom (a violation of the LLBO regulations) to open solicitation. In March 1951 alone, inspectors made six unannounced visits to the hotel, reporting that "conditions were very bad," with the women's barroom "filled, both afternoon and evening," with prostitutes. Reports of customers staggering around drunk, "raucous" singing around a poorly played piano, and coed mingling and dancing were common at the Blue Water and other hotels and bars in the downtown core.[61] There Canadian and American men and women could meet, enjoy drinks together, and solicit sexual services with the tacit acceptance of the establishments' owners. The ease with which these unofficial tourists could find the illicit services they desired and the growing visibility of the trade on city streets prompted Windsor magistrate Arthur Hanrahan to assert that the city was destined to become a "border brothel for Detroit."[62]

Detroit, though, had its own booming commercial sex trade, one that also relied on the influx of customers into the city. Given the large population of Detroit, Canadian visitors made up a comparatively small percentage of customers in the city's sex trade, yet they still had a noticeable presence. During the 1940s and 1950s, Canadians were by far the largest

The Blue Water Hotel was a favorite hangout for sex workers as well as American tourists. (Blue Water Hotel, Windsor [between 1927 and 1961], RG 36-8, barcode B335026, © Archives of Ontario, 2015. Reproduced with permission)

number of non-U.S. offenders arrested on prostitution charges.[63] The fact that these numbers reflect those arrested and booked rather than the number of people actually engaging in prostitution suggests that although they were far from the majority of customers, Canadians had a visible presence. As Joe Zaneia (whose family owned the Majestic Theater in Detroit) recalled, in the city's swinging north end, "Canadians would raise holy hell [on the weekends]. . . . Then on Sunday morning they would end up back in Windsor and go to church, saying, 'I'm never going back to that Sin City.' But they were back [there] the next week."[64] In Detroit, Canadians hoping to circumvent Windsor's blue laws, which mandated that places of entertainment remain closed on Sundays, as well as liquor laws that shut down the city's bars by 10:30 P.M., could drink, dance, and purchase illicit services well into the early hours of the morning.

If Windsor's sex trade functioned largely as a cross-border business, Detroit's became a distinctly urban trade that relied on the city's status as a major metropolitan center. Toward this end, American men from other suburbs, cities, and states were a key customer base for the city's working girls. Though Detroit lacked an official red-light quarter, prostitution took place across the city's expansive entertainment districts, making it easy for tourists to find the services they desired. Prostitutes often worked the streets that bordered the famed Woodward Avenue, hoping to draw customers from the large crowds of visitors who came each night to enjoy the city's many downtown hotspots.[65] Brothel-based prostitution and street-walking were also common on streets that separated Detroit from the neighboring suburbs of Royal Oak, Highland Park, Ecorse, and Hamtramck.[66] These spaces reflect both the urban nature of the trade and the fact that many of their customers crossed into Detroit from nearby cities and states. As one local community group noted, there was an "appalling number of prostitute-seekers, many of whom can be observed driving autos with out-of-state license plates, who prowl the inner city streets [of Detroit] on weekends."[67] Just as Americans crossed the national border into Windsor for illicit leisure, so, too, did tourists prowl the streets of Detroit in search of sexual pleasure and urban adventure.

Detroit's sex trade relied on a range of people and businesses that helped visitors solicit sexual services in the city. In bars, jazz clubs, and dance halls that bordered Woodward, illegal transactions took place under the cover of legal forms of leisure. The city's three taxi-dance halls—Tree Studios, the Hollywood Ballroom, and the Trianon Ballroom—were located within two square blocks along Woodward in an area full of tourists.[68] At the halls, men would purchase tickets and exchange them for dances with women of their choice. Occasionally the halls would hold "costume parties" in which the workers would dance with the men wearing "no more than a 'strip-tease entertainer.'"[69] Often referred to as "pink-light districts," the halls blurred the line between risqué commercial entertainment and outright prostitution by creating public spaces in which women and men could exchange a wide range of sexualized services. Legally, these were limited to dancing and flirting between workers and patrons. Open solicitation, though, also took place, and women sometimes serviced men in the back rooms of the clubs or made arrangements to meet their customers off-site after work.[70]

In 1948, a reporter from the *Chicago Tribune* embarked on an investigative mission to find out whether Detroit lived up to its wide-open reputation. After an evening of gambling at bars off Woodward (within close proximity to the police station, he noted), the reporter ended up at a mixed-race "Black and Tan" bar. There he listened to the five-piece band and inquired of one of the patrons, "Where is there to go for the romantically inclined at such an hour?" He was taken to a building where for an hour he watched taxicabs drop off customers and pick them up a short while later. He was unable to get in because the brothel was "only taking its old list" of regular customers that night. His unofficial tour guide then drove him to a hotel where he was told he could get a room for $2.50 a night and the bellhop would set him up with a girl. If it was not after-hours, the man explained, they could have hit up the taxi-dance halls, where he would have "no trouble" finding the services he desired.[71] This type of open solicitation made it easy for men from outside the city to locate places where they could purchase illicit sexual pleasure. In the city's core, prostitution, gambling, and drinking went hand in hand, enabling visitors to participate in multiple forms of entertainment simultaneously.

While prostitution took place in neighborhoods throughout the downtown core and along the city limits, Detroit's working-class black neighborhoods hosted a disproportionate share of the illicit trade. Hastings Street in the Paradise Valley neighborhood continued to function as a center of vice throughout the late 1940s. Many local residents, though, noted the changing nature of the East Side district, which slowly saw its status as the center of black business (both legal and illegal) slipping away. As the editor of the black-run *Michigan Chronicle* declared in 1946, "No longer is the Valley the gay, charming, and alluring young lady she once was, instead she is a withered, ugly old hag who no one likes and who everyone is beginning to forsake for a younger, more beautiful companion."[72] Those "younger companions" were emerging on Detroit's West Side, where the influx of large numbers of black migrants from the South helped transform all-white neighborhoods into largely black communities. The Twelfth Street neighborhood, a formerly Jewish community that attracted large numbers of black migrants, began to fill the role once held by Hastings Street. Jazz clubs, bars, and other spaces of entertainment began to emerge and, along with them, illicit economies.[73] This spatial transformation correlated with a shift in the demographics of women working in the city's vice trade. White women had made up the majority of sex workers in the city through the end of the 1930s, but by the mid-1950s, African American women accounted for more than half of those working in the trade.[74] As one contemporary sociologist explained, "The 'area' of the streetwalking prostitute is, of course, the area commonly called the slums. The percentage of Negro [prostitutes] per Negro population living in these areas is greater than the corresponding percentage of whites."[75] The fact that many of their customers had come to Detroit from other suburbs and cities began to highlight the increasingly complex social role that vice played in neighborhoods across the city. Prostitution would not only challenge the lines between licit and illicit activities but also come to reflect the contested meaning of race, space, and community in the border region.

Pushing Boundaries in the Postwar Sex Trade

Although boosters attempted to distinguish between licit and illicit economies, framing them as wholly separate ventures, in many ways both depended on fantasies of spatial and cultural difference. Like official definitions of the border spirit, vice was about selling affective experiences. It was about exploring new spaces, experiencing pleasures, and engaging in interactions that one might not have access to at home. Vice, though, also pushed the bounds of social interactions in important ways. At the center of its appeal was the commodification of illicit sexual pleasure, which allowed participants to cross sexual, spatial, and racial boundaries simultaneously. Contemporary reports emphasized that the trade allowed customers to purchase illegal services as easily as they would any other form of entertainment. As one *Windsor Daily Star* article explained to its readers, the Canadian border city attracted so many customers because it was a place where "anything in the way of diversions for the 'tired businessman'" was available. There, men had their choice of women "who were typed like brands of whiskey. Some good, some bad. You get what you pay for."[76]

Framing women's sexual labor as a readily available commodity ran counter to normative conceptions of healthy sexuality that developed in the early postwar years. In an attempt to achieve a sense of normalcy after years of depression and war, many North Americans began to place a growing importance on the home, family life, and "traditional" gender roles, touting the heterosexual, monogamous marriage as the bedrock of society.[77] The renewed emphasis on marital sex and family life meant that nonmarital sexual expression, which had gained a degree of acceptance between the 1920s and the 1940s, once again came under attack by reformers intent on asserting a Cold War moral order. *Deviance*, a term linked to the concept of sexual perversion, dominated psychoanalytic theory, marriage manuals, and popular representations of sexual relations, helping to establish strict lines between normal and abnormal interactions. Prostitution, homosexuality, premarital sex, and masturbation were all framed as specific social threats and therefore publicly condemned by psychologists, social workers, politicians, and moral reformers. As contemporary experts warned, prostitution, in which sex was "largely indiscriminate, without affection, and frequently anonymous," was "a severe deviation from the explicit or stated sexual mores . . . of American society."[78] It was, in short, in direct violation of the social codes that upstanding North Americans were supposed to hold dear.

While experts denounced prostitution as a dangerous activity that catered to the dark side of human sexuality, the appeal of purchasing stigmatized activities drew many customers into these exchanges. As early as the 1920s, researchers working for the Social Hygiene Association in Detroit noted that prostitution provided an outlet for what they considered to be deviant sexual practices. One investigation of prostitution in the city found that "perversion" was "extremely prevalent" in the local sex trade. In fact, the investigators declared that there were far more perversions in the Detroit sex industry than in any other American city, in part due to the city's wide-open nature that arose during Prohibition. For an additional fee of fifty cents to two dollars, women would perform these sexual acts, which nine times out of ten meant "French" or oral sex.[79] Sociologist Glen Seymour Taylor's 1933 interviews with local working women similarly identified oral sex as the most commonly performed "perversion," and the researchers noted the frequency with which women agreed to perform "French" sex for the price of a 'straight trick.'"[80]

By the 1940s, the perception that men could pay women to perform deviant sexual acts was deeply entrenched in the trade. Sex workers were keenly aware that the illicit nature of these exchanges drew customers in, and many worked hard to capitalize on this appeal. In her autobiography, Helen McGowan explained that she offered "frenching, straight, and fancy screwing," all to satisfy the needs of individual customers. McGowan's recollections—salacious by contemporary standards—described a wide range of requests made by her customers, which included woman-on-woman sex, rape fantasies, urophilia, role-playing, voyeurism, and group sex. One regular customer, for example, paid her to "snap his sex organs with a towel many times until the penis and testicles were red and swollen." Another man would bring an outfit of a ten-year-old girl with him and have the prostitute don the clothing while pretending to resist his sexual advances. Others still paid to just watch, like her customer of three years who hid in her closet and observed as she gave other men "vigorous-screwing[s]." As McGowan explained, "Not being a psychologist, I never attempted to analyze why a man wanted to do this or that to satisfy his sex wants. All I knew was that if a customer used my body without harming me it was all right with me and it didn't matter how wild the request."[81]

McGowan's autobiography speaks to some of the larger trends that shaped women's experiences in the local trade, offering important insight into the industry from the perspective of someone who actually worked within it. She describes how she got into the business, her attitudes toward her work, and her interactions with customers, pimps, and police. Born January 23, 1911, in Malden, Missouri, McGowan was the daughter of poor white sharecroppers. She moved north to Flint, Michigan, at the age of fifteen to escape the shame of an unwanted pregnancy (and correlating rumors that the father was a black man). She lived there with her sister for a brief period, but when her brother-in-law began making sexual advances, she was forced to again leave town. McGowan made her way to Chicago, where she worked a series of low-paying service jobs for several months. Frustrated with the lack of work options available for a poor, uneducated young woman, she hitched a ride to a place she heard was full of opportunities: the Motor City. There she befriended a young woman working as a streetwalker and decided to give prostitution a try. As McGowan explained, "I was sick of poverty, sick of being kicked around, and here was a chance to rise in the world, to become respectable, for respectability, I had learned, was mainly a matter of money."[82]

Over the next thirty years, McGowan worked at all levels of the industry. She began by picking up customers on the streets, moved to brothel-style prostitution, became a madam in charge of several of her own houses, and ultimately spent several years in the Detroit House of Corrections. Through these various experiences, McGowan came to view the sex trade not as a dangerous scourge inhabiting the nation's cities, but instead as an important form of both labor and entertainment. For some of the women she worked with, selling sex offered an avenue out of abject poverty. This was especially true for her employees who had moved from the rural South, where poverty rates could reach as high as 80 percent.[83] While McGowan is careful to detail the very real dangers these women faced—including harassment by police, violence at the hands of customers and pimps, and drug and alcohol addiction—she also frames their decisions to work in the trade as rational choices. In McGowan's estimation, her business catered to working-class clients in Detroit, the "hundred-dollar-a-week boys," providing important social outlets for customers and much-needed income for workers.[84]

Throughout the text, McGowan refers to the political motivations behind her decision to write about her life. The author makes it very clear that she sees the problem not in prostitution, but in prostitution's illegal status. Citing the wide range of desires among seemingly ordinary men, she explains that she was "convinced that most of these deviants would be a menace to society if they were baulked in their perversions. My house offered a comparatively harmless outlet to their abnormal desires. A few were as normal-appearing as your bank teller. Remove all prostitution and the streets of Detroit, or any other city, would be more fearful after dark."[85] Though couched in contemporary language that reinforced binary categories of normal and deviant sexuality, McGowan's assessments also demonstrate that participants saw prostitution as a means through which they could act out their sexual fantasies, especially ones that fell outside the normal categories of proper sexual behavior. Despite the sometimes self-righteous tone of her memoir (indeed, she tends to position herself as the savior of both the girls who ended up at her houses and the customers who just needed some comfort and affection), the way she chooses to convey the social meaning of prostitution to her readers is significant. For McGowan, this was an important service that catered to the realities of human sexual desire. It was both a job and a source of entertainment, and as such it played an important role in the lives of both sex workers and their customers.

Other contemporaries noted the social role that prostitution played in the border cities, providing opportunities for otherwise unacceptable forms of sexual intimacy. Mackie C. Johnson, a former street cop in Detroit, recalled that he was always "fascinated" by what he saw on the street. One case in particular stood out in his memory. He used to see a woman, who he assumed was between the ages of sixty and seventy, "hanging out on the streets" of Detroit in the early hours each Sunday. Though well-dressed, the woman was up too early to be attending local church services. He was shocked when one day he saw a young, attractive man stop and solicit her services. Dumbfounded, Johnson approached the woman, explaining that it was "really amazing" that someone her age would attract such a customer. The woman's response to the young cop was telling: "That's what's interesting about our society," she explained to him. "Sometimes people are attracted to the older folks."[86] Like McGowan, the woman pointed out that sexual desires were diverse and sometimes surprising. What Johnson considered beyond the normal bounds of sexual intimacy—in this case, a young, attractive man paying for sex with an older woman—was precisely what enabled women to make a living in the trade. Pushing normative boundaries was part and parcel of the business.

In the border cities, deviance took on a spatial meaning, as entertainment districts gained reputations as places where out-of-towners could pay to engage in a wide range of sexual acts. Part of this experience was the actual process of crossing the border, which contemporaries noted often made travelers feel they could engage in activities they might not do in their hometowns. The 1950 *Saturday Night* article that described the "border spirit" in Detroit and Windsor also argued that Americans and Canadians "in search of sin" made up a substantial portion of travelers crossing between Detroit and Windsor. As the authors explained, "When there is a raid on a bookie, bootlegger, or bawdy house, a sizeable percentage of the clientele hails from the neighbor city." It was, according to the journalists, the intrigue of crossing into a new space for otherwise unseemly activities that brought these "legions of afterdark" across the borderline.[87] A 1946 *Windsor Daily Star* editorial put it more bluntly: "Windsor is a bad spot for sex perverts, because in addition to the local rash of perverts there are the ones who cross the river from Detroit seeking greener pastures."[88] The anonymity, excitement, and appeal of "doing bad" in urban vice districts could also be compounded when they crossed the national line separating the border cities. For some tourists, greener pastures awaited them on the other side.[89]

Prostitution also drew explicitly on the appeal of crossing racial and ethnic boundaries and of engaging in otherwise stigmatized interactions in the segregated border region. In Windsor, the fact that many prostitutes were not only Canadian but also *French* Canadian added to the allure of the city and served as a clear marker of difference between tourists and locals. Requests for French-style sex predate the postwar years, but the association between French women and prostitution was solidified in the wartime environment. The American military's antiprostitution campaigns often focused on the supposed hypersexual nature of French women, warning soldiers and civilians about the dangers of "pick up" girls and other women of "loose morals."[90] Local papers' discussion of the large number of French women working in Windsor's vice districts was likely not lost on their American readers. In the words of one former customer, Windsor's French women "were beautiful, rob you as soon as [they] look at you, and *of course* they performed well in bed."[91] It turns out one did not need to go abroad to meet women of "loose morals"; French Canadian women could fulfill this fantasy for American men living near the border region.[92]

Yet Windsor's sex industry was not open to all Americans. With the exception of three women, everyone arrested on prostitution charges between 1945 and 1960 was listed in the police registers as "white."[93] This is significant given that Detroit's African American population more than tripled during this period, making up almost 30 percent of the population by 1960.[94] Clearly, though crossing the national border enabled white men to traverse sexual, moral, and legal boundaries, it did not offer men of color the same possibility. In fact, the number of American men arrested in brothels in Windsor began to increase in 1943, correlating with riots that took place in downtown Detroit. For many, the riot was a reminder that even seemingly harmless activities like hanging out on a beach could turn deadly in a city where racial tensions were running high.[95] In one sense, it appears that the Windsor sex trade was a form of white flight, wherein white Detroiters could enjoy the comforts of white male privilege without the overt challenges to this position that took place in the racially charged city of Detroit.

It would be a mistake, though, to view the segregated nature of Windsor's sex trade as simply a response to racial tensions on the American side of the border. The whiteness of the illicit industry also demonstrates the strong presence of de facto segregation in the Canadian city. Demographically, Windsor was a predominantly white town, with African Canadian and Chinese residents making up less than 1 percent of the total population in the postwar years.[96] Though racial discrimination in public accommodations was officially outlawed at the provincial level in 1953, for minorities living in Windsor, segregation in housing, employment, and entertainment continued to be a daily reality.[97] African Canadians were often turned away from the city's bars, restaurants, and nightclubs in what were often humiliating confrontations between would-be customers and business owners.[98] When one Windsor resident tried to take his wife for dinner and a drink at the St. Clair Tavern in the winter of 1957, for example, they were asked to leave by the bar owner with the simple explanation that they "just don't serve mixed-race couples." The man wrote a complaint letter to the LLBO explaining that, as a veteran of the Canadian army, he was appalled by this experience. "Sirs," he explained, "I am from Trinidad (BWI). I came to Canada thinking it was a wonderful country. I served three years in the Cdn Army (in Essex Scottish Reserves now) [*sic*] and have my Canadian Citizenship Papers. Now I'm thinking maybe it isn't so wonderful a country when a man and his wife can't be served in a Public Place, because his face is a bit darker than hers. . . . I am very hurt and deeply insulted about this matter."[99] For residents like Wupperman Alexis and his wife, full citizenship was determined by the color line, and entertainment and leisure establishments were sites in which these unofficial barriers were enacted on a daily basis.

The color line also shaped freedom of movement across the national border for leisure purposes, calling into question the open and easy nature of cross-border travel touted by local boosters. According to a Detroit Urban League study, white Detroiters visited Canada almost twice as frequently as black residents.[100] When black residents did cross the national line, they often faced an additional level of discrimination that made these trips increasingly difficult. For example, though Jim Crow did not formally exist on Bob-Lo Island, a popular American-run amusement park on a Canadian island in the Detroit River, the company that ran the steamships from Detroit excluded "all negroes and disorderly persons." As a result, black residents were barred from visiting the Canadian island and from participating in drinking, dancing, and live music shows on the "moonlight voyages" run by the company.[101] For many local black residents and prospective tourists, there was little reason to cross into the largely white Canadian border city where segregation was a common practice.[102]

If Windsor's sex workers were able to capitalize on the appeal of ethnic and national difference, all within the context of a largely white entertainment district, across the river the color line was more ambiguous. In many ways, men's and women's experiences in Detroit's illicit economy reflected the shifting social patterns emerging in the early postwar years. Throughout the 1940s, the Second Great Migration continued to bring thousands of African Americans north both in search of employment and as a reprieve from stifling racial systems in the South. Once settled in Detroit, though, many black migrants found that they were still subject to both structural and interpersonal forms of racism. Acute housing shortages and restrictive covenants forced many African Americans to live in old, dilapidated neighborhoods. At the same time, many whites, angered by the influx of what they saw as unwanted outsiders, began to move out of the city and into nearby suburbs. Discrimination in employment kept black residents in some of the lowest-paying jobs in the city, exacerbating the divides between suburban and urban residents.[103] A shortage of recreational facilities in downtown neighborhoods, rising police brutality, and escalating interracial violence helped to further the divide between black and white Detroiters.[104] By the mid-1950s, residents from diverse backgrounds asserted that racial antagonism was one of the most pressing problems in the city. Many white residents complained that black Detroiters were too militant in their demands for social equality; many black residents pointed to the violence and intimidation they experienced on a daily basis as one of the key features of their lives in the northern city.[105]

Within this context, the city's sex trade played contradictory roles of both reflecting the growing inequality between black and white residents and providing opportunities for men and women to cross the color line in the most intimate of ways. The disproportionate number of African

American women working in the city's sex trade by the mid-1950s was, in part, a sign of the limited job opportunities available to them in the segregated city. The interactions between black workers and white customers likewise signaled the growing racial and economic divides that separated the suburbs and the city core. The fact that working women's business relied heavily on white men who traveled into the city for a night of fun became a source of frustration for many black residents.[106] The rowdy nature of Detroit's vice districts, many insisted, was due not to the influx of poor blacks (as white city residents often asserted), but instead to the "overwhelmingly white clientele which supports Negro prostitutes."[107] For some black Detroiters, the fact that their neighborhoods became the stomping grounds for suburban white men was just another symptom of the inequalities they faced on a daily basis.

For working-class and poor residents of neighborhoods like Paradise Valley and Twelfth Street, though, vice brought much-needed money into the communities. In the process, it also provided moments of social transgression when men and women could mingle in interracial settings. At night, local businesses hosted large mixed-race crowds who filled the streets and nightclubs. In black and tans like Club B & C, the Crystal Lounge, and Club Zombie, the appeal of interracial mingling was so central to attracting customers that their owners made sure to advertise the interracial makeup of their clientele in local newspaper ads.[108] As Detroit jazz musician Thomas "Dr. Beans" Bowles recalled: "The Flame [club] was black and tan and more white than black. On the weekends the traffic would line up; you could not drive down Canfield or John R. That was hustle night, girls were on the street, pimps were out, everybody was makin' money. It was like Las Vegas. People would come from everywhere. It was the center of entertainment. . . . White people would come from all over."[109] Another woman who grew up near Hastings Street remembered the visible nature of interracial street solicitation. On many a night, if she stayed out on the streets after dark, she would see prostitutes and pimps "pulling the 'Murphy'" on white men who had come into the city. They would take the men's money and send them up to an apartment where they claimed a woman was waiting. By the time customers realized they had been duped, the prostitute or pimp was long gone.[110] Others noted that licit and illicit industries went hand in hand in the city's black neighborhoods and became embedded in the cultural life of those communities. As one resident explained of her neighborhood on Detroit's East Side, the streets where she grew up were "part carnival side-show, with hard-drinking dudes and loud street ladies, and part close community, with people who looked out for each other."[111] In this way, vice served as both a reflection of the mounting racial divides in the city by the mid-1950s and a strategy through which some local residents attempted to deal with those divides in the postwar years. For brief moments in the city's vice districts, the borders between black and white residents, licit and illicit industries, and suburban and urban residents became a bit less stark.

Conclusion

The years immediately following World War II brought a renewed sense of optimism and growth to the border region, allowing both licit and illicit economies to flourish. Across Detroit and Windsor, tourists, travelers, and local residents helped to forge vibrant entertainment districts in the cities' downtown neighborhoods. For city officials and tourism boosters, cross-border travel became an important tool that could bolster the local borderland economies, as well as a larger symbol of the freedom and mobility enjoyed by North Americans. These various interests placed the border spirit at the center of their promotions, presenting Detroit and Windsor as unique cities in which tourists could come to celebrate the culturally distinct, yet closely intertwined, borderland community. Whether to shop, dine, dance, or attend the various cultural shows offered across the border cities, by the late 1940s and early 1950s, boosters seemed to welcome tourists with open arms.

This narrow vision of entertainment and tourism, though, failed to reflect the complex ties that linked Detroit and Windsor residents in the postwar years. Alongside legal forms of travel emerged illicit cross-border economies that forged important connections between borderland residents. Prostitution in particular attracted men and women who wanted to capitalize on the booming local economy. In brothels, bars, and jazz clubs and on the streets, participants built alternative forms of both labor and entertainment. Like the formal tourist economy, the sex trade offered its participants affective experiences in the bustling downtown neighborhoods. It marketed the appeal of crossing into a new space and of experiencing something one might not have been able to access in their hometowns. Vice, though, also allowed participants to cross sexual, social, and spatial boundaries in a way that formal tourism did not. Prostitution provided illicit forms of sexual interaction that depended on the appeal of doing bad in the urban vice districts. In doing so, it not only provided an important source of income for those working in the illicit market but also openly challenged the conception that heterosexual, monogamous marriage was the only legitimate form of sexual expression in the postwar years.

Perceptions of racial and ethnic difference were central to the local sex trade and shaped men's and women's experiences in complex ways. While French Canadian women were able to market ethnic and national differences to their American customers, this had limits. Indeed, the predominantly white nature of the city's sex trade demonstrates the impact of de facto segregation in Windsor. Though contemporaries framed the "race problem" as a distinctly American problem, segregation in Windsor's sex trade suggests that we need to rethink this narrative. The color line also clearly shaped social relations in the Canadian border city and helped to determine who was or was not able to participate in illegal economies during the early postwar years.

The confluence of sexual, spatial, and racial boundaries is also clearly evident on the American side of the border. Detroit's sex trade provides an important example of interracial mingling during a time when historians have documented rising segregation and racial tensions in the city. By looking at social interactions in the city's leisure districts, we see a booming underground economy that violated the strict segregation codes in the larger region. These were, however, by no means even exchanges, and, as we will see, the concentration of vice in predominantly black neighborhoods would lead moral reformers and the police to blame black communities, and especially black women, for the rise of crime in the city in the late 1950s and 1960s. In this way, lines separating licit from illicit activities, suburban from urban residents, and welcomed visitors from unwanted outsiders were never static and would take on renewed political importance as moral reformers worked to eliminate illicit economies from the border cities.

3

MAINLINING ALONG THE LINE

Building a Transnational Drug Market

In 1938, *Maclean's* magazine printed an article about the growth of illegal drug networks across North America. After explaining that there were as many as "8,000 dope addicts in Canada," it told its readers the story of two Americans who smuggled drugs into Ontario. In January of that year, George De Bozy and his girlfriend crossed into Windsor via the ferry in Detroit. Once through border inspections, the couple "got into [their] car . . . and drove off, apparently innocent tourists out to explore Canada." A few minutes after leaving the docks, though, members of the Royal Canadian Mounted Police (RCMP) pulled them over and searched their car on the "main street of Windsor." Under the dashboard they found twenty-five marijuana cigarettes and "the makings for 1,000 more in a cleverly concealed cache beneath the rear seat." These supposedly "innocent tourists" were, as it turns out, anything but; they were importing large quantities of illegal drugs from the United States. The article warned that this growing problem, if ignored, would increasingly give "North American narcotics squads plenty to worry about."[1]

By the late 1940s, it appeared that the *Maclean's* article's prediction had come to fruition: Americans and Canadians were regularly crossing the border in search of both illegal drugs to purchase and potential markets in which to sell them. This transnational industry had a direct impact on the nations' bordertowns, which served as connecting points for the drug market on both sides of the border. By examining the drug cultures that emerged in Detroit and Windsor during the 1940s and 1950s, as well as the larger trade that enabled those subcultures to grow, we gain important insight into the multiple roles illegal drugs played in the lives of border-land residents. Like commercial sex, the drug market provided important forms of both entertainment and income and shaped the cultural and economic lives of the border cities in multiple ways.

The bustling downtown neighborhoods that facilitated the growth of prostitution in Detroit and Windsor also enabled a transnational drug market to grow. Along Woodward, Hastings, Goyeau, and Ouellette streets, Americans and Canadians bought and sold narcotics and mingled with other users in the cities' bars, clubs, pool halls, and rooming houses. The men and women who engaged in these illicit transactions were building an alternative urban subculture based on the consumption of illicit and pleasurable substances. For some, taking heroin and marijuana provided access to an emerging hipster culture that ran counter to images of clean suburban living touted by postwar boosters. In jazz clubs, at house parties, and on city streets, participants pushed the boundaries of what counted as acceptable forms of consumption and leisure. "Doing bad" in the border cities could in fact feel very *good*, as illicit networks enabled users to experience both intense physical pleasure and the sense that they were part of a broader community of people.

As a transnational industry based on the sale of illicit commodities, the drug market also provided an important source of income in neighborhoods increasingly facing economic decline. As boomtown conditions leveled off in the early 1950s, and as capital flight and suburbanization began to remake urban neighborhoods, illegal forms of moneymaking became even more important. For some residents, the drug economy offered an alternative form of labor that provided both much-needed income and a sense of social mobility. This was particularly true for the largely working-class and African American residents who turned to the illicit economy when few legitimate work options materialized. For some, the choice to sell drugs in the border cities became one tangible way in which they could counter the impacts of suburbanization, segregation, and economic decline on their daily lives.

By examining the experiences of men and women most intimately involved in the drug trade—the users who frequented local hotspots, the street-level peddlers who worked in downtown neighborhoods, and the high-level importers and distributors who trafficked drugs in an expansive global market—it becomes clear that illegal economies served multiple and often contradictory roles in the local community. The drug economy was an expression of the postwar preoccupation with consumption, leisure, and mobility. Partaking in the drug market showed that even the most marginal city residents could participate in the thriving entertainment districts in the cities' downtown neighborhoods. Yet, divides within the illicit economy itself—which usually left poor, working-class, and black residents working at the lowest and least profitable levels—show how drug use also became embedded in the larger structural forces shaping the region. If participating in the illegal drug economy provided moments of social mobility and a sense of community belonging, it often did so unevenly and sometimes at very high costs. In this way, postwar expressions of boom and bust, growth and decline, and hope and despair were manifest in the illegal drug cultures that emerged as World War II came to a close.

"If I Could Feel Better, I'd Rather Feel Better": Using Drugs in the Detroit-Windsor Region

At first it seemed that the *Maclean's* article's warning of a growing illegal drug trade was a miscalculation. Not long after its publication, the outbreak of World War II closed international trade routes, resulting in a drastic reduction in illegal drug supplies across North America. Drug prices, which had been increasing throughout the Great Depression, skyrocketed, putting drugs like morphine, codeine, cocaine, and heroin far beyond the average person's reach. Those determined to secure narcotics turned to unscrupulous doctors or robbing pharmacies as a way to obtain drugs, though these methods were not able to sustain a large user population.[2] Across both Canada and the United States, federal officials claimed that the drastic reduction in the supply of drugs had virtually eliminated narcotics addiction in their respective countries.[3] Like other forms of cross-border travel and trade, the international drug market was not immune to the disruptions of war.[4]

This drastic drop in drug use across North America, though, proved to be a temporary aberration, as cross-border smuggling resumed in full force as the war came to an end. While major cities like New York, Los Angeles, Vancouver, and Montreal emerged as the centers of the illegal drug economy in their respective countries, border cities like Detroit and Windsor were uniquely situated to act as connecting points within the growing North American market. Much like the formal economy, there was a significant size disparity between the drug markets in Detroit and Windsor, a disparity that actually bolstered the transnational nature of the industry. By the late 1940s, Detroit's user population was the fourth largest in the nation, behind only New York, Los Angeles, and Chicago.[5]

Law enforcement officials estimated that there were about 2,000 to 5,000 "addicts" in the city in the mid-1950s.[6] In contrast, Canadian officials estimated that Ontario's "addict" population was between 400 and 450, with Toronto making up about 90 percent and Windsor and Hamilton making up the remaining 10 percent.[7] Though Windsor's using population remained small in relation to that of its American neighbor, its position between Detroit and Toronto—two of the largest drug markets in the region—meant that it functioned as an important hub through which both users and traffickers traveled on a regular basis.

There were many similarities between the drug cultures that developed on both sides of the national line. Prior to the war, Americans and Canadians consumed a wide variety of drugs, including cocaine, opium, heroin, morphine, and codeine.[8] This changed in the late 1940s, as heroin became the primary drug of choice on both sides of the border. According to Edward Piggins, the commissioner of police in Detroit, by 1955 heroin made up 90 percent of the "drug problem" in the city.[9] Similarly, the National Health and Welfare Department in Canada consistently reported that heroin comprised more than 90 percent of illegal drug use in the country.[10] Though drugs like cocaine and marijuana were also available, heroin consistently dominated the international market into the 1960s. Injecting heroin directly into the vein, or "mainlining," became the most popular method of use.[11] In the United States, "outfits" (an eyedropper, a hypodermic needle, thin or absorbent paper, and a spoon) could be rented through an illicit market; in Canada, all these items were legal and available in drugstores. It was common practice to share outfits, though most users usually shot themselves up.[12] Heroin was also available in powder and pill form, but these were often less potent and therefore offered less of a "kick" than mainlining.[13]

Like the commercial sex market, the illegal drug economy was concentrated in the cities' downtown leisure districts, where it relied on the cover of seemingly legitimate businesses. In Detroit, users and sellers met in bars like Uncle Tom's Cabin and the Ebony Bar, as well as jazz clubs, hotels, and rooming houses.[14] As one Detroiter explained to the Michigan Legislative Committee, anyone who wanted to purchase drugs in the city could simply patronize one of the many all-night theaters, taxi-dance halls, beer gardens, or music venues, where they could easily locate peddlers looking to sell their products.[15] This was particularly true in the neighborhoods bordering Twelfth Street and Paradise Valley. As another local resident recalled, "Numbers, dope, prostitution . . . everything! You could get anything. You could go to any barbershop on 12th Street and get anything you wanted. You just come in and make your order and come back in twenty minutes and pick it up . . . whatever it was."[16] While the sale of illegal substances was more covert in Windsor, largely because of the smaller user population in the city, men and women bought and sold drugs in the bars, dance halls, and hotels along Ouellette, Pitt, and Goyeau streets. By the early 1950s, establishments close to the Detroit River, such as the Border City Hotel, were known for their rough-and-tumble clientele who came to buy a range of illegal substances and services.[17]

The fact that drug users tended to be concentrated in particular downtown neighborhoods meant these spaces often elicited a degree of intrigue from visitors intent on a night of fun. Like other forms of vice, engaging in the illicit drug market offered an affective experience that blended both excitement and danger. This was especially true for young suburban residents who came to the city to enjoy its nightlife. Betty, for example, a suburban Detroiter looking for some adventure on her sixteenth birthday, decided to head downtown. She "went to a beer garden in the northwest section of [Detroit], and, while there, her curiosity got the best of her and started her first shot of narcotics." She enjoyed the experience because she found the drug "helped her listen to the band, sort of give a boost to the music."[18] One young woman from small-town Ontario similarly recounted that when she first used heroin, she "thought it was wonderful." She testified before the 1955 Senate Committee on Narcotic Drugs in Canada that she often went to the nearest urban center, Toronto, to play "hookey." She recalled that there was only one place to go, "and that is to the worst part of the city. There you run into people. I was *fascinated* by them."[19]

The mystique surrounding urban leisure districts was heightened when one crossed the national line. In the border cities, rumors often spread about the purity of heroin and the ease with which one could obtain the drug in the neighboring town. One *Star* article explained that while the number of known "addicts" in Windsor was actually quite small, the population frequently increased due to the number of users who traveled through the city in search of heroin on the American side of the border.[20] The testimony of the head of the South-western Ontario division of the RCMP confirmed this pattern. "We have got a floating population," he explained. "If there is a panic, let us say, in Hamilton—and by 'panic' I mean in short supply—we will have them up from Hamilton, until the supply eases there. There have been times in the past where there has been a panic here, and they headed to Hamilton or Windsor, or wherever they can get it."[21] Those users, according to Corporal Kelly LaBrash of the Toronto

RCMP, included Americans crossing into Ontario border cities in search of stronger drugs. "Jazz groups, beatniks, and musicians" were becoming more visible in the border cities, he explained, as Americans increasingly crossed into Canada "for stronger kicks."[22] One such woman, interviewed by the 1955 Senate Committee, told the senators that she used to cross from Detroit into Windsor to purchase heroin because the drugs sold in the Canadian city were much more potent than what she was used to in Detroit.[23] While users certainly faced an added level of regulation when crossing the national border, the perception that they could attain drugs more easily once they made it across encouraged some to take the risk.

Americans and Canadians were attracted to the heroin subcultures for similar reasons, viewing them as a way to achieve both intense physical pleasure and a sense of community belonging. Men and women who hung around bars and clubs where heroin use was common recalled being intrigued by the "obvious enjoyment" of those around them.[24] One former user, upon trying his first shot, found it brought him a powerful sensation unlike anything he had felt before: "Well, it's very difficult to describe, even the way I felt. Some people have said it's the way to . . . one of the great sexual experiences one might have. It's been also compared to a man having a climax with a female possibly at the same moment. It's one of those highly sensual types of feelings."[25] Similarly, at a conference on addiction in Toronto, one researcher noted that heroin users across Ontario regularly described the feeling they got from heroin as an "orgiastic climax," a bodily experience that could only be compared to the most intense sexual encounter.[26] Another former heroin user explained that he began using heroin because he did not very much care for alcohol or marijuana. Heroin, though, gave him a unique and powerful boost. When asked why he preferred heroin over sobriety, he explained that he did not mind sobriety, but "if I could feel better, I'd rather feel better."[27]

Others began using heroin and marijuana as a way to gain access to the hip subcultures developing in the cities' leisure districts. The perception that the drugs were taken by a cultural elite of sorts—the "jazz groups, beatniks, and musicians" that patronized the cities' bars and clubs—became part of their appeal in the late 1940s. One former user explained that he began using heroin when his "curiosity" got the best of him. As he recalled, "It became a fad. . . . Most of the young people started using it after so many top bands and stuff like that, they found out they were using it . . . [and] it more or less became a fad from then on with the younger generation."[28] A 1953 study commissioned by Detroit Mayor Albert E. Cobo also concluded that young people in particular were drawn to heroin use because they saw it as a way to fit into a hip group of people visible in the city's downtown leisure districts. In those neighborhoods, the committee argued, drug use often provided a "path to prowess and distinction for the user among his fellows," since it showed daring, guts, and a willingness to defy authority. Once men and women were accepted among other users in the city, the report argued, they tended "to become more or less part of a definite sub-culture" that used slang, expressions, and styles of dress "understood only by those who are part of the sub-culture."[29]

Significantly, the mayor's report concluded that drug use enabled young men and women to participate in an alternative consumer culture that contrasted sharply with the images they came across in magazines, television, and other forms of popular culture. Participating in illicit commodity cultures provided a different path for those unable (or unwilling) to purchase luxury goods and fit into middle-class visions of respectability. As the researchers explained, being part of the drug subculture appeased "the individual's feelings of lack of status because he has no good job, house, car etc." It allowed users to show that they, too, had money to spend and were part of the thriving illicit communities. This was not a complete rejection of consumerism itself, but rather a reimagining of what consumption could be. It became an alternative form available to even the most marginal community members. As a Detroit study explained, "Since the war the earning ability, while not large, of even those often considered least employable has put drug purchases within the reach of many group-members."[30] The perception that postwar prosperity enabled the growth of a using culture was echoed by the Canadian Department of National Health and Welfare, which claimed that "addiction increased [in 1951] . . . partly due to the generally high level of prosperity and consequently increased earning power of addicts and potential addicts."[31] Using heroin, at least initially, became a way of expressing an alternative vision of prosperity and community belonging, one that was a far cry from suburbia, white-collar work, and family vacations.

Perhaps nothing signified this cultural break more than the jazz scene that emerged after the war. The rise of bebop in particular breathed new life into cities' clubs, bars, and dance halls. In Detroit establishments like the Flame Show Bar on John R Street, the Blue Bird Inn on Tireman, the Twenty Grand on Grand River Avenue, and Klein's on Twelfth Street, locals and out-of-towners gathered to listen to the complex improvisation that gave bebop its character.[32] By the late 1940s, this New York style had taken the region by storm, bringing both big-name musicians and local talent together in the cities' music venues. For two weeks in the summer of 1947, for example, Dizzy Gillespie played the El Sino Club in Paradise Valley, infecting Detroit with what one reporter called "Be Bop fever."[33] By 1953, a *Chicago Defender* article declared that "the Motor City can easily be called 'Jump City,'" as crowds "invade" the Paradise Valley and Twelfth Street neighborhoods seeking out these live jam sessions.[34] Given its close proximity to Detroit, Windsor also attracted American musicians to play at local establishments. While the Liquor License Board of Ontario (LLBO) attempted to limit the type of music allowed in the city's bars, taverns, and hotels, local owners often violated the board's strict mandates to profit from the growing popularity of jazz. The owners of the Arlington Public House, for example, were reprimanded by the LLBO when they began to host "a following of local and Detroit jazz musicians that play all the taverns and roadhouses in the border cities." Eventually, they ended up shutting down the live entertainment because "jazz was starting to bring in a young crowd" and they were starting to have "difficulties with the minors."[35] While the smaller number of clubs and bars in Windsor made oversight easier for organizations like the LLBO, even their close regulation and undercover inspection tactics could not prevent the jazz craze from spreading to the Canadian border city.

Toward this end, bebop not only transformed a musical genre but also helped to create a hipster culture among a generation coming of age in major North American cities. Forged largely by African American musicians who saw themselves first and foremost as artists, the style was fashioned as a response to the overwhelmingly commercial nature of swing bands.[36] Musicians and their followers wore their own fashion style—"cardigan jackets, horn rimmed glasses, and goatees"—and began to use heroin and marijuana as part of this cultural scene.[37] The mobile nature of the jazz community meant that musicians across North America shared similar cultural experiences, including drug use. In Canadian cities like Windsor, Hamilton, Toronto, and Montreal, American and Canadian musicians came together to enjoy "marijuana cigarettes" and heroin as part of their late night "jam sessions."[38] Musicians who traveled through major American cities likewise began using drugs with their fellow band members. Ted Stewart, a musician and former heroin user, recalled that he "was introduced to marijuana [in 1955] by a friend of mine. Both he and I were musicians. He offered me a marijuana cigarette. . . . I didn't want to show I was the least bit square, because at the time I wanted to be hip, we used to call it then. I smoked marijuana and I got high off it, and to be truthful about it, I enjoyed the feeling at the time." He further recalled that he "played tenor saxophone, and most of my professional playing was right after I got out of the army. This was a reason also for me to be drawn more to narcotics, because all of the people I admired were musicians like Charlie Parker and Miles Davis, and they used narcotics."[39]

For some local musicians, using heroin became a way of proving authenticity among their peers, allowing them to fit into the expansive jazz networks that were quickly spreading across major North American cities. Rodger Moyer was fifteen years old when, in the late 1940s, he left Detroit with his band and headed to New York City, a center of both jazz and heroin use. There he met members of another band from Detroit who introduced him to heroin: "We were all in a room together, and they asked me if I wanted to get high. Rather than say no, for fear of being ostracized, or being looked upon as a square, I said yes. And that's when I took my first shot of heroin. . . . I was just wanting to belong to a certain group of people, to my peer group." Moyer explained that he continued to use heroin when he returned to Detroit because, unlike alcohol and marijuana, it allowed him to perform as a musician: "I functioned for a while as a musician," he recalled, "and I did a lot of traveling around the country. And for a while I was making a pretty decent buck. But then all good things come to an end. Big bands went out. Jazz became sort of out of fashion. And by this time, I was deeply into the drug subculture."[40]

Moyer's description of his descent into the "drug subculture" points to the very real challenges faced by men and women who began to use heroin on a regular basis. Indeed, just a few years after heroin's reemergence, a divide began to develop within the using community itself. In his study of heroin use in New York City, historian Eric Schneider found that people who began using in the 1940s were often considered "neighborhood 'cool cats'—hustlers, gamblers, and pimps who made their living on the street." These figures conveyed the message that heroin was hip and that its users were an elite distinguished from the ordinary working people of the neighborhood. This generation of users was perceived as respectable; they never passed out in the streets, and they never left home without being presentable. As users transitioned from casual to habitual use in the early 1950s, though, they began to take on the image of the drug-addicted street "junkie," a far cry from the "cool cat" image that often drew users into the drug scene.[41]

Similar hierarchies developed in the border cities, as members of the using community began to distinguish between those who seemed to control their habits and those who descended into a life of addiction. One former Detroiter described the difference between respectable users and junkies, noting that the method and frequency of use determined how one was viewed by fellow users. He explained that a person snorting heroin attempted to act the same as they did before they began using—they kept up their jobs, their personal appearance, and their social ties. In contrast, the intravenous user "sever[ed] all his ties . . . and would not be conscientious about his dress or his personal appearance or personal hygiene. They just don't seem to care anymore, the majority of them." As a result, he found that "the people who are involved indirectly or directly with drugs sort of look down on a person who shoots. Whereas a person who snorts is . . . higher on the hierarchy."[42]

Helen McGowan, whose position as a prostitute and madam brought her into contact with users and sellers on a regular basis, also described the class differentiation that developed among the using community. While McGowan herself never became a user, she recalled talking to hundreds of women and men over the course of her life who all cited the same reasons for using: "It gives them a sense of power, of well-being; it puts them above and beyond their everyday existence for a short while, at least." Yet she, too, noted the devastating impact addiction had on many of those around her. While "pros and pimps" during the late 1920s and 1930s had used opium, cocaine, and morphine, which she characterized as "'high class' drugs," the rise of heroin as the primary drug of choice after the war created new divides within the using community. By the early 1950s, McGowan explained, the "main-liner" who shot heroin on a regular basis was only "vaguely respected by the rest of the addicts who only use the capsule method."[43] Thus, many contemporaries began to draw a fine line between engaging in the using subculture and alienating oneself when his or her heroin habit spiraled out of control. The risks that many took trying to prove their membership in the illicit community often had unintended effects that made it increasingly challenging for some users to function within even the city's illicit communities.

Making It Work: Selling Drugs in the Border Cities

As the recollections of former users suggest, using heroin and other drugs was about much more than simply attaining pleasure, particularly for those who found themselves using for extended periods of time. The drug economy became an important source of income as well as a coping strategy for residents living in neighborhoods facing economic decline by the mid-1950s. Like the women who sold sex in the cities' leisure districts, the men (and, less often, women) who sold drugs built alternative forms of labor in an increasingly volatile market. Participating in the illicit economy could bring a sense of sociability, enabling participants to feel that they were part of a larger community in the cities' downtown neighborhoods. The drug market, though, was highly stratified and began to reflect patterns of race and class inequality developing in the border region. For those working at the lowest level of the drug economy, this would limit the amount of money they could make, as well as the mobility they could attain, through the illicit market.

When people bought drugs in Detroit and Windsor, they most likely did so through street peddlers, individuals who operated at the lowest position in the underground economy. They usually sold drugs on a relatively small scale, sometimes to supplement their own habits.[44] On both sides of the border, street-level sellers tended to be male, to come from poor or working-class backgrounds, and to live in the cities' downtown cores. In his study of drug arrests in Ontario, Clayton Mosher found that 66 percent of users and sellers were from working-class backgrounds, with an additional 15 percent listed as "unemployed." Though Windsor was the fourth-largest city in terms of population, it had the third-largest percentage of arrests. He attributed this to the city's position as a bordertown, which put it into close contact with the U.S. drug market.[45] Toward this end, arrests were concentrated in the downtown leisure district and in the areas bordering the bridge and tunnel that connected the city to the neighboring American city.[46]

In Detroit, street sales were also concentrated in the city's downtown core. According to the 1953 Mayor's Committee, which interviewed seventy-six heroin users in the city, more than 90 percent came from the first and thirteenth police precincts. These districts were bounded by the Detroit Terminal Railroad tracks, the Detroit River, Hamilton Avenue, and Russell Street, covering three and a half square miles in the city's core. The Council of Social Agencies placed that area in the lowest quintile rank in the city with respect to public assistance, aid to dependent children, violations of the juvenile code, court cases, and total deaths. As the study put it, "Generally speaking, this is an area of economic and social deprivation."[47] Across the city, African American men were by far the most likely to be arrested and prosecuted for low-level drug offenses, and this racial divide grew exponentially over the course of the 1950s. For example, the number of black and white men prosecuted for narcotics offenses in 1949 was sixty-two and twelve, respectively. By 1958, the divide was even starker, with 355 black men prosecuted versus just 31 white men.[48]

Arrest and prosecution records are problematic, as they often tell us more about the proclivities of the police department than they do about actual patterns of use. The rising number of arrests and prosecutions in both cities grew, in part, out of changes to laws and policing tactics in the early postwar years. In Windsor, as in other Canadian municipalities, the 1950s ushered in the professionalization of its police department. They began to use informants, surveillance and raids, and undercover work much more extensively than previous generations. Local police also received more active cooperation from the RCMP, the agency tasked with enforcing the federal Narcotic Drug Act.[49] The relatively small size of the drug economy in the city, combined with these increased policing efforts, meant that sellers and users tended to come into contact with law enforcement on a regular basis.[50] In Michigan, where the drug economy was much more extensive, changes to state laws similarly made it easier for police to bust men and women for small-scale drug offenses. In 1952, the state of Michigan passed Senate Bill No. 144, which increased the maximum sentences for the possession and sale of narcotics. A change to the state constitution that year allowed police officers to conduct searches and seizures on the streets and in private vehicles (rather than simply in private residences).[51] Thus, the rising number of arrests is probably as reflective of these new policing tactics as it was an actual growth in the number of people involved in the drug trade.

The fact that African American men bore the brunt of intensified policing in Detroit (by 1955, black residents accounted for about 89 percent of those arrested for drug offenses in the city) also reflected the deep racism that pervaded the local police force.[52] Of the 4,200 police employed by the city, only 107 were African American, a staggeringly low figure, given that the city's black population had been rising since the war years. Black neighborhoods were largely policed by white officers, many of whom commuted from the city's suburbs. Black and white policemen rode in separate squad cars and walked separate beats. By the mid-1950s, city residents and civil rights activists regularly complained about the systemic racism and police brutality that were part of their daily experience.[53] The problem was so severe that organizations such as the local chapter of the National Association for the Advancement of Colored People spent much of their time filing complaints against the force.[54] Their calls for a reorganization of the department to reflect the demographic realities of the city would continue to go largely unanswered until the Coleman Young administration in the 1970s.[55]

Changes to policing tactics and racism within the force were not isolated developments; instead, they reflected larger economic and spatial shifts in the border cities. The economic gains made during World War II did not remain steady, and by the mid-1950s, capital flight and suburbanization began to remake the cities' downtown neighborhoods. Automation displaced thousands of workers on both sides of the border, and companies moved their plants to the newly developing suburbs and Sunbelt.[56] This was devastating for residents in the Detroit-Windsor region, whose main source of employment was industrial manufacturing.[57] In the winter of 1949–50 alone, sudden layoffs in the auto industry put 127,000 Detroiters out of work, many of them black.[58] Among the men and women who remained employed through the economic downturn, many found employment in jobs that paid significantly less and had little job security.[59] Further exacerbating the problem was the rising rate of suburbanization by the middle of the decade. In Windsor, "poverty pockets" developed in areas where industries were no longer operating and middle-class residents had moved to peripheral neighborhoods in South Windsor, Sandwich East, and Riverside, leaving low-income, depressed neighborhoods behind.[60] In Detroit, prosperity and poverty were directly linked to class, race, and geography—as white workers continued to move to the suburbs in large numbers, conditions for African American workers in particular rapidly deteriorated.[61]

In an attempt to counter some of the worst effects of capital flight and suburbanization, some local residents turned to the illicit economy as a way to make ends meet. Like the decision to work in the commercial sex trade, local residents sometimes saw selling drugs as one solution to the problem of underwork in the blue-collar cities. One former Detroit user explained that it was easy for him to turn to illicit economies because of both the few choices available to him and the ease with which he could integrate into the illicit community. He explained that the "environment" that he grew up in during the 1950s and "the people that I was closely associated with at that time and most of my life had been directly or indirectly involved in narcotics. And our neighbors, and our neighborhoods, almost in every other block there was some form of dope house." Therefore, when few appealing licit forms of employment materialized, illicit economies provided an obvious alternative.[62] Rodger Moyer similarly recalled that selling heroin provided an important outlet for young men, especially African American men, who had few work options available: "When I was young, I was raised in a culture where if some guy went to school he got to be a Pullman Porter. And I didn't relish the idea of going to school to be a Pullman Porter. At this time, a young black man, if he

This photograph shows a man walking in the business district in Detroit sporting a "zoot suit." Flashy clothing was a key sign that one was making good money in the local illicit economy. (Photo by Arthur Siegel, courtesy of the Library of Congress, Prints & Photographs Division, FSA/OWI Collection, LC-DIG-fsa-8d25384)

went to school and got an education, you couldn't do anything with it."[63] Instead, Moyer found the culture of using and selling to be an alternative to the bleak outlook he found as a young black man with little formal education.

Underemployment was only part of the motivation behind an individual's decision to work in illicit economies. Selling drugs and other illicit services provided alternative working environments where the jobs one performed and the schedule one kept differed significantly from those in the formal labor force. Sellers had a sense of mobility, as street-level peddlers worked in a wide variety of spaces to drum up business. As one seller told the Michigan Legislative Committee, "The peddler, now, he changes places so often. He might be at dances and, again, he might be in beer gardens, in a show. He might be anywhere." Though this invokes the specter of the dope peddler lurking around every corner, it also highlights the various spaces in which drug sellers operated, which included the "beer joints, all-night theaters, dime-a-dance places, [and] dances halls" across the city.[64] Toward this end, there was an element of sociability to the business, based in part on the necessity to remain undetected by legal authorities. As one Detroit report explained, "The circle of acquaintances" for sellers is often "tremendous," with their business relying on "well-defined relationships" that helped them avoid undercover agents and police informers.[65]

Lower-level sellers were also likely to have some combination of licit and illicit employment, blurring the lines between acceptable and unacceptable forms of labor in the cities' downtown neighborhoods. Sellers often worked a variety of blue-collar jobs on a part-time basis—inspecting factories, welding, and assembling cars in the Ford plants.[66] This not only helped them supplement their incomes from the drug trade but also provided important cover for their illegal activities. Flexibility was crucial, and users and sellers tended to work jobs that accommodated their daily routines and physical needs. One former user described his work unloading trucks as an ideal position because he could pick up work on a truck-by-truck basis, leaving him time in between to take a cab across town, buy dope, and return to the job. He could earn $25 for unloading a truck of frozen chickens, and this money was paid to him in cash right away, enabling him to purchase drugs when necessary throughout his week.[67]

Yet the physical effects of the drugs and the legal prosecution they faced on a regular basis made it difficult for many to keep their dual lives separate. John Hammond, for example, moved to Detroit when a friend got him a job at the Detroit Edison Company in the midst of the company's attempt at racial integration. According to Hammond, "They wanted a black fellow to come out there, you know, just like Jackie Robinson in baseball. . . . I went to work for the Detroit Edison Company, working four days a week and then going to school one day a week at Wayne University, taking Steam Engineering at the expense of the company." While Hammond was able to keep this job for four years, he lost the position when his employers found out about a televised raid on a drug house in which he was busted. That was the last formal job he held while using heroin.

Rather than risk getting fired from another position, Hammond saw this as his "best opportunity" to begin selling in what he assumed was a lucrative illicit market.[68]

The perception that selling drugs was easier and more profitable than low-paying factory or service jobs did not match many sellers' actual experiences. The illegal nature of the industry makes it impossible to know with any certainty exactly how much money individuals made, but contemporary evidence suggests that few local peddlers became wealthy through the illegal drug market. In 1951, the Michigan Legislative Committee interviewed Larry, a man serving time in a Michigan penal institution for crimes committed in order to obtain drugs. When, over the course of the interview, the legislators continued to use the terms "trafficker" and "peddler" interchangeably, Larry responded with confusion: "I am not quite clear on what do you mean by the peddlers . . . because a lot of the peddlers that I know—what I call a peddler—is little men who have nothing and they're just pushing the stuff to keep up their own habits, more or less." Instead, he perceived a clear distinction between traffickers at the top and local sellers trying to make ends meet: "All I know is that it is a vicious racket, a million dollar racket for whoever is behind it."[69] Another Detroit seller claimed that he barely made enough money to break even once his own heroin habit was covered for the day. He paid $1.25 for pills of heroin and sold them for about $2.50, "but his own habit necessitated ten heroin capsules a day. This man had earned a substantial income through dealing, but it was not fabulous, and he was a large-volume operator."[70] Rodger Moyer recalled that it was "only a very small percentage who make a big profit off narcotics. The ones who make a great profit don't use [heroin] and the ones who do use don't make too big of a profit. They might maintain a home or maybe keep a small family, even buy a car now and then, but I think most of them sell it for their own convenience."[71]

While selling drugs could bring some profit for local sellers (enough to buy a car or help take care of a family for a while), few made large sums of money through their drug sales. Instead, the intensification of policing, combined with the damaging effects of long-term addiction, often made life increasingly challenging for peddlers working in the border cities. In this way, there were limits to the social mobility one could achieve through the illicit market, and poor, working-class, and black residents often had to deal with the underside of the illicit economy most directly.

Organized Crime and Transnational Smuggling

While street peddlers played the most visible role in the local drug trade, interacting with users on a daily basis, their business depended on higher-ups who were responsible for importing heroin through an expansive global market. For many large-scale operators, the Detroit-Windsor region was a desirable place to set up shop due largely to the border. Working in close proximity to the national line enabled them to make connections between the using communities in the United States and Canada and to move their illegal products between cities on both sides of the "49th parallel." By and large, local importers hoped that they could capitalize on the border's fluid nature. The expansion of the local drug market in the late 1940s and 1950s suggests that many were successful in this endeavor.

Importers and distributors were responsible for bringing large quantities of drugs into the United States and Canada and for transporting them to major cities across both countries. These mid-level workers became adept at moving their products in resourceful ways, often creating secret compartments in cars or their clothing in which they would stash the illegal goods. In contrast to marijuana, the compact nature of heroin meant that it was often easier to smuggle. "There are numerous ways," explained one Canadian enforcement officer, "depending on the ingenuity of the distributor. Drugs are often sent through the mail in small parcels, in a talcum powder tin, or hidden in other types of cosmetics; it may be in rubber containers in the gas tank of a car; it may be secreted in the false bottom of a suitcase or other type of baggage."[72] Like alcohol smugglers in the Prohibition Era, importers worked hard to adapt as customs officials and narcotics agents changed their enforcement techniques. When the policing of port cities like New York and San Francisco began to heat up in the early 1950s, for example, smuggling across land borders became more common.[73]

As the busiest crossing point between the two countries, the Detroit-Windsor region provided an important opportunity for importers and distributors. Many attempted to blend in with the large volume of tourists and commuters that crossed the border daily. Some traveled in extensive networks that linked cities like Chicago, Cleveland, New York, Toronto, and Montreal.[74] Peter Devlin, for example, was busted by Windsor authorities while attempting to move large quantities of heroin between major cities in the Great Lakes region. Stories of his arrest and trial were covered by the *Windsor Star*, and for months local residents could follow the sensational exploits of the transnational dope peddler.[75] Others, like Giuseppe

Indelicato of Windsor, came to the public's attention when they were caught moving heroin between major cities in Ontario and Michigan. When customs agents discovered a large amount of white powder in Indelicato's car, he attempted to convince them, unsuccessfully, that it was merely cake frosting. In the end, it turned out he was carrying more than $300,000 worth of heroin.[76] While men like Devlin and Indelicato were ultimately busted by law enforcement officials, American and Canadian agents were quick to concede that the large numbers of travelers crossing the border on a regular basis made it impossible to apprehend the majority of travelers who brought illegal goods with them. Countless others, they estimated, were successful in their illegal undertakings.[77]

Some operators tended to work more locally, integrating their cross-border smuggling networks into the larger vice economies in the border cities. In the late 1940s, Barbara La Prad (known in Detroit as "Mother Bee") came to the attention of George H. White, district supervisor for the Bureau of Narcotics.[78] He suspected that this gray-haired woman in her sixties, along with her son Fred Dupree, was running an extensive dope-smuggling ring in the border region. White first became aware of the mother-son team when he rented a room in La Prad's Detroit rooming house. One night, over a few drinks with a fellow renter, White learned that the man had seen La Prad pulling contraband, probably heroin, out of a tire after she returned from a visit to Canada.[79] White began to watch the mother and son closely and became increasingly troubled by their associations. Dupree was well-known by people who frequented local Detroit saloons, where he seemed to have a knack for getting into trouble (in part the result of his alleged affairs with at least a dozen married women). By 1947, Dupree was running "around with a [married] woman named Beverley, who worked at the Avenue Burlesque Show." White observed that every time he saw this former showgirl she was "higher than a kite." He figured that Dupree was using the burlesque club to make connections with narcotics users.[80] The fact that the man drove a Packard car and had nice clothing, without any legitimate means of income, pushed White to conclude that he must be involved in dope peddling.[81] His suspicions were confirmed when he discovered that several "lake workers" were staying at La Prad's rooming house for extended periods. White deduced that these men, who worked on boats that crossed between the United States and Canada, provided the means by which this mother-son team could move their illegal products.[82]

The case of La Prad and Dupree demonstrates how smuggling rings became intertwined with other vice economies in the border region. This duo worked in the local leisure districts and made connections with men and women who frequented the city's bars, clubs, and rooming houses. They concocted elaborate stories to cover their tracks, often speaking of their extensive inheritance money, the lavish houses and boats they owned in other states, and the celebrities they hobnobbed with on a regular basis, stories too fantastic for even the most gullible to believe. Most important, they were able to maintain a successful cross-border smuggling ring by using the cover of supposedly legitimate undertakings (the rooming house, the shipping business, and the burlesque club). It is unclear whether the Narcotics Bureau ever charged the mother-son team with anything, but White's deep-seated resentment for the brazen way they broke the law pours off the pages of his investigative report. To him, their open flouting of the law was dangerous, irresponsible, and damaging to the community.

Since they dealt with large quantities of drugs, importers and distributors tended to be more mobile than street-level peddlers and to have access to more expendable cash. They did, however, still have to answer to the highest level of the drug trade: members of organized crime. By the late 1940s, crime syndicates had taken over the international heroin trade and were carving out territory across North America. In the Detroit-Windsor region, crime families, drawing on their experience during Prohibition, began to rebuild illicit networks based on the traffic in narcotics. In an interview on the Canadian Broadcast Company's TV show *TBA*, Charles Siragusa, who was a narcotics agent throughout the 1940s and 1950s, explained the important position the Detroit-Windsor region played in this process. "The proximity of Toronto to Windsor, to Detroit," he explained, and "the presence in Detroit for many, many years of professional dope peddlers, the affinity between Canadian gangsters and Detroit gangsters, this is a situation which has prevailed for many years."[83] The gangsters and smugglers who took over the narcotics market in the postwar years, though, were not simply extensions of Prohibition Era gangs. By the 1950s, crime syndicates had worked their way into legitimate businesses that provided an important cover for the vice activities that were their real moneymakers. By the early 1960s, investigators had identified at least ninety-eight local businesses that showed "significant Mafia infiltration, ownership, or influence."[84] In the words of historian Stephen Schneider, "organized crime was now more widespread, more sophisticated, more entrepreneurial, more consensual, more transnational, and more Italian."[85]

Law enforcement officials estimated that six or seven large-scale smuggling rings were working along the Michigan-Ontario border by the early 1950s.[86] These were run largely by white ethnic smugglers who imported heroin directly from Europe. Italian gangs rose to the top of the local market, serving as the main importers of heroin. Investigators estimated that local members of what law enforcement dubbed La Cosa Nostra (the Sicilian Mafia) made at least $150 million yearly in various illegal enterprises.[87] Narcotics became their chief moneymaker, but crime syndicates continued to skim money off other vice industries, including prostitution and gambling. Like importers and distributors, women working at the higher levels of the commercial sex trade often found themselves having to negotiate with members of organized crime. As Helen McGowan recalled, "Every madam has two bosses: Mr. Citizen and Mr. X, who represents the rackets. It's like steering a boat between two jagged rocks in an ebb tide and it's not easy."[88] Like their predecessors of the 1920s, rackets continued to use intimidation and violence to get residents and business owners to comply with their demands. Local authorities had identified at least sixty-nine "gangland murders" between 1929 and 1962 that, while decreasing in frequency by the 1950s, continued to serve the purpose of intimidating those unwilling to comply with the Mafia's dictates.[89] "Fear," the commissioner of the Detroit police proclaimed, remained their "principal product."[90]

In Detroit, men like William "Black Bill" Tocco, Peter Licavoli, and Joseph "Scarface Joe" Bommarito ran their illegal operations from suburban estates (many in the wealthy suburb of Grosse Point), using the money they made from urban vice economies to pay for their lavish lifestyles.[91] The U.S.-based Mafia families increasingly turned their attention to the Canadian side of the border, hoping to expand their power across North America. As early as the 1930s, the infamous Charles "Lucky" Luciano had devised a plan to divide the United States and Canada into twenty-four separate regions, each under the jurisdiction of different families. Southwest Ontario was placed under the control of the Detroit-based mob, and the remainder of the province was held by Buffalo's Stefano Magaddino.[92] While these power holdings would diversify in the 1950s, the American Mafia continued to exercise considerable control in Canada.[93] Canadian-based crime families like the Agucci brothers in Toronto and the Papalia crime family in Hamilton attained their status, in part, through the support of American crime families.[94]

By the mid-1950s, Italian gangs were working with French smugglers running what became known as the French Connection. This was, in part, a result of intensified policing in New York City, which encouraged smugglers to look for new points of entry into the North American market. "With Quebec's cultural, commercial, and linguistic ties to France, the subservience of the mafia in [Ontario] to the American Cosa Nostra, as well as Montreal's inviting seaports and close proximity to New York," the French Canadian city was ripe to become a major entry point for heroin.[95] Officials assessed that four main French organizations were involved in heroin smuggling, and they often used French Canadian connections to bring drugs into North America. Dominick Venturi, for example, whose brother Jean Venturi resided in Montreal, would pay Corsican seamen to bring heroin through the St. Lawrence Seaway, into the Great Lakes, and eventually across the U.S.-Canada border.[96] By the late 1950s, officials estimated, 150 kilos of French-produced heroin were smuggled into North America monthly and distributed across the two countries.[97]

Perhaps the most significant player in the local narcotics market was Joseph Zerilli. Born in Sicily in 1897, Zerilli began his criminal career during Prohibition, when he worked with other Italian gangsters to unseat the Jewish-led Purple Gang in Detroit. He was tapped as the head of the city's La Costa Nostra in 1936, when Black Bill Tocco was sent to prison for tax evasion. Over the next forty years, he built an expansive vice network in the region. Zerilli's key contributions were his quiet takeover of the local narcotics trade (which included working with associates in nearby Canadian cities) and his ability to gain control over African American–run vice industries.[98] Increasingly, even small-scale vice operators in the region had to answer to higher-ups like Zerilli. A raid on Detroit's Gotham Hotel, which had been a staple institution in the African American community since 1925, confirmed this transition. By the early 1960s, the Gotham had turned into a gambling den catering to the local black community. When authorities raided it in 1962, they found records indicating that the Mafia had been supplying the establishment with numbers pads and was skimming money off the top of their profits.[99] In business after business, be it gambling, numbers running, liquor sales, or prostitution, white ethnic gangs worked their way to the top, capitalizing on urban vice districts while maintaining an important distance from their everyday operations.

While the postwar heroin subculture and street-level markets were born, in many ways, on the streets themselves, they were also subject to the decisions made by those at the top. Drawn to the border region with the hope that the fluid nature of the national line would allow them to capitalize on the drug market in both the United States and Canada, importers, distributors, and their Mafia bosses helped to grow what became a truly transnational economy. Since senior-level figures like Zerilli rarely got their own hands dirty, they could make large sums of money in what was an expanding illegal market. Unlike arresting the street peddlers who worked the illicit economy on a daily basis, apprehending large-scale dealers took a much more coordinated effort from authorities working across multiple legal jurisdictions. The border cities, while not free of risk for large-scale importers and members of organized crime, provided a fruitful space in which they could grow the illegal economy.

Conclusion

The drug market that emerged in the wake of World War II had multiple social and economic impacts on the borderland communities. People from a wide range of backgrounds participated in the illegal trade, helping to build what became an extensive transnational economy. Users and sellers gathered in both public and private spaces across the city. They met in the bars, gambling dens, and brothels where locals and out-of-towners congregated, as well as in apartment buildings, rooming houses, and hotels that served late-night visitors. For some men and women who hung around the cities' leisure districts, taking heroin and marijuana became a way to fit into the hipster subculture emerging in the late 1940s. Consumption and mobility were key facets within this community, as the image of the wealthy hustler, the hipster, and the cool jazz musician helped draw some people into these illicit exchanges. For those unwilling or unable to participate in broader cultural definitions of consumption, travel, and leisure touted by postwar boosters, the illicit drug subcultures could serve as an important alternative.

The drug market also provided an important source of income for residents of the cities' downtown neighborhoods. By the mid-1950s, a slowing economy, compounded by the effects of suburbanization and segregation, left many poor and working-class residents struggling to make ends meet. Within this context, selling drugs became one viable alternative, particularly for those who lived in neighborhoods where vice was most visible on a daily basis. By providing not only income but also a sense of sociability and community belonging, the illicit drug market helped to blur the lines between legitimate and illegitimate forms of moneymaking in the border cities. Yet, race and class stratification within the drug market demonstrates that the social mobility one could attain through the illicit market was limited. Unlike white ethnic dealers who worked at the top of the international industry, and who found it easier to avoid arrest and prosecution, street peddlers made little monetarily, were more likely to come in contact with the police, and often struggled with the effects of long-term drug addiction. In this way, by the late 1950s, the illicit economy had begun to mirror the race and class divides within the formal economy. For those working at the bottom, the drug market could indeed be a very risky business.

While the drug market was clearly stratified along race and class lines, one thing remained a constant in local users' and sellers' experiences: the importance of the national border in the illegal drug market. People at all levels, from users to traffickers, tried to use the border to their advantage. Canadians and Americans crossed into the neighboring border city in search of excitement and adventure, coming together in their search for stronger kicks. Street-level sellers, importers, and distributors also built cross-border networks that enabled them to meet users on both sides of the border and make connections through which they could sell their products. While the added surveillance at the border sometimes foiled their plans—as people like De Bozy and his girlfriend found out the hard way—the perceived fluid nature of the national line continued to encourage users and sellers to take the chance. Frustrated by the rise of such open flouting of national and local laws, some residents began to wonder how long authorities would continue to allow this to go on.

4

SIN, SLUMS, AND SHADY CHARACTERS

Fighting Vice in the Detroit-Windsor Region

On a sunny afternoon in August 1960, thousands of African Americans crossed into Windsor to attend the city's annual Emancipation Day festival. Founded to celebrate the abolition of slavery in the British Empire, the event was one of the few Windsor festivities that catered specifically to the black community. That evening, at a jazz concert attended by approximately 4,500 people, the majority of whom were African American, a fight broke out between rival Detroit gangs. As part of the scuffle, one man was stabbed in the chest and at least fifty others were wounded, including several police officers. Local, national, and international headlines were quick to dub the incident a "jazz riot" and to denounce the emergence of a violent and disorderly youth culture. Though the use of the terms *jazz* and *riot* had racial connotations, local papers made sure to indicate the racial nature of the incident.[1] As the *Windsor Star* pointed out, "Police said all the rioters were Negroes from Detroit."[2] Local Emancipation Day supporters were horrified by the incident and worked hard to separate their celebration from the violence at the concert. Walter L. Perry, Windsor's "Mr. Emancipation," accused Detroit crime "syndicates" of exploiting the festivities for their own personal gains and consequently giving the Emancipation celebration a "bad reputation." For Perry, the jazz riot only confirmed his fears—that disorganized and rowdy Detroit criminals would reinforce negative racial stereotypes during the very festivities meant to celebrate racial equality and promote racial harmony.

Windsorites and Detroiters alike viewed the jazz riot as an unsettling indicator of the moral decline that had been occurring across North

America since the close of World War II. These fears were national in scope, and many North Americans used the incident as an occasion to express their concerns about urban decline and the deterioration of key social institutions. One Alabama resident responded to the "riot" by asserting that it fit a clear pattern. "In at least all the Western world," the author explained, "the pattern is a sickness of moral chaos and lack of discipline. Overlaying this disorder is a fabric of tensions which seek outlets in senseless destruction and transitory excitements." According to the editorial, the young people involved were "products of a tense and chaotic age. . . . For this is an age which no longer practices or cherishes discipline or manners. Wrong-doing and rudeness and sloppy performance are no longer penalized but shrugged off." The result was violent events like the jazz riot—incidents that occurred on both sides of the border.[3] No longer were Canadians safe from the challenges embedded in the neighboring society. Instead, Canadians and Americans alike grappled with an "urban problem" that seemed to be spreading rapidly across North America.

In the Detroit-Windsor region, residents, social agencies, and community groups alike struggled with how to understand the problems of the postwar city at a time when North Americans prided themselves on attaining a standard of living unparalleled in both its own history and that of nations worldwide. It was difficult for many to reconcile images of urban poverty, violence, dilapidated houses, criminals, heroin addicts, and streetwalkers with the belief that the American dream was alive and more attainable than ever before. Similarly, titles like "Toronto the Good" that enabled Canadians to purport that their cities fared considerably better than their U.S. counterparts were harder to defend, given the many problems faced by residents of industrial Canadian cities.[4] The reality was that the prosperity experienced by many North Americans and the narrow middle-class vision of a North American consumerist society did not fit with the experiences of many residents in urban centers across the two countries. Drug use was on the rise, prostitution operated openly in city centers, and vice networks generated millions of dollars annually in illegal markets that clearly defied normative definitions of labor, leisure, and consumption.

In response, community groups, activists, newspaper reporters, and city residents actively attempted to change the moral trajectory of North American inner cities. Their combined efforts produced a complex process of moral regulation in which they sought to define the parameters of proper conduct and to provide explanations for—and solutions to—illicit industries in the border cities. The language and conclusions put forward by reform societies, researchers, community groups, and the media overlapped on both sides of the border and suggest a unity of purpose across the Detroit-Windsor border. This took place through the deployment of three main themes: a fear of transient individuals, the development of urban renewal programs as distinctly antivice projects, and the rise of juvenile delinquency. On both sides of the border, these themes were formulated through particular class and racial perspectives, which tended to frame urban issues in terms of decay and decline while simultaneously promoting the growth of suburban living, middle-class consumption, and social order.

Tracing the discursive constructions of vice in the border cities makes clear that moral regulation was about much more than simply eliminating unwanted activities. It also functioned as an unofficial form of nation building wherein "average citizens" sought to define who did or did not belong in their community. Questions about citizenship became particularly acute in Detroit and Windsor, as residents struggled with the implications of both internal and cross-border flows of people throughout the region. While racial politics played different roles in Windsor and Detroit, in both cities black-white color lines were reinforced through moralizing discourses that defined communities along the lines of "insiders" and "outsiders." In this way, nation-building projects were also explicitly racialized projects that reflected the anxieties many local whites—Americans as well as Canadians—felt about the shifting racial dynamics in the city of Detroit. Incidents like the jazz riot became the ultimate expression of what would happen if residents were not vigilant against the corrupting influences of urban vice and crime. For reformers, the moral imperative to rein in vice activities was about more than saving North America's cities. It was also about saving the broader nations from moral decay.

Crossing Lines: Transience in the Borderland

As local residents read stories about or saw firsthand the rise in vice in the border cities after the war, they began to look for answers as to who or what was to blame for this phenomenon. One cultural figure that emerged in public debates was the transient—an individual who drifted through town to indulge in illicit activities, subsequently challenging the physical, social, and moral character of the areas he or she passed through. The opposite of the rooted citizen, these individuals had no permanent place but rather functioned parasitically, descending on the cities when it suited their desires. The image of the transient that emerged in the postwar years was in many ways an extension of the "tramp," a figure that dates back to the late nineteenth century. Tim Cresswell argues that the tramp became associated with individuals and lifestyles that challenged the sedentary metaphysics ingrained in North American society. In their ability to traverse place and all that was associated with it (ideas of home and roots, for example), mobile individuals were defined by a number of absences—a lack of commitment, involvement, and attachment—and subsequently became intimately linked with notions of shiftlessness, deviance, and disrepute.[5]

Cresswell argues that the cultural resonance of the tramp died out during World War I, but a close examination of moral discourses surrounding vice reveals that in many ways this figure reemerged in the form of the transient. In public debates about the state of urban life in the 1940s and 1950s, the transient came to represent the underside of mobility in North American society. Sparked by anxieties over large-scale migrations in the United States and Canada during the war years, North Americans began to express concerns about the impact of the war on their communities at home. Families torn apart, people on the move, and uncertainty about the future were all linked to North Americans' ambiguous romance with mobility.[6] As wartime turned into peacetime and Americans attempted to put the upheaval of those devastating years behind them, the rootless individual became even more problematic. While postwar boosters celebrated a controlled type of movement—the legally sanctioned tourism trips and family vacations at the heart of their campaigns—transients pushed these boundaries in key ways. They had no stable home, job, or means of income; overall, they fell short of the markers of middle-class respectability so central to rebuilding the nation in the early postwar years.

In the border cities, public debates about transients portrayed them as perilous individuals who threatened the health of the communities they moved through. This danger was couched in gendered terms, with transient men presented as immoral and nefarious and transient women as young, naive, and vulnerable. One 1944 *Star* article, titled "Girls Who Leave Home for Larger Cities Face Dangers," warned its readers that young women who were "lured from the farm, village, or small town" for wartime employment in larger cities were at great risk of moral and physical danger by "men who don't respect them." Though the author acknowledged that many girls were able to make the trip unharmed, he lamented the "good many tragic letters [that] are coming to me about the teenage girl" who came into contact with dangerous men when she arrived in the big city.[7] Michigan residents were also warned that young women who were allowed to hang out on city streets after dark were likely to turn to prostitution. According to one report, any observer could find countless "saddle shoe, sweater girls standing in dimly lighted, recessed store and shop entrances 'necking' with the youthful service man or civilian as late as 1 or 2 o'clock in the morning."[8] The image of these innocent young women engaging in sexual activity with older men encouraged the Juvenile Delinquency Study Committee to recommend that teenagers be banned from being in the street between the hours of 10 P.M. and 6 A.M.—the hours synonymous with streetwalking.

By the mid-1940s, reports of vulnerable young women falling victim both to nefarious men and to the temptations of prostitution inspired groups like the Women's Local Council of Windsor to take action. Established in 1934 under the name Border Cities Local Council of Women, its goal was to provide women with a stronger voice in community policy making and other activities. Among their focuses were the issues of post-war readjustment and social services within the cities, placing the issue of vice and crime firmly in their sights.[9] Their renewed focus on these issues began with a 1946 campaign designed to make city parks safer, which ultimately led to swearing in parks caretakers as constables that year. If they could protect young women from the wiles of dangerous characters in the city's public spaces, the group insisted, it would go a long way toward discouraging transients from making their way to the border city.[10]

The growing visibility of vice at the end of the war also encouraged thousands of local Canadian women, including members of the Young Women's Christian Association, the Roman Catholic Church, and various Protestant churches in Windsor, to join together in a drive to eliminate sex crimes from the city. In 1945, their vocal efforts resulted in a meeting between staff members at the *Windsor Daily Star*, the police department, and Mayor Reaume. In an effort to dissuade men and women from participating in the sex industry, the *Star* agreed to publish the names of those arrested for prostitution-related offenses. Emboldened by this modest success, these organizations continued their crusade against vice in the border city. At the Women's Local Council of Windsor's 1948 annual meeting, members expressed concerns that "delinquency and crime were getting out of control." In response, the vice president of the council pushed the mayor to call a "broadly representative conference of the religious, social, educational, and recreational bodies, the law and law enforcement agencies, the press and radio, to consider and deal with a serious problem."[11]

Through public campaigns—which combined media attention, political capital, and grassroots organizing—middle-class women brought public attention to the effects of transients and vice on their communities.

Across the river, many middle-class Detroiters also became concerned with the rise in vice, transience, and prostitution as the city transitioned from wartime to peacetime. There, too, protecting girls and young women became a primary concern. Organizations like the Girl's Work Council, the Girls' Protective League, the Detroit Council for Youth Services, and the Girls' Service Clubs were established with the purpose of overseeing and regulating young women living unsupervised in the city. These organizations shared the goal of getting girls off the streets and into homes where they could be properly supervised. They also operated on the assumption that the longer young women were without formal oversight, the less likely they were to become integrated into society as productive citizens. When the United Community Services organization conducted a study of the conditions of wayward girls in Detroit, their report affirmed the belief that society would eventually end up paying for these girls in one form or another. As it explained, "The girl with unresolved problems can add to the community tax burden by involvement in prostitution, illegitimacy, or long term dependency upon the public social welfare." It further argued that "most of the girls-with-problems were the products of broken, disorganized, or demoralized families" and that service programs geared toward strengthening the family and local communities were vital. If given a chance at a proper home life, the girls just might be able to make a valuable contribution to society one day, thus saving tax-paying citizens their hard-earned money.[12]

Reformers and local residents did not limit their disdain to the most obvious figures—the prostitutes, drug users, pimps, and other people who frequented the cities' vice districts. They also began to target legal forms of leisure and entertainment when they felt they crossed moral lines. Traveling carnivals in particular drew the ire of local residents who became concerned about the questionable characters they brought to town. When the W. G. Wade Carnival show passed through southeastern Michigan in May 1953, for example, a group of residents informed the Michigan State Police that there was illegal gambling going on. When Officer Charles Frank arrived to investigate, he found more than just gambling. While canvassing the carnival grounds, he entered the "Jezebelle Show" around 11 P.M. and noted a large number of teenage boys gathered there. As the officer watched, a man named Rex Allen entered the stage and introduced the act, performed by Margareta Pagan: "Well boys, we all know what you came here for," he belted. "Of course you'll have to pay something. You know you never get anything in this world for nothing. If you do you want to be damn careful." He continued to entice the young viewers: "Now if you never saw pussy before, you will see it to-night [*sic*]. Also there is a snake in the act and to-night is a cold night. Those snakes like warm holes, so don't be surprised what you will see." According to the officer, after this titillating introduction, Pagan proceeded to "completely disrobe to the extent of being nude and then perform various dances" in front of the crowd.[13] The officer arrested Pagan and Allen (after he observed the show, of course!), who each pled guilty to "Indecent & Obscene Exposure" and served sixty days in the county jail—the maximum penalty for the offense.[14]

Traveling shows also drew public criticism from Windsor residents, and local media explicitly drew connections between vice, transience, and moral decline that took place as part of these spectacles. One *Star* article warned its readers of the connection between venereal disease and transient people such as carnival workers and prostitutes, arguing that both were a major problem because they brought disease and disrupted otherwise wholesome communities. According to the report, of the prostitutes that traveled to Windsor to take up the sex industry, many were "unaware of [VD] infections" and some had been only "partially treated," making them a risk to local residents.[15] The author further explained that traveling people such as "the hangers-on and camp-followers of traveling shows" also put a community in danger. They "constitute a grave menace to the cities where they travel. I do not refer to the acrobats and others who must maintain a high level of physical fitness," the author clarified, "but to the concessionaires."[16] The connection between carnival workers and prostitution was the mobility of their occupations. Importantly, this instability was portrayed as necessarily linked to immorality. This had strong class undertones, as acrobats were necessarily healthier than the lower-status concessionaires. The "hangers-on" and concessionaires working traveling carnival shows attracted people of loose morals, and therefore moral reformers and concerned citizens took action to try to protect their communities from these unseemly characters.

In the border cities, concerns over transience were often framed as a problem of noncitizens preying on local community members. This was particularly acute in Windsor, where Canadian residents expressed anxieties about Americans crossing into their otherwise quiet community to commit crimes. For many local residents, news of criminals like convicted felon Leo Thompson proved their anxieties were well-founded. In 1941, Thompson was charged under the White Slave Trade Act of the United

States with trafficking a Windsor girl into Detroit. Though a Canadian national, he had been living in the Detroit area on and off for twelve years and was wanted by federal authorities on both sides of the border. On November 21, 1940, he reportedly abducted a fourteen-year-old girl from her Windsor home. He brought her to a Detroit hotel, where he kept her locked in a room and "repeated[ly] assaulted" her. He was discovered in the Windsor area by police because he had been seen frequenting the Blue Water Hotel, a place where prostitution and other illicit activities were common.[17] For many, the Thompson case provided a clear example of the dangers presented by outsiders who came to the city for illicit purposes. Transient strangers could use their cross-border mobility as a way to avoid arrest, and unsuspecting local residents would be none the wiser.

Unlike earlier images of tramps, hobos, and vagabonds, the transient was not necessarily completely rootless. The specter of hordes of American tourists crossing the national border for illicit forms of entertainment, even if they would eventually return home, was enough to spark some Windsor residents' concern. Near the end of the war, government bans on the production of alcohol in the United States encouraged many Detroiters to travel to Windsor in search of beer, which a front-page *Windsor Star* article termed the "thirsty invasion." Reporting on beer shortages in Windsor, the article lamented that "Americans could be spotted driving through all sections of the city on exploratory trips. . . . And even in neighborhood hotels in residential areas, where everybody usually knows everybody else, groups of strangers walked in [to bars] and everyone knew, after listening to their distinctive dialects, that they were Americans."[18] In this way, American visitors challenged the familiarity of leisure spaces in the city of Windsor, and their verbal markers delineated their outsider status within the local pub culture.[19] As the number of American tourists continued to climb after the war, so, too, did complaints about rowdy Americans frequenting the bordertown. By the late 1940s, Windsorites regularly complained about "curb cruisers," American men who drove around the city trying to pick up young Canadian women.[20] Warnings that the border brought hordes of "sex perverts" rang true to many local residents, who became increasingly frustrated with the brazenness with which Americans walked their city in search of illicit adventure.[21] As it turns out, there was an underside to border tourism, and, for some Canadians, the money to be made from cross-border trade was not worth the risks.

Detroiters certainly read their share of stories about criminals, transients, and smugglers using the border to evade arrest, and occasionally large-scale busts at the border would remind Detroiters about the potential dangers of living along the national line. It was, however, another border that dominated debates about transience and vice in the Motor City during the 1940s. For many white middle-class Detroiters, the border between the North and South and, by extension, blacks and whites, came to symbolize the dangers of the transient on the move. While southern whites, or hillbillies as they were called, were hardly welcomed with open arms, the influx of the "Southern Negro" sparked the most outrage from white residents.[22] Contemporary sociologists who studied the migration of African American southerners to the city of Detroit termed this phenomenon "ecological invasion."[23] Challenging racial lines through this process was thus described as unnatural, an infiltration of the rightful order of the "ecological" environment of the neighborhood.

Stories of urban decline, poverty, and vice blamed transient migrants for many of the problems in Detroit's shifting urban neighborhoods. One national magazine article described Detroit as "a kind of transient hotel," a city whose culture was being transformed for the worse by "white and negro" migrants from the rural South. As the author explained, "The collapsing frame houses, with sagging porches and window frames askew, which dot Paradise Valley, Detroit's worst Negro slum, are open sores that indicate the kind of decay which must be present even in the brick buildings, two-family homes and small apartments, where too many people are forced to live together." According to the author, "The white slums, usually called the hillbilly slums, are of much the same quality, have much the same look about them. Only the color of the faces at the windows and the kind of music coming from the bars and hash houses (rock and roll in the Negro slums, country music in the white) indicate the racial character of a neighborhood, and on many slum streets the two races meet in a common squalor."[24] In such articles, authors linked the transient nature of southern migrants to the growth of both slum and vice districts, blaming the city's ills on what they saw as a temporary population. By frequenting bars and hash houses and hanging out on city streets, many believed the southern migrant was changing the moral trajectory of local communities for the worse.

Concerns about transience were not limited to residents who opposed the influx of southern migrants. Even groups working to better race relations in the city blamed the problem, in part, on transience. In its study of the Twelfth Street neighborhood, the Detroit Urban League (DUL) argued that as long as the neighborhood continued to be defined as a "bad" place to live, "the high rate of transiency will continue, causing the area to remain an intermediate point between the 'worst' and the 'best areas.'"[25]

Though the DUL report was sympathetic to the issue of changing neighborhoods and worked to counter attitudes that linked black communities with crime and vice, their own report suggested that transience was a key part of the problem. As long as people remained unsettled and moved in and out of the neighborhood, outsiders would continue to perceive it as a slum area that facilitated neighborhood blight and illegal activities. Thus black southern migrants who "invaded" local communities were viewed as the main reason for the rapid deterioration of Detroit's downtown neighborhoods and came to represent a particularly problematic figure in the border region.

Although the carnival worker, the prostitute, and the "negro invader" were perceived differently according to the social and legal codes they violated, they all also simultaneously invoked fears of shiftlessness and the spread of immorality. The movement of these men and women into the border cities during the 1940s challenged beliefs in the rooted community in which active citizens played a key role in protecting their families and social institutions. Especially in the years immediately following the war, residents sought to bring some order back to their lives and their communities. Fear of invasion by outsiders, whether temporary travelers or long-term migrants, led many middle-class North Americans to openly attempt to protect their communities from this infiltration. Outsiders also provided useful scapegoats on which they could pin many of the problems they saw developing in their community.

Renewing the Postwar City

If the people traveling into the cities' cores sparked moral reformers' concern, so, too, did the very neighborhoods that were attracting this transient population. Like many northern cities, outdated infrastructure in Detroit and Windsor made it difficult for the cities to accommodate the economic and demographic changes that took place during World War II. By the end of the 1940s, overcrowding, rundown neighborhoods, and the visibility of poverty made it clear that the city centers were falling far short of the prosperity promised by local boosters. In response, to counter blight and all its related issues, the cities began to undertake expansive urban renewal projects. Though municipal leaders approached renewal in different ways and on different scales, the various projects that fell under the umbrella of "urban renewal" had similar objectives on both sides of the border. Central to their goals was the desire to remake rundown neighborhoods with the hope of eliminating poverty and crime. No longer simply a problem of postwar maladjustment, by the 1950s, the problem of vice came to symbolize the problems of the postwar city writ large.

Perhaps no city demonstrates the newfound faith municipal leaders and local residents placed in urban planners as well as Detroit, which emerged at the forefront of urban redevelopment in the postwar years. Its 129-acre Gratiot Project, which identified twelve locations for the development of public housing, was the nation's first attempt at residential redevelopment under the Federal Housing Act of 1949.[26] Municipal leaders turned to such large-scale redevelopment projects to achieve three particular goals: stopping the exodus of business from the inner city, turning slum areas into better housing, and growing the city's tax base, which dwindled as suburban communities drew both businesses and families out of the city core.[27] These goals were outlined in "The Detroit Plan: A Program for Blight Elimination," a groundbreaking report released by Mayor Jefferies in 1947.[28] Under its general framework, by 1963 the city had more than ten urban renewal projects under way. More than 10,000 structures had been demolished or were scheduled for demolition, and 43,096 people, 70 percent of them African American, had been or were soon to be displaced.[29] As part of its planning efforts, the city also enacted an ordinance specifically designed to eliminate vice in "skid row" districts along the Detroit River. "The purpose of the ordinance," according to a Canadian study hoping to mirror its effects, was "to prevent a re-concentration of these uses in other areas of the City once they were forced out of the downtown area by the urban renewal project."[30] In other words, not only were urban renewal projects aimed at displacing vice and crime in downtown neighborhoods but also they were designed to prevent them from spreading to middle-class neighborhoods within and adjacent to the city limits.

Given these objectives, urban renewal tended to have a disproportionately negative effect on residents living in neighborhoods defined as "slums." Though aimed at improving housing conditions in particular, these projects often destroyed low-income housing in exchange for middle- to upper-income residential areas, leaving many poor Detroiters without affordable places to live. In the lag between the time an area was designated for urban renewal and when the actual process began, many renters and owners had no need to keep up their properties, further encouraging blighted areas.[31] Although groups like the United Auto Workers maintained that new low-income housing needed to be created *before* "slum areas" were cleared, renewal projects generally ignored these warnings.[32] Once the demolition process began, vandalism and violence often increased in the area, and the lack of oversight by community members provided cover for a wide range of illegal activities.[33] Critics of urban renewal projects noted that the results were often only "structure-deep" and failed to give attention to "improving *cultural* values" in the areas under redevelopment. As a DUL report put it, "Too much attention is given to the structural elements and too little attention is given to the human elements of redevelopment."[34]

In Detroit, class and race were intimately intertwined and shaped how residents responded to renewal projects. Stereotypes associating African Americans with vice and crime left many white residents unable to distinguish between rundown vice districts and working-class black neighborhoods. When the DUL surveyed city residents about their perceptions of the Twelfth Street community, for example, they found that the majority perceived it as exclusively African American, as the area with the city's highest crime rate, and as the "only place on the Westside with 'poor-type' people, structures, and facilities."[35] The study argued the rapid influx of large numbers of black residents had fostered these perceptions, which did not in fact reflect the actual conditions in the neighborhood. The community was not exclusively poor and black, nor did it have the highest rate of crime in the city. Researchers also found that both middle-class African American and white leaders were deeply concerned that this perception of the neighborhood would invite additional transients and crime that might eventually leave "*their areas*" open to "invasion." "Therefore," the study concluded, while urban renewal projects were supposedly aimed at improving the Twelfth Street neighborhood, "the latent interest is to *contain the residents*."[36]

Significantly, the DUL argued that the link between poor African American residents, crime, and urban blight was often most vigorously enforced by black middle-class residents who attempted to dissociate themselves with the stigma of the city's slums. "In fact," the study found, "sometimes it is difficult to determine: who is the fastest in leaving an area which is being invaded by lower class Negroes—the white or the Negro middle class resident?"[37] The result of the mutually reinforcing class and race divides would continue to ensure that the cycle of movement and urban decline would "begin anew: the middle class Negroes, fearing a loss of status and property values, will attempt to run to the better white areas; the white residents, fearing a loss of status and property values, will run closer to the suburbs. And, in their haste to 'escape,' too few people are objectively aware of either what they are escaping from or where they are escaping to."[38]

The study of the Twelfth Street community demonstrates the complicated nature of urban renewal and the multiple lines that worked to define particular neighborhoods as desirable or undesirable places of residence. The reputation of an area could have as large an impact as the reality on the ground. If a particular space was perceived as a place where crime, violence, and blight were rampant, that in and of itself was often enough to encourage those conditions to develop. The process of fleeing one area and attempting to contain undesirable community members in the spaces left behind was central to urban renewal projects. Further, the association between crime and vice was directly linked to racialized and class perceptions of a given neighborhood. The fact that illegal activities were so widely associated with African Americans meant that black middle-class residents had to work even harder to dissociate themselves from areas perceived as slums. This went beyond simply moving away from those areas; it also meant becoming vocal proponents of urban renewal projects in poor neighborhoods, thus pitting African American residents against one another along class lines.

Ultimately, the fate of Paradise Valley demonstrates the extent to which municipal leaders hoped to use urban renewal to wipe out vice from the city. The neighborhood that had for decades functioned as the center of black businesses—both legal and illegal—was slated for demolition under the "Detroit Plan." Hastings Street, the cultural center of the Valley, was razed to build I-375. By the end of the 1950s, the haunts where jazz and blues greats like John Lee Hooker, Bobo Jenkins, Ella Fitzgerald, and Count Basie had played on a regular basis were torn to the ground. Though the Valley had struggled with economic decline since the war, the construction of the expressway still destroyed at least 409 businesses, "including forty-nine eating places, sixty-eight markets, twenty appliance and furniture stores, fifteen drug stores, eighteen bars, and twelve churches."[39] By the early 1960s, the street once described as "a place where everything is happening" was no more.[40] To the north, massive housing projects like the Jefferies Project demolished what remained of the neighborhood. In this way, "renewal" projects not only destroyed homes and businesses but also worked to erase the memory of what was once a vibrant neighborhood, a place where black and white residents had come together in search of leisure and community. Displacing Paradise Valley would not eliminate vice from Detroit and, in many ways, simply sped up the process of transforming neighborhoods like Twelfth Street into new spaces where illegal economies could flourish. Renewal, however, was more successful at demonstrating who did and did not count as a full and welcomed citizen in postwar Detroit. For some, the destruction of Paradise Valley became a symbol of municipal efforts at "containing" poor and black residents in

Hastings Street, the central corridor of Paradise Valley, before and during the urban renewal process. (Courtesy of the Walter P. Reuther Library, Wayne State University)

the worst parts of the city and of destroying neighborhoods they saw as a threat to the wider community. As a result, many Detroit residents would come to know urban renewal programs under a much more descriptive term, "negro removal."[41]

Across the river, Canadian municipal leaders looked to the example set by their American neighbor and began to take steps to fight vice, blight, and transience in Windsor. A bit late to the game, in 1959 the city of Windsor commissioned the foremost urban renewal expert in Canada, E. G. Faludi, to propose a project that would address the city's key problems. The resultant Faludi Study focused on trends common across the border region, including an emphasis on suburbanization and the corresponding deterioration of industrial neighborhoods. Central to the study was the desire to redevelop so-called blighted areas and to rezone neighborhoods to facilitate a desirable mix of residential, commercial, and manufacturing spaces. According to the report, one of the main goals was "to save the City and the fringe areas from further deterioration and to reduce blight by the application of an urban renewal programme consisting of protective, preventative and curative measures."[42] This was, in part, a response to the fact that by the late 1950s, many industrial sites sat vacant, and the land was deemed not only unsightly but also dangerous because it provided locations where illegal activities could take place. The closing of many factories also had a negative impact on the surrounding communities, the report noted, and residential properties began to suffer because of the owners' lack of income.

The Faludi Study concluded that two developments were at the heart of Windsor's urban problems: the city's inability to attract the necessary level of industrial development and the increasing rate of suburbanization. As residents moved to the suburbs in large numbers, services deteriorated in the downtown core. According to the study, "In contrast to the rapid suburbanization . . . the central parts of the City, residential, commercial, and industrial, are declining and give little incentive for improvement."[43] Significantly, "the pattern of the outward growth is disorderly and haphazard but the inward decline is continuous and uniform. Undoubtedly much of the urban blight in the central core of the City is due to the functional defects in many parts of the structure of the City." Maps the researchers created further demonstrate that blighted areas tended to develop along industrial sites near the Detroit River and on streets within the downtown core. It also made clear that the economic disparities between suburban and downtown neighborhoods were directly linked to the upkeep of properties and the conditions of local infrastructure.

Contemporaries asserted that there was a direct link between the trends identified in the Faludi Study and the issues of vice and social welfare. To appease these concerns, the report asserted that its fifteen-year program, if undertaken, would have a direct impact on the social conditions of the city of Windsor in four main ways: first, by "eliminating slum conditions"; second, by "reducing incidents of crime, disease and fire hazards"; third, by "halting the trend of decline all over the Metropolitan community"; and finally, by "providing up to date rental housing accommodation for an income class which cannot pay economic rents."[44] In effect, the study promised, like the Detroit Plan, to both prevent and cure issues of crime and vice by gutting slum neighborhoods and replacing them with more distinctly modern, middle-class housing. This in turn would aid the economic growth in the city and lead to a generally upwardly mobile trend for city residents.

The connection between vice and rundown slum areas was echoed in the local media, helping to bolster the public's faith in renewal programs as a way to clean up the city. The same news reports that drew attention to the rise of prostitution and other forms of vice after the war were quick to link those developments to the deterioration of the city's core. One *Maclean's* article, for example, directly linked urban decline to the rise of illegal economies, noting that the rundown and dilapidated neighborhoods provided the necessary fronts for the illegal activities. "For a $2 ride in and out [of] the compact blocks of Windsor's business section," it explained, "any cab driver would point out which of the dingy rooming houses, pool rooms, and tobacco stores on Pitt, Sandwich, Assumption, and Pellissier Streets, behind whose false fronts you could get a girl, buy a drink, or place a bet."[45] These "backroom sin-bins sandwiched between factories and tumble-down shops" were precisely the type of spaces urban renewal was supposed to eliminate. In this sense, the study's recommendation of razing entire city blocks adjacent to the commercial district also promoted a reorganization of Windsor along class lines. By eliminating symptoms of poverty and lower-class leisure and entertainment, such as prostitution and numbers-running, the Toronto-based firm purported to not only eliminate crime but also reinvent the city of Windsor as a solidly middle-class, suburban border city.

The recommendations of the Faludi Study were enacted in two phases, both of which focused on what contemporaries termed "redevelopment." Unlike the competing strategies of rehabilitation or conservation, *redevelopment* was defined as the "drastic surgery of cutting out slums and replacing them with new housing or other developments."[46] Both phases were concentrated in the city's core and included eliminating older structures to build row housing, apartments, and an esplanade that would connect City Hall to the waterfront. Relying on a mix of municipal, provincial, federal, and private funding, city planners advertised their renewal project in major cities across the United States and Canada. Presenting it as a unique opportunity to invest in a thriving borderland community, advertisements for investors emphasized the close relationship between Detroit and Windsor, the busy waterway that connected the two nations, and the city's position as an important cultural center. The city specifically called for department stores, retail shops, apartment buildings, and hotels or motels, the very businesses that were at the heart of the tourist boom of the 1940s and 1950s.[47] Hoping to expand cross-border tourism while eliminating the most unsightly elements of their city, municipal leaders seemed to want to revitalize the boosterism of the recent past to build a brighter future. As in Detroit, though, this project relied on their ability to erase the unsightly elements of the city and eliminate the underside of the borderlands economy, a project that would prove too great for even the most well-funded renewal program.

By the end of the 1950s, municipal governments in Detroit and Windsor had enacted urban renewal projects as one solution to the problems of vice, transience, and urban decline in the border region. In many ways, the goals were parallel in the two cities: they attempted to remake blighted neighborhoods by rebuilding structures and discouraging the settlement of undesirable characters. In Detroit, this became an explicitly racialized project, and urban planning in Windsor similarly signaled the class and geographic divides in North American cities. Hoping to stem the flight of industry and tax dollars from city centers into the surrounding suburbs, urban planners attempted to rebuild what they saw as the essential elements of middle-class living: stable homes, vibrant business districts, and modern transportation systems. As symptoms of poverty, decay, and economic downturn, vice districts were framed as diametrically opposed to healthy communities. Ironically, on both sides of the border, renewal projects tended to displace poor communities without rebuilding them in any functional way, therefore perpetuating some of the economic impetus behind the illegal economies they were hoping to eliminate. While urban renewal projects were able to disrupt some vice patterns, they often served to merely shift the spaces in which vice took place from one neighborhood to the next—much to the chagrin of middle-class and suburban residents in the region, and at the cost of much upheaval for the poorest residents.

Juke Joints and Jazz Riots: Juvenile Delinquency in the Borderland

Concerns about transients and urban decline encouraged reformers to turn their attention to those deemed most vulnerable: the cities' youth. On both sides of the border, North Americans saw what was happening to young people as a sign of the larger problems facing the countries. Like the drifter and the transient, the young delinquent became a symptom of the moral decay growing in the nations' urban centers. In juke joints, dance halls, and soda shops teens seemed to be turning to a dangerous youth culture in which sexual promiscuity and drug use were becoming common. For Windsor and Detroit residents alike, the problems of the delinquent symbolized the ultimate consequences of vice, crime, and urban blight in the postwar years.

Concerns about juvenile delinquency began to grow during the 1940s, as many North Americans worried about the long-term impact that the war years would have on the nations' youth. One 1944 newspaper declared that juvenile delinquency was "the nation's No. 1 problem" and described the hordes of young people flocking to American cities. These "young drifters," who could be seen sleeping in "hallways, on subway trains, in parks, theater balconies, and in garages," were presented as a dangerous and growing "menace to law-abiding citizens."[48] A 1945 article, titled "Crime Wave—Hangover from War," explained that a "general unrest" was sparking a "rising tide of lawlessness now sweeping the country as criminals big and little are giving harried police [the] most hectic time in years."[49] Articles published in cities across the United States and Canada warned that if steps were not taken to help people adjust as the war came to a close, delinquency would continue to rise and eventually reach crisis proportions.[50]

Experts posited psychological and environmental explanations for delinquency, tending to avoid the belief—prevalent in earlier decades—that these teens were inherently bad or immoral. Instead, psychologists and other experts most often located the causes of deviance in both bad home lives and bad social environments.[51] In part, this reflected faith in the nuclear family, which was supposed to act as a grounding principle around which North Americans could rebuild their personal lives and their society as a whole.[52] The family was framed as a "psychological fortress" that would protect its members from an uncertain and potentially dangerous world; in the absence of this emotional protection, children would necessarily turn into delinquents.[53] As James S. Plant explained in a 1945 study of youth gangs in Ontario, a juvenile delinquent was "a person striking back at society's failure to give him what he wants out of life. He is the sensitive member of a community who is trying to tell us what is wrong. . . . Juvenile delinquency is a thing that *happens to* an individual, not a thing that he does."[54]

Within this context, one of the most troubling developments in inner-city neighborhoods was the increase in matriarchal households, which disrupted normative gender patterns by challenging the authority of the male-headed household. An in-depth report issued by the Mayor's Committee for Community Action for Detroit Youth (MCCADY) determined that single mothers were a leading cause of crime and delinquency among the city's young people, especially in African American families living in downtown communities. According to the working papers of the committee, "The development of personalities among lower class Negro children [was] largely determined by broken homes and the influence of maternal authority."[55] In their families, mothers were more likely to be the breadwinners because work geared toward women (such as domestic and retail positions) was often more readily available than industrial work. Due to their frustration with their inability to fulfill their proper male role, men often left their families. In cases where the father remained with his family, the children saw a weakened male figure, which worked as a disincentive for black boys imagining their future careers. Therefore, according to the study, black male youths were more likely to turn to the illicit economy and nonnormative gendered patterns of interaction within their communities.[56]

In addition to diminishing boys' desire for gainful employment, the committee argued, the dominance of female-led households caused two interrelated issues: the development of homosexual tendencies and hypermasculinity that often turned into violence against women. "Because of the dominance by women and lack of adequate males as models," it concluded, "we are not surprised that a clinical psychologist, listening to the tapes of our interviews suspected a good amount of latent homosexuality among the males." The researchers provide no additional evidence to support this claim but rather rely on the expertise of a psychologist who never actually met the boys. Apparently, just by listening to the way they talked and the views they expressed in their taped interviews, the unnamed psychologist could detect deviant sexual and character traits linked to homosexuality. Alternatively, this perceived crisis of gender identity also took the form of violent heterosexuality. The male interviewees regularly "talk about pimps beating up prostitutes, fathers hitting mothers, and so on. Sexual behavior for the boys has more elements of aggression related to it than elements of affect." The committee concluded that "the style of life, then, is perceived to be female-centered and aggression against women by males would seem to indicate that such a matriarchy is not a preferred and valued cultural phenomenon at all, but rather a mode of adjustment to the blocked opportunity for males."[57]

The MCCADY report reveals several key ideologies that permeated postwar discourses of domesticity and family. First and foremost, the committee demonstrates the primacy of the patriarchal family order and identifies the female household head as a key factor in a youth's turn toward delinquency. According to the report, one's decision to join the illicit economy was made both out of a lack of proper male role models in the family and as a rebellious act against the improper authority role played by the mother. The fear that female breadwinners led to weakened father figures was further linked to deviant forms of sexual and gendered interactions, encouraging young boys to either pursue homosexual relationships or act violently in their relationships with women. These conclusions led the study to reject the possibility that matriarchal families could be a "preferred" family structure, instead viewing it as a phenomenon that developed out of the limited opportunities for men in industrial cities like Detroit— it represented a *lack* of opportunity rather than a positive choice made by residents in the downtown neighborhoods. Further, this placed much of the blame of delinquency on African American women who, in their attempts to take care of their families by taking on the breadwinner role, were subverting proper gender roles and creating an environment where young boys in particular grew up without a sense of a well-ordered household. The racialized image of the aggressive black matriarch was a prime example of the consequences of the increase in poor, single-parent households in the city's urban slums.

Canadian reformers also emphasized the problems caused by single-parent households, and across Ontario parents read about the potential dangers awaiting children from "broken homes." A 1952 report on a board meeting of Evangelicalism and Social Service of the United Church of Canada claimed the problems of the "poor, the alcoholic, the aged, the unmarried mother, and the homeless" were a much greater threat to Canadian society than Communism, a claim with particular resonance given the Cold War climate in which it was made.[58] According to a *Globe and Mail* report, "74 per cent of delinquency cases arise out of broken homes."[59] The ultimate consequence of the single-parent household was explained in a 1954 article, which told the story of "a 13-year-old boy" who "hanged himself at the Cobourg Training School for Boys this week. He was the product of a broken home, where he felt himself unwanted." The author warned that "before people with children consider a divorce . . . they should think of their offspring." When a child comes from a divorced family, "something that was fine in him dies for lack of the nourishment of love." Significantly, these unhappy children were repeatedly said to be from lower-class and minority families, reinforcing the divide between the middle-class suburban family and poor families living in the nation's major urban centers.[60]

In the border cities, moral reformers were able to use the image of the teenage delinquent to gain public support for their antivice measures. They did so by publicizing stories that linked gender deviance, racial transgressions, and dangerous urban spaces. In 1944, the Canadian Minister of Health, John Howe, announced the start of an intense campaign aimed at ridding Windsor of its houses of prostitution and other places that facilitated commercial sex in the city. According to the *Windsor Star*, this campaign grew out of the "civic indignation" that ensued after "two teen-aged boys were found in a Windsor disorderly house."[61] The article claimed that "the problem" of prostitution was "brought to a head here by the frank testimony given by the boys, one 15 and the other 16 years old, who were picked up by the city police morality squad in a raid." The author of the article seemed particularly concerned that "the youngsters made no attempt to conceal the purpose of their visit to the raided house." "Prostitution," the minister warned readers, "comes directly under the scope of the health department's work because it spreads disease and *cannot* be made sanitary. In addition, it corrupts morals and bankrupts families, and provides a haven for petty criminals and is always associated in one way or another, with alcoholism and the drug traffic."[62] Though the issue of youthful customers drew the attention of authorities, they situated these concerns within broader discussions about transience, the family, and moral decline.

Similarly, a handbook published by Detroit Public Schools provided a dire warning for parents and teachers to be on the lookout for the symptoms of drug use and delinquency among teens. It explained that unsupervised boys and girls were likely to turn to narcotics to alleviate the pain that resulted from their family problems. It included a quote from one young addict: "I just didn't care after my parents were divorced, and started to take heroin to forget my feelings."[63] According to the booklet, teens started by sniffing or snorting powders and progressed to intravenous drug use, aided in part by the drug peddler who gave them drugs for little or no money to get them hooked. "Their favorite meeting places . . . are rooftops, basements, school and movie lavatories, and in their own homes if they have the opportunity there. . . . During the course of the addiction there is a progressive narrowing of interests. They give up their interests in school, in sports, in their friends." Eventually, according to the handbook, boys who became physically addicted to drugs turned to a life of crime to pay for their habits, perpetuating the cycle of delinquency.[64]

Just as unsupervised boys were likely to turn to illicit and delinquent activities, poor parental supervision of girls left them susceptible to the corrupting influences of delinquent boys. These narratives echoed the gendered discussions of transience, wherein girls were susceptible to the corrupting influences of nefarious men. They also reinforce the fact that deviance and delinquency among young women was explicitly linked to sexuality—the ultimate violation of gender norms being sexual promiscuity and public expressions of illicit sexuality. In 1951, the U.S. Senate Crime Investigating Committee received international press attention when it reported on the rise of interracial prostitution among teenagers in cities like New York, Chicago, and Detroit. News reports that covered the investigation included an excerpt from the testimony of a fourteen-year-old Chicago boy who claimed that white girls were prostituting themselves to black men to get narcotics. When the chairman of the committee asked the African American boy how he "knew about the white girls," the boy replied, "There is no segregation in using dope," a statement that no doubt frightened many middle-class white parents.[65]

Canadian papers also reported on the rise of interracial sex among young American teens, warning Canadians that if they failed to take decisive action, they, too, would face similar problems in their own cities. One such report, titled "Juvenile Junkies," successfully deployed all the signs that middle-class Canadians feared most: sexually promiscuous single mothers raising children in drug-infested "ethnic" neighborhoods. It began by claiming that "happy youngsters wrapped in love and security of a home do not become addicts"; instead, juveniles become addicted in "an attempt to escape from their wretched lives." The author focused on Harlem, painting a disturbing picture for its Canadian readers: "[Harlem] is a district where sexual promiscuity is the normal behavior. A man and a woman will set up a shabby household without benefit of clergy; then in a year or two the man will move off with another woman, leaving his original partner to support the children he may have fathered."[66] According to the article, these children then turned to gangs and drug use, joining the growing ranks of juvenile delinquents. For middle-class Canadians, the message was clear: sexual promiscuity, broken homes, race mixing, and poor neighborhoods would weaken the moral fabric of Canadian society and create an environment in which juveniles would become unproductive, drug-addicted delinquents.

American and Canadian reports on delinquency united competing concerns about unsupervised urban leisure, race mixing, and violence, arguing that the problem among the nations' youth seemed to be spiraling out of control. One local publication explained to readers that in "Hell's Half Acre," a neighborhood in north Detroit, unsupervised young people struggled to deal with the social tensions that were emerging in their ever-shifting neighborhoods. "From areas where race and religious hatreds smolder," it explained, "from too crowded homes come today's delinquents. In poolrooms, on street corners, they will become tomorrow's criminals—unless something is done." The article was accompanied by a photo of teens hanging out on a dimly lit corner, unsupervised and up to no good. Similarly, throughout the course of its interviews with local Detroit teens, the MCCADY researchers were shocked at the level of violence articulated by the interviewees. When researchers asked them to "tell me about your neighborhood," the vast majority of girls and boys commented on the high level of violence around them. Many of the respondents saw this as a normal day-to-day experience, using expressions like "this is the world, man, and that's where it's at."[67] The interviewees also noted that interracial fighting among young people was commonplace and expressed the opinion that white and black groups were not supposed to mingle to any great degree.[68] Records of the Detroit Police Department's Youth Bureau confirm these patterns. The police regularly responded to calls from local residents who reported when interracial clashes between teens broke out on city streets.[69] Significantly, this violence often began at leisure spaces and other sites where teenagers hung out. With the memory of the 1943 race riots fresh in many residents' minds, fears about unsupervised teens clashing in the city streets had important resonance. Unsupervised boys and girls in the city's downtown neighborhoods were not only at risk of delinquency; they were also susceptible to violence when gangs of black and white teens came into contact in the racially charged streets.

As interracial tensions heated up on the American side of the border, Canadian residents expressed concerns that the "American" race problem would spill over onto their side of the border. Local reports provided racialized descriptions of American ruffians who purportedly took pleasure in violent confrontations with Canadian boys. A 1943 article, for example, claimed that "four zoot-suited Detroiters" were arrested in the early hours of the morning as they made their way back to the Ambassador Bridge. The officers picked up the boys after reports of "an orgy of horseplay and zoot-suit terror tactics which left a wake of battered youths behind them in the resort section of Kingsville [Ontario]." Earlier in the evening, after throwing the son of the local police chief into Lake Erie, the Americans headed to a dance at the Kingsville Casino. There they got into a skirmish with some local boys. The Canadians begged the Detroit teens to put down their rubber hoses and have a "fair fist fight," which they refused to do. "This is how we fight," they apparently told the Canadian boys; "this is how we handled those colored guys in Detroit!"[70] Though this quote suggests that the Detroit boys were themselves white, the headline presents them as "Zoot Suit" terrorists, an image that drew on contemporary tropes of urban African American and Mexican American youths. It also presents an image of rough Detroiters who were unwilling to have a fair fight with the Ontario boys—this was the violent style of fighting they learned on the racially charged streets of Detroit. The fact that the boys had almost made it to the Ambassador Bridge when they were picked up by authorities further suggests that they were going to cross back into Detroit (and out of Ontario legal jurisdiction) to evade arrest.

At their arraignment, Magistrate J. Arthur Hanrahan reminded the boys that they were merely guests of their Canadian neighbors and reprimanded them for acting in a way unbecoming of those who held American citizenship. "As guests of this country," he scolded them, "you violated the hospitality that was extended to you, by boorish rowdyism in which you displayed cowardly conduct similar to what we have come to expect from groups of youths in another country—but not the youths who are privileged to live in the United States."[71] In other words, the young men were not only in violation of local law but also guilty of actions morally unbecoming of border city residents. These young zoot-suiters were precisely the type of individuals reformers feared. They engaged in fighting and violence in illicit leisure establishments, they broke local laws, and they eventually fled the scene of their crimes in an attempt to disappear in the streets of Detroit. It is not incidental that Magistrate Hanrahan—the very judge who seven years later would plunge Windsor into a firestorm of antivice investigation—invoked the concept of citizenship when sentencing the boys. Their violent and disrespectful actions, in direct contradiction to the society reformers attempted to create, were the ultimate expression of what would happen if North Americans did not vigilantly enforce the moral line between productive citizens and immoral outsiders.

By the end of the postwar period, fears about American criminals and delinquent teens came to a head in the 1960 "jazz riot." For many, the incident seemed to be yet another sign of urban decline and the deterioration of key social institutions that had taken place since World War II. Ironically, while reports of the incident continued to blame the violence on Detroit criminals who had crossed the national line, confirming for many Windsor residents that their fears of an invasion by American criminals was well-founded, the incident also helped to embolden a sense of racial solidarity between white residents in Detroit and Windsor. For whites living on both sides of the national line, events like the riot supported earlier claims that the in-migration of poor, southern, and black migrants would have long-term consequences on the border cities. The free and open border touted by boosters in the early postwar years was thus increasingly becoming problematic, and some began to worry that the Negro ruffian, the teenage prostitute, and jazz riots might be signs of troubles to come.

Conclusion

Though the early postwar years are often remembered as a time of prosperity and material abundance, they were also a time of great uncertainty and a rising gap between the rich and poor, particularly in industrial urban centers like the Detroit-Windsor region. Discussions about vice in the urban borderland reflected this tension, as local residents, social organizations, city planners, activists, and the media all grappled with how to best eliminate the signs of the emerging inequalities. Because contemporaries considered vice to be both a cause and a symptom of the urban problem, it consequently became central to various agendas aimed at reshaping urban spaces. Vice industries became one of the most obvious targets of these campaigns, since activities like prostitution and drug use came to symbolize all that was wrong with the postwar city. Attempts at moral regulation brought a broad group of actors together across the border cities who, despite differing political positions, were united toward similar ends. The resulting antivice movements were one approach to addressing sin in the cities, and reformers joined together in nation-building projects designed to demarcate the lines between productive citizens and unwanted outsiders.

The moral programs enacted in the 1940s and 1950s spanned the national border, and similar narratives developed on both sides of the national line. Detroiters and Windsorites alike worried about the influx of newcomers to the region and about transient individuals corrupting otherwise healthy communities. They formed social agencies and activist groups aimed at addressing the issues of poverty and crime in the downtown neighborhoods and mobilized a wide array of legal, expert, and lay forces to deal with these issues. At the heart of these reform efforts was the question of citizenship, of who did or did not belong in the postwar city. This was particularly acute in the borderland, as residents grappled with the meaning of their position along multiple boundaries. While Windsor residents blamed their vice problem, in part, on rowdy Americans crossing into their town for a night of fun, white residents on both sides of the border could agree that vice was also a result of the shifting race and class dynamics in the city of Detroit. As the number of southern black migrants increased and as racial tensions between Detroiters seemed to escalate in the 1950s, white Windsorites began to worry that their Canadian town would be susceptible to the effects of what many saw as the American "race problem." By the end of the postwar years, Canadian fears of an "American invasion" had explicit racial undertones and became increasingly aligned with the language expressed by white middle-class American reformers. In this way, reform projects on both sides of the national line became distinctly racialized projects that pitted the healthy, middle-class, nuclear (i.e., white) family against the deteriorating conditions that characterized life in the nations' urban communities.

Ultimately, in viewing illicit economies as wholly disruptive to the communities in which they took place, reformers were unable to understand the important social and economic roles that these industries played in the lives of local residents. As a result, though sometimes successful at temporarily slowing vice activities or shifting them to different parts of the cities, reformers were largely unsuccessful at eliminating prostitution, drug economies, and other unseemly activities from the border cities. By the late 1950s, the continued growth of underground economies would also ignite national debates about the meaning of citizenship, the need for border enforcement, and the relationship between residents living in communities that straddle the national line. As debates about vice in the borderlands reached the national stage, the tension between fostering a close cross-border relationship and keeping out undesirables would become even more acute.

5

PROHIBITION, ENFORCEMENT, AND BORDER POLITICS

Debating Vice at the National Level

On January 5, 1952, a front-page *Washington Post* article reported on a nationwide crackdown on narcotics trafficking in the United States designed to put at least 500 peddlers behind bars in what was termed "the greatest criminal roundup in the Nation's history." "The raids stretched from Canada to Mexico," the paper reported, and included border cities like Detroit and Buffalo, which acted as "key gateway[s]" to the drug market in Canada. In this massive federal raid, American authorities attempted to "break the backbone" of the illegal drug trade that, by the early postwar period, stretched across North American borders and beyond. While the scope of this investigation was exceptional, its goals and the publicity it received were not. Throughout the late 1940s and 1950s, national publications in the United States and Canada printed stories about international drug-smuggling rings that used the border as a way to sneak illegal drugs into the country. The porousness of the national line, and the gall of the criminal underworld that congregated around it, led Americans and Canadians to worry that these "swashbuckling criminals" were increasingly making life difficult for federal authorities and dangerous for law-abiding citizens.[1]

As the *Washington Post* article suggests, borderlanders were not the only ones concerned with the rise of vice along the national line. By examining media and pop culture narratives on the issue of drug trafficking in particular, as well as federal investigations into the "drug problem" in the United States and Canada, this chapter traces the cultural meanings of antivice discourses as they emerged across both countries. In publications ranging from nationally circulated papers like the *New York Times* and the *Globe and Mail* to local papers like the *Windsor Daily Star* and the *Detroit Free Press*, Canadians and Americans regularly read about drug traffickers and crime syndicates bringing large quantities of narcotics into North America. Blaming the smuggling problem on the rise of organized crime and communist conspiracies from abroad, contemporary media and pop culture images portrayed bordertowns as vice towns, where the forces of good and evil collided and where otherwise good citizens came into contact with dangerous outsiders on a daily basis.

As Americans and Canadians heard more and more about the domestic drug problem and its connections to global criminal conspiracies, they began to wonder what their governments were doing to protect law-abiding citizens. In 1955, the American and Canadian federal governments took up this question when they formed special senate committees to investigate the drug problem. These investigations, which were large-scale and national in scope, were aimed at assessing the extent of the drug economy and finding the best ways to eliminate it. Though there were significant differences in the size and scope of the markets in Canada and the United States, the goals and objectives of both committees dovetailed in important ways. The Canadian and American senators were able to work together because they shared a belief in a prohibitionist ideology that emphasized the need to enforce a clear line between acceptable and unacceptable drug use through legal means. The expert testimonies presented before the committees, which included law enforcement officials as well as medical experts, strengthened the role of the state by formulating a complex moral schema in which ideas of addiction, disease, and danger were interwoven. They also served to define the lines between productive citizenship and weak or damaged individuals, often by infusing these categories with particular race and gender codes. The prohibitionist goals thus helped to define who did or did not belong in postwar society and how to best eliminate the contaminating elements deemed so damaging to North American urban centers.

Yet a close look at the complex representations of bordertowns and border enforcement in the senate committee debates also highlights the contradictions inherent in attempting to control spaces that operate simultaneously as barriers and as connecting points. While the simplistic dualism of heroes and villains sometimes enabled federal enforcement officials in the United States and Canada to work together to fight an identifiable other (such as a member of the Mafia importing heroin across national lines), it also often led local enforcement officers to blame the trafficking problem on the lax policies of their neighbors. Despite lofty attempts to present a unified front in the fight against cross-border smuggling and crime at the federal level, the realities of life in border cities often blurred the line between good guys and bad guys that was so central to postwar antivice rhetoric. Ultimately, the exclusive definitions of citizenship that allowed the public and government officials to blame vice and illicit cross-border activities on dangerous others also at times undermined the effectiveness of nation-building projects, diplomacy, and border enforcement in the postwar years.

Bordertowns as Vice Towns: Debating the Illicit at the National Level

If public debates about vice in the Detroit-Windsor region were shaped by the local borderlands context in which they emerged, they were also embedded in larger national discussions about crime and delinquency.[2] By the late 1940s, politicians, law enforcement officials, social organizations, and the media across the United States and Canada were expressing serious concerns about vice in general and about illegal drug economies in particular. Within these debates, Chinese Communists and European smugglers became the central "villains" in the fight against vice, and contemporary media reports reinforced the image of racial and ethnic outsiders sneaking across national boundaries to harm otherwise healthy citizens by spreading addiction. Thus emerged the hero-villain binary in which legal authorities and the media framed federal enforcement agents as the first line of defense against unscrupulous outsiders who sought profit from the demoralization of North American citizens.

Growing fears over the rise of the two international conspiracies in the postwar years—the Mafia and Communism—transformed national antidrug narratives into global struggles against much larger sinister forces. This transformation was bolstered by high-ranking federal officials who stressed the need to remain vigilant against the infiltration of North American society by these menacing forces. Organizations like the Federal Bureau of Narcotics (FBN) and the Federal Bureau of Investigation (FBI), under the direction of Harry Anslinger and J. Edgar Hoover, respectively, misleadingly depicted both the Mafia and Communism as coherent and centralized international conspiracies and argued that they were the two most dangerous threats facing North American society.[3] Their claims were reinforced by several government investigations into the growing power of organized crime and its negative effects on North

American life.[4] The most publicized hearing was the Special Senate Committee to Investigate Organized Crime, or the Kefauver Committee as it came to be known. These televised hearings, which took place over the course of 1950, were watched by millions of North Americans and became a useful tool in mobilizing the public against organized crime.[5] The hearings documented extensive interstate and international criminal activities, which included illegal wire services, gambling rings, and other forms of illicit activities in Detroit, Windsor, and other cities along the northern border. The committee argued that these large-scale ventures were run by an extensive network of organized criminals who set up shop along the national line to evade arrest. No longer were drug dealers the street thugs of the Prohibition Era; the hearings portrayed figures like Detroit's Joseph Zerilli as sophisticated individuals whose tactics had evolved to allow them to blend in with corporate leaders and use legitimate businesses and unions as fronts for their illegal activities.[6]

Throughout the 1950s, newspapers, magazines, films, and television shows created sensational stories about the connection between the illegal drug trade and transnational syndicates. Anslinger and FBN agents collaborated with journalists who printed pieces based solely on the information they received from the enforcement officers. They regularly leaked stories about their agents standing bravely alone against the Mafia and the People's Republic of China, suggesting that the objective of both was to speed up the moral degeneration of the American people through the spread of drug addiction.[7] National publications in Canada, such as the widely read *Maclean's* magazine, published similar stories of large-scale syndicates trafficking dope across the national border and subsequently harming thousands of Canadian citizens. "The individual racketeer has gone," one 1954 article explained, "and the traffic is controlled today by 'syndicates' headed by [men who are] clever, suave, outwardly well-mannered, but inwardly as vicious and dangerous as the old-time gangster."[8]

Widely circulated media representations of the Italian mobster shaped public perceptions of the clever and cunning, yet extremely dangerous drug trafficker. One 1950 article, written by investigative reporter Drew Pearson and reprinted in newspapers across the country, explained to the American public that "a total of 50 men control most of the big rackets in the United States. All are members of the mysterious Mafia, and all but one are either Italian-born or of Italo-American descent. . . . Like a plate of spaghetti, the connections of the Mafia members are tangled and twined together."[9] In a similar tone, a *Chicago Defender* article provided a brief history of the organization, explaining its transition over time from a group of Sicilians forming an underground economy in the eighteenth century to a sophisticated organization that used violence and intimidation to infiltrate even legitimate businesses and unions across North America. Ethnicity and bloodlines were key, with pedigree "being handed down from father to son in the strict baronial manner." "Essentially," the author explained, the Mafia was "just one big law-breaking family."[10] Contemporary reports noted that this violent, patriarchal "family" controlled the narcotics traffic in North America by relying on lower-level peddlers who would do the actual work of moving the illegal products. The higher-ups rarely got their hands dirty but instead relied on a series of mid-level dealers who would push drugs in designated urban neighborhoods, especially among racially segregated African American and Latino communities.[11] As a result, federal officials had to use increasingly sophisticated tactics to pin narcotics, racketeering, and prostitution charges on them.

The danger of the white ethnic mobster could be matched only by Chinese Communists, who, according to the media, trafficked dope into North American cities in an effort to undermine the moral and physical health of its citizens. Reports regularly drew clear connections between North American men of Asian descent, illegal drug trafficking, and Communist subversion.[12] One *Spokane Daily Chronicle* article told the story of Pon Wai, a "smiling 64-year-old operator of the Fragrant Flower Garden shop in San Francisco's Chinatown," who "was peddling the white death called heroin." The article explained that "day after day" the FBN had watched the florist in an effort to ascertain how he was moving his illegal products. When a search of one of Pon Wai's messengers revealed that he was smuggling "pure heroin" in green capsules attached to the stems of the roses, the FBN agents finally had the evidence to arrest Wai and eight of his messengers on smuggling charges.[13] Similarly, a *Saskatoon Star-Phoenix* report described a bust of a smuggling ring in Vancouver's Chinatown that uncovered a sophisticated network of individuals illegally bringing jade, diamonds, and opium into Canada from China. "In Market Alley, a dingy section of Vancouver's Chinatown, with its rabbit-warren dwellings," the article explained, "law enforcement agencies swooped down to uncover the existence of the ring after months of intensive investigations. The officers had to battle their way down the alley, finally overpowering four Chinese armed with meat cleavers who guarded a house doorway, leading to the Vancouver headquarters of the ring."[14] In these media narratives, federal agents emerge victorious over the smugglers, who used sophisticated and violent tactics to evade arrest.

Contemporary publications also stressed the interconnected nature of the drug trade between Canada and the United States, explaining that traffickers often used the legal divide that separated cities along the national line as a way to evade arrest. As one South Carolina newspaper warned, "Good neighbor Canada will wake up any day [now] with as hard a headache as ours, over a national dope and crime scandal." Claiming that cities across Canada were seeing a rise in drug use, especially among young people, the author wrote that the problem was caused by the extensive smuggling networks that successfully brought heroin into Canada from either Mexico or the "Orient." "The reason is," the article explained, "the executive (mobster controlled) work of the Canadian underworld is done in Detroit and Buffalo, which are beyond the jurisdiction of the Mounties and other law enforcement agencies north of the border. And the parallel executive affairs for much of Buffalo, Detroit, and other nefarious traffic are headquartered in Canada, beyond the jurisdiction of the U.S. Federal and other policing." This was "shrewdly operated in this fashion so that books, witnesses, collateral data, etc. can't be subpoenaed on either side of the line."[15]

If global criminals were the central villains in postwar antidrug narratives, the media portrayed teenagers as innocent victims uniquely susceptible to their illicit intentions. Like local antivice narratives, national newspapers provided lurid stories of drug traffickers actively courting teens in cities along the northern border. One well-publicized case occurred when Buffalo police were led to Crystal Beach, a small Canadian town just across the border on Lake Erie, which was apparently functioning as a "marketing centre for heroin and marijuana." According to the report, Buffalo's infamous "West Side Gang" was using the Ontario city "to sell drugs exclusively to teen-agers." Their operation was run out of a cottage called "the Bebop" and included "a group of teen-age peddlers organized to sell heroin and marijuana cigarettes at various dance halls and amusement places" throughout the Canadian beach community. In this case, even the seemingly innocuous Canadian beach town, when situated on the national line, could become a site where transnational drug sellers set up shop and subsequently turned otherwise good teens into "really sick junkies."[16]

Accounts of vice and crime along the U.S.-Canada border also emerged in films and television shows. These pop culture representations functioned in tandem with contemporary media reports, expressing the anxiety many North Americans felt about the rise of global crime networks and the porousness of the national line. Like media narratives, they presented the issue of drug smuggling as a battle between heroic male officers and nefarious drug traffickers, wherein the former struggled to protect innocent citizens (usually white female protagonists) from the latter. The 1949 film *Johnny Stool Pigeon* follows the story of FBN agent George Morton and convicted felon Johnny Evans as they go undercover to expose a heroin-smuggling ring. The unlikely duo track the smugglers from San Francisco north across the Canadian border to Vancouver, then back south across the Mexican border to Nogales. By contrasting the cold northern frontier city of Vancouver with the rugged, wide-open spaces of Tucson and Nogales, the film depicts the expansive transnational networks through which smugglers operated. The white ethnic traffickers in Vancouver worked in tandem with the Mexican smugglers, and both used seemingly legitimate nightclubs, tourist resorts, and import-export businesses to hide their shady transactions. Ultimately, though, these operations were no match for the "skill, intelligence, and courage" displayed by narcotics and customs officers. In the end, the officers successfully foiled the smugglers' plans to kill Agent Morton in Nogales and arrested them before they could flee their Tucson hideout. As the final narration concludes, "Within a matter of hours the greatest international narcotics ring since the war was stopped cold before it ever got started. In simultaneous raids Martinez and his gang were rounded up by Mexican authorities, and 1,700 miles away in Vancouver, British Columbia, the McCannis mob was taken into custody." *Johnny Stool Pigeon* thus portrays the very real dangers posed by transnational drug smugglers while also reinforcing the power and moral authority of federal officers who, in the end, are able to protect the North American public from the wiles of these shady individuals.[17]

Two television shows helped perpetuate North Americans' fascination with cross-border crime in the postwar years. In 1959, CBS released a series called *Border Patrol*. As the name suggests, it followed the exploits of a fictitious deputy chief of the Border Patrol, Don Jagger, as he crossed the U.S.-Canada and U.S.-Mexico borders in search of dope dealers, illegal immigrants, gun runners, and other criminals.[18] The show, which aired for only one season, was overshadowed by *The Untouchables*, a popular TV series that debuted the same year. Set in Prohibition-era Chicago, it followed Special Agent Eliot Ness and his investigative team as they attempted to fight organized crime and vice. Episodes like "The Canada Run" and "White Slavers" brought viewers into the worlds of dangerous criminals who ran cross-border enterprises based on drugs, bootleg liquor,

numbers running, and prostitution. They allowed North American viewers to enter the seedy bars, brothels, gambling dens, and other illicit spaces
that made up the underworld, all from the comfort of their own homes.
Viewers were also assured that, whether on the hunt for heroin or Canadian Gold whiskey, the protagonists of these shows would continue to
emerge successful and to stunt the nefarious intentions of the global criminals working in the nations' border cities.

Building on cultural stereotypes that perceived of bordertowns as vice
towns, these various representations mirrored media narratives in which
unscrupulous transnational criminals threatened to harm innocent North
American citizens by undermining the power of federal authorities and
the efficacy of national boundaries. While there was no one monolithic
reception of these shows or films, their focus on bordertowns and transnational criminals suggests that these stories resonated with a North
American public.[19] Simultaneously mixing danger, intrigue, and adventure,
they fit within a narrative in which the good guys fought vice lords and
attempted to secure the border from their international crime networks.
In these representations, the plight of the bordertown in many ways became an urban problem writ large—no neighborhood was isolated from
the harmful effects of transnational crime and vice. Set in locations as disparate as Tijuana, Detroit, Vancouver, and a small fishing village on the
shores of the Great Lakes, these multiple representations reminded Americans and Canadians that they needed to remain vigilant against the powerful criminals who sought to undermine national authority and threaten
law-abiding citizens.

Policemen, Doctors, and Deviant Addicts:
Debating the Drug Problem at the Federal Level

Within the context of these animated public debates, the Canadian and
American federal governments set out to determine the extent and causes
of the drug problem in their respective countries. On February 24, 1955,
the Canadian Senate adopted a resolution to form the Special Senate Committee on the Traffic in Narcotic Drugs in Canada, which subsequently
conducted investigations between March 9 and June 7 of that year. Tom
Reid acted as chairman of the committee, which had twenty-three additional senators. Hearings were held in the major cities across Canada and
received testimony from physicians, drug researchers, social welfare agencies, private citizens, federal officials, police representatives, and Harry J.
Anslinger, the commissioner of the American FBN.[20] Its focus on the

major urban centers reflected the committee's assertion from the start that drug use in Canada was overwhelmingly an urban problem.

Following closely on the heels of the Canadian Senate Committee, on June 2, 1955, the U.S. Senate commenced its own investigation into the nation's drug problem. Like its Canadian counterpart, the U.S. committee concentrated on major urban centers across the country.[21] As a testament to the close relationship between the two countries, the U.S. committee invited two members of the Canadian committee to join their investigative team. Senator Tom Reid and Mr. Curran, the Canadian committee's chief counsel, were warmly welcomed by the American senators in the opening hearing. Senator Reid was asked to provide the first comments, in which he spoke of the significance of the drug problem, the common situation facing Canada and the United States, and his appreciation for being invited to sit on the U.S. committee. After all, Reid asserted, this was "the first time in the history of the two countries that a Canadian Senator has had the privilege of sitting in with the Senate of the United States."[22] The congenial remarks were shared by the Americans, who offered their Canadian counterparts a warm welcome. As Senator Welker of Idaho put it, "The committee realizes that we have a touching human-interest problem to solve. Probably no greater problem will ever rest upon the shoulders of any members of this committee. . . . With the cooperation of the great neighboring visitors who are here and the members of their staffs and their committees, I am sure that we will come up with something realistic, which in effect will help . . . both countries."[23]

In explaining their goals and intentions, the Canadian committee asserted that it would take as "comprehensive" an approach "as possible." Accordingly, "the Committee decided to hear evidence on all the ramifications of the drug problem," which would include not only experts from a variety of fields but also "views of the addicts and of society in general."[24] Similarly, the U.S. committee asserted that "the purpose of the investigation is to hear, as far as possible at our initial meetings, the extent and the concentration of the narcotic problem in the United States, with breakdowns by cities and states, and then to have a review from the Federal officials as to what is being done under present law to cope with the problem."[25] Thus both committees began with an attempt to elucidate the drug problem at the national and local levels, examine the laws currently in place, and interview a combination of expert and nonexpert witnesses to help provide a nuanced understanding of the many issues at hand.

Despite their expansive goals and lofty rhetoric, a detailed reading of the senate committees reveals that they fell far short of a comprehensive approach. While the committees interviewed a wide range of witnesses, they ultimately reinforced a prohibitionist ideology by treating legal and medical authorities as the foremost experts on the drug problem. Not only were law enforcement officials and medical experts almost always the first witnesses interviewed in each city but also they made up the majority of witnesses across both committees.[26] Since law enforcers and the medical profession "have at least one objective in common—effective and knowledgeable control of deviant behavior," their approaches to the drug problem often overlapped in important ways.[27] Law officers drew on the language of sickness in discussing their subjects, and the medical profession advocated treatment approaches that had punitive effects. Together, medical and legal authorities created binary categories to define drug users and attempted to frame the problem in terms of "villains" and "victims," with some users in need of help and others in need of punishment. Doctors retained their control over the licit realm of drug administration while legal authorities continued to arrest and punish those who engaged in recreational drug use. In this way, their combined approach to the drug problem ultimately supported the states' prohibitionist agendas designed to eliminate illegal drug use and its corrupting influences on North American citizens.

Over the course of their many testimonies, legal and medical witnesses proved their knowledge about drug addiction by providing statistical, quantitative, and seemingly objective data. In fact, collection of statistical information was one of the key goals of the committees, reflecting an increasing belief in empirical, quantitative analysis during this period and the idea that experts could provide unmediated knowledge on a particular subject.[28] According to the first witness of the Canadian Senate Committee, Minister of National Health and Welfare Paul Martin, these proceedings were designed to be "sober, factual, and objective examinations" of the drug problem. The use of the word *sober* here is telling—the committees would collect their information in large part from authorities who had attained their knowledge of the drug problem through education, training, and professional experience rather than through actual drug use.

Members of law enforcement agencies were called upon to testify on a wide range of issues related to illegal narcotics. Perhaps not surprisingly, they were asked to provide data on arrest numbers, convictions, and jail sentences. Significantly, though, they were also expected to provide information that was not directly linked to their role as law enforcement officials, ranging from the social life of users prior to their involvement with illegal drugs to their lives after arrest, incarceration, and treatment. In answering the senators' wide-ranging questions, many officials provided anecdotal evidence that served a particular moralistic objective. When Senator Welker encouraged Harry Anslinger to provide testimony as to the effectiveness of "cold turkey" treatments for narcotics addictions, he seemed more than happy to oblige. Though the senator acknowledged that Anslinger was "not a medical man," he still insisted that his long history of law enforcement work (he served as commissioner of the FBN for thirty-two years) made him a foremost expert on drug-related issues. Despite his lack of medical training, "Thousands of Americans, all of us, would be interested in your recommendation—yes, your *enlightenment* for the American people—as to the treatment of drug addicts." In his response, rather than focusing on the medical reasons that the cold turkey approach worked, Anslinger emphasized the moral reasons. He argued that forcing users to undergo this method made them less likely to seek out drugs again—they would remember this terrible experience and in the future would choose to forgo taking the drug that had caused it. Though Anslinger had no actual medical evidence to support his opinion, he felt confident making such a claim because it fit within his broader objectives of curing an addict's drug habit through a means that would simultaneously punish the addict and work as a deterrent.[29]

Some law enforcement officials were more reluctant to attempt to explain the causes behind drug use to any considerable degree and dismissed this information as incidental to their goals of regulating a criminal class of people. As Commissioner Nicholson of the RCMP asserted, "Psychiatrists and sociologists may explain the fundamental reasons which led to the unhappy condition these people are in. From the standpoint of the police, who see them from day to day, they are a dreary lot of parasites."[30] He also asserted that law enforcement officials maintained a unique authority on drug-related issues because they interacted with users on a "day to day" basis, experience that medical and sociological experts were supposedly lacking. For officers like Nicholson, it was not necessary to understand what caused addiction; they knew all they needed to know through their daily interactions with users. They were parasites who infected otherwise healthy neighborhoods and led to degraded conditions in inner cities across North America.

Medical and legal experts employed moralistic classifications of drug addicts, relying on binary definitions of "villain" and "victim" to determine how to treat users. Officials viewed traffickers in particular as morally corrupt because they sold drugs to make a profit, and as a result, virtually no witnesses showed any sympathy for large-scale peddlers. The testimony of Reverend Dr. J. Hobden of the John Howard Society (a Canadian organization that helped criminals readjust after incarceration) typified descriptions of traffickers on both sides of the border. He described the illicit traffic in Canada as "a vicious criminal movement, promoted for personal and selfish gain, without any regard whatsoever for the bodies and souls of its victims. The chief promoters, who usually remain far enough in the background to avoid any evidence of actual unlawful distribution, are . . . foes of Law and Order and Decency. They deserve very little pity when apprehended for their wrong doing."[31] Defining traffickers as "enemies of the State," Hobden's words suggest that through breaking social and legal codes, traffickers were undermining the very order and structure necessary for a well-functioning nation. This perception encouraged many witnesses to view the trafficker as simply a criminal in need of punishment rather than as a victim in need of rehabilitation. As Nicholson of the RCMP explained, "I think [traffickers] are criminals and that is all there is to it, and they should be jailed as criminals."[32]

In contrast, many witnesses believed that addicts, though morally weak, could perhaps be cured and reintegrated back into normal society. While officials like the Detroit commissioner of police were quick to assert that the narcotics trade was responsible for a large portion of the crime in North American cities (going so far as to call it the "greatest breeder of crime" in cities like Detroit), they also often framed users as *victims* of the large-scale, nefarious traffickers.[33] For example, the assistant attorney general in the Criminal Division of the Department of Justice described the difference between the "vicious, despicable, big time racketeering violator" and the "pitiful victim of the sordid business who has become ensnared by it."[34] Nicholson likewise asserted that "while the addict as such may be deserving of sympathy and because his motivation is a drive of his addiction rather than the profit, he cannot be regarded as being in the same vicious class as those criminals who traffic solely for money." In this instance, the head of the RCMP was making a clear distinction between people who used drugs because of a physical addiction and people who sold drugs purely for profit. Though both were considered morally corrupt, the scale was different. Tellingly, Nicholson further argued that "the addict . . . forfeit[s] much of this sympathy when he becomes involved in distribution."[35] He could feel some sympathy for individuals who broke the law to satisfy a physical addiction; as soon as they started selling, even if only to pay for their own habit, they gave up their status as victim and instead joined the ranks of the "vicious class."

The language used to distinguish between traffickers and peddlers took distinctly racialized tones in the United States, since white ethnic dealers tended to operate at the top of the drug market and African Americans and Latinos tended to work at middle to lower levels of the trade. Though members of transnational syndicates were considered morally depraved because they made money off other people's habits, they were also viewed as sophisticated and cunning criminals. Their ability to capitalize on the transnational drug market, while incredibly dangerous, also suggested that they were highly organized and intelligent individuals who used creative means to skirt federal enforcement authorities. As one district attorney explained, "They are professional criminals. They have lots of money. They have powerful allies. They have expert knowledge as to how to evade the law and to escape detection." They were never addicts themselves and rarely handled the drugs. Instead, they had scores of henchmen who carry out their bidding.[36] Thus while enforcement authorities viewed them as the most dangerous elements of the drug trade, they simultaneously provided these criminals with some degree of agency. They were in many ways the white ethnic elite of the criminal world, whose intelligence, expert knowledge, and power enabled them to rise to the top of the illicit market.

Small-scale peddlers, by contrast, were lowly, degraded citizens whose weak wills left them susceptible to a life of addiction and crime. Indeed, if the problem of smugglers was a transnational problem, the issue of users and small-scale peddlers became a distinctly racialized urban problem. The drug addict turned small-time dealer, someone increasingly associated with black communities—with "the Negro sections of the city"—was denied the modicum of entrepreneurial respect that even the most vicious traffickers received.[37] Instead, the small-scale dealer and the local dope addict "[is the] carrier; he is the individual who spreads this insidious death known as narcotic-drug addiction," and he did so within his own community and among his peers.[38] In city after city, especially those in the North and the East Coast, senators questioned interviewees as to why men and women of the "Negroid race" made up such a high percentage of those arrested for drug crimes.[39] The answers they received ranged widely and wildly—from arguments that poverty in black neighborhoods bred crime, to suggestions that the high wages in the North allowed more blacks to afford drugs, to accusations that "liberal" judges in the North (who showed sympathy for newly settled black residents they believed had never been given a fair shake) meted out lenient sentences and therefore failed to deter crime among black residents.[40] Regardless of the supposed causes, what is clear is that in city after city, the senators continued to draw connections between black neighborhoods, addiction, and crime. In their view, the poorest drug addicts (read African American addicts) were the weakest members of society who would even go so far as to infect their own neighborhoods with this deadly habit.

The belief that drug users and sellers were participants in a dangerous economy that could spread like a disease throughout the nations' cities led the majority of witnesses to advocate suppression of both cross-border trafficking and domestic use through the implementation of punitive measures. Law enforcement officials drew on the language of sickness to describe addiction and argued that since it was a self-induced disease, the person needed to be punished. In his testimony before the U.S. Senate Committee, Judge W. McKay Skillman of the Detroit Recorder's Court insisted that drug addiction was "like a contagious disease" and therefore addicts needed to be "gotten off the streets." In his exchange with Senator Daniel, Skillman again emphasized that this was a sickness that did not deserve sympathy. Daniel explained that he did not "like to look on addicts as sick people alone. They are not only sick because of something that *they have done to themselves*, but most every one of them either were in crime to start with, or at least are continuing and violating the law to keep up their habit." Skillman replied, "Oh yes; we can waste a lot of sympathy on people who probably don't deserve much sympathy . . . they are a menace to society and should be dealt with. And if they don't want to voluntarily take the cure, they ought to be compelled to do so." Skillman then suggested that state or federal hospitals were the right place to do so, but if this was not feasible, perhaps they should be sent to a "farm colony, home, or something to keep them in, so they will not get back and spread the addiction to society." After all, he concluded, "we quarantine people for other diseases, I don't know why we shouldn't quarantine people for this disease."[41]

This blending of medical and legal language demonstrates the increasingly blurred lines between the two discourses. Many witnesses believed that punishment could actually work as a form of treatment and that the state needed to exert a high degree of control over users to facilitate their transition from criminals into productive citizens. According to George McClellan of the RCMP, if addicts were to be rehabilitated, they needed to be placed "under conditions of complete control." To achieve this, he recommended removing addicts from their community, placing them in isolation, and keeping "him under" the "thumb" of the state, since "any attempt to rehabilitate or treat the addict under the squalid conditions in which he lives is doomed to failure."[42] In similar language, Melville Anthony, chief constable of the city of Edmonton, blamed addicts for their state of addiction and argued that they had to be removed from city streets. He recommended that they be held financially responsible for their own treatment and argued that "the greater percentage of addicts become addicted through their own mental weakness, and if they can be cured, they should in some manner be required to pay for their cure." Anthony also asserted that once released from treatment facilities, addicts should be further monitored through a work program in which they would earn credit money that parole officers would hold and distribute to them when necessary.[43] When asked if addicts should be isolated on an island until cured, a suggestion that came up in several previous testimonies, he agreed that it was one possible approach because "if we are going to try to help these people we have to be ruthless about it."[44] The chief constable of Toronto further advocated whipping for traffickers, and Senator Hodges went so far as to suggest large-scale traffickers be hanged, "but apparently it was not thought to be practicable."[45]

While the senators and interviewees tended to refer to drug users as male (reflecting, in part, the fact of the higher number of male users in both countries), the image of the drug-addicted prostitute came to epitomize the disease, devastation, and delinquency associated with drug addiction. Medical and legal authorities framed drug use and prostitution as mutually reinforcing activities: women often turned to prostitution to pay for their drugs, but prostitution often also encouraged women to begin using drugs to cope with the requirements of their profession.[46] In this way, causal explanations for deviant behavior among young women living in urban centers were often interchangeable. Further, if addicts brought disease into a community through their addiction, this was doubly true for prostitutes who also spread "social diseases" within inner city neighborhoods.[47] Following this logic, the senators grilled female users about their home lives growing up, how they began using, how they paid for drugs, and their sexual and social relationships with men. Asking these particular questions helped draw out a narrative that would confirm the image of the drug-addicted prostitute whose life had spiraled out of control. Since the committee had the ultimate say over whom they interviewed, they were also able to choose women whose life stories fit this narrative. Shirley Aiston, who was interviewed by the Senate committee in Detroit, provides just one example. When asked about her upbringing, she explained that she had been orphaned at the age of eleven and was subsequently sent to a girls' home. She ran away at fifteen and began working a series of low-paying service jobs, including a stint as a cashier and a candy girl in a Detroit theater. Around the age of sixteen, Aiston began working as a prostitute and, encouraged by one of her friends, started using heroin about a year later. To pay for her habit, she told the committee, she eventually began stealing money from johns and selling heroin that she bought wholesale in cities like Windsor, Chicago, Cleveland, and New York. Significantly, the committee pointed out that she had married a "Negro" man who worked as a bellboy on the west side of the city, but that her marriage had ended because of her addiction. In short, Aiston's testimony confirmed the cultural trope of the drug-addicted prostitute: she came from a broken home; she was introduced to heroin through her associates in the urban underworld, eventually selling her body to pay for her habit; and she had intimate relationships across the color line (including her own marriage), which she destroyed through her addiction.[48]

Not all interviewees fit so easily into this narrative, and some pushed back against the moralizing questions posed by the senators. Virginia Eddington, also interviewed during the Detroit session, rejected the senators' characterization of her as a common prostitute. She told the committee that at the height of her addiction she was spending more than $100 a day on heroin. When she explained that she had to "increase her number of boy friends [sic]" to pay for her habit, the senators assumed this was an admission that she had sold sex to pay for drugs. Eddington, however, saw this as more nuanced, rejecting their attempts to define her actions as prostitution: "Well I still don't feel I turned to prostitution," she corrected the senators. "I don't feel that having a boy friend that supplies you with money on a weekly basis is prostitution. I just had a lot of boyfriends who were generous with me, that's all. I mean, I don't go out in the street or work in any house of prostitution." In fact, she told the committee, the two times she had "altercations" with the law, they had failed to lay prostitution charges on her.[49] The exchange between Eddington and the senators demonstrates the clear power dynamics that shaped the interview process. The senators were able to ask questions in a way that would allow them to elicit a particular narrative from the interviewees. Although Eddington attempted to push back against their moralizing descriptions of her actions, in most interviews the senators were able to frame women as slaves to their addictions, weak individuals whose actions led to the moral decay of their family lives, their bodies, and ultimately their communities at large.

In discussions about how to treat female addicts, legal and medical experts made it clear that they believed they were dealing with many interrelated problems that needed to be addressed, including sexual abnormalities and other deviations from respectable womanhood. While treatment facilities were recommended for men, some witnesses thought that women should be housed in home-type foster care that would mimic forms of domestic surveillance. As one witness explained, "Because of their previous immoral habits it seems undesirable that women should be living fifteen to twenty in one house as was recommended for the men." Their feminine natures meant they would be much better suited to foster care facilities where an authority figure could keep a close watch over them. Their assumed sexual transgressions left officials concerned that if housed in one large room, their immoral tendencies might spread to the rest of the women.[50] This invokes contemporary perceptions that delinquent women were susceptible to both sexual promiscuity and lesbianism, and housing them together in large numbers would enable these behaviors.[51] Their deviant personalities, as indicated by their drug addiction and prostitution, could snowball into multiple social transgressions if not treated with the utmost care and by the proper authorities.

Thus, despite their stated intentions of finding complex solutions to a public health problem, the senate committees ultimately ended up reinforcing a prohibitionist framework that relied on punitive measures to fight addiction. Men and women who chose to use drugs were presented as weak individuals who forfeited their right to remain in the wider society by their choice to engage in illegal drug use. Medical and legal officials argued that quarantining drug addicts and separating them from decent citizens was key to stopping addiction. After all, this was a sickness that spread across communities much like a communicable disease. Punishment and treatment approaches often worked hand in hand. Law enforcement drew on conceptions of sickness, and medical experts increasingly promoted correctional treatment methods such as forced institutionalization. The measures became increasingly punitive for traffickers, who were the ultimate villains in the moral crusade to rid the countries of drug addiction. The victims, however, were often vilified as pathetic individuals whose failure to function as productive citizens meant they needed to be subjected to close regulation by the state. In this way, the legal and medical authorities both perpetuated a moral agenda that served to keep the power out of the hands of actual drug users and maintain it firmly within the realm of the states and the authorities that carried out their prohibition policies.

Powders, Pills, and the Porous Border: The International Implications of the Drug Problem

If the senators were concerned with the extent of the domestic drug problem and its impact on urban communities across North America, they were equally interested in *how* addicts were securing illegal drugs in the first place. Toward this end, both committees entertained detailed investigations into where drugs were being produced, how they were imported, and who was in charge of these activities. Enforcement officials provided evidence that heroin was produced externally in Mexico, the Middle East, the Mediterranean, and China and trafficked through various trade routes, usually through European countries like France and Italy or Asian trade routes based in Hong Kong.[52] There was some evidence that the main sources of heroin had shifted from the Middle East in the early postwar period to mainland China by the mid-1950s, in part the result of the opening of trade routes following the war. In the case of marijuana, American officials asserted that most supplies originated in Mexico and were smuggled across the border and, occasionally, up to Canada.[53] The committees certainly acknowledged the role of organized crime in these networks, but unlike the Kefauver Committee of 1950, they were not particularly interested in the internal workings of crime syndicates.[54] Instead, they mainly sought to understand where the drugs were coming from and how they were smuggled into the United States and Canada on such a large scale.

Witnesses argued that these global networks had important political implications within a Cold War framework, linking them directly to the global struggle between Communist and "free" nations. The link between dangerous outside influences, political subversion, and drug enforcement had been solidified in the United States in 1951 with the passage of the Hale Boggs Act. The law (which established the first mandatory minimum sentences for narcotics offenders) was passed within the context of the early McCarthy era, growing fears of Soviet aggression, and the rise of Communist China, creating a clear connection between domestic drug policies and perceived threats of Communist influence.[55] Four years later, testimonies before the senate committees reinforced the link between the use of illegal substances and Communist subversion, framing the problem as one of both international influence and domestic infiltration. In his testimony before the U.S. committee, Assistant Secretary of Defense Frank Berry, M.D., articulated the fear that Chinese officials were "purposefully encouraging the sending of these drugs to members of the armed services of our country and of the other free nations, and to the people of the free nations to try to demoralize them, and also to try to make money for Communist China." According to Berry, the United States had "sworn statements from communists that they were directed to sell this material to finance their own party organization."[56]

By pinning the importation of heroin on Communist China, American and Canadian authorities were framing the drug problem as an international one, linked to the problem of porous borders and the precarious place of free states within a global, Cold War context. They were also drawing on a long history of racialized perceptions of drug users that treated them as immoral outsiders who threatened the health and welfare of North American cities. The association between Chinese immigrants and opium that developed in the mid- to late nineteenth century had ingrained the conception that the Chinese represented a distinctly demoralized race that would ultimately devastate North America.[57] What connected earlier discussions about Chinese opiate use and postwar fears of Communist subversion was the belief that importing opiates was an act of imperial aggression that ultimately would lead to deteriorated North American cities.[58] The growth of Chinatowns in the late nineteenth century seemed to embody this threat, and Americans and Canadians pointed to these neighborhoods as dangerous spaces that spread sin, disease, and other debilitating problems in urban centers.[59] In the postwar years, the supposed imperial aspirations of the Chinese were much more covert. Rather than sending hordes of migrants, the Communists chose instead to send dangerous and deadly forms of heroin. The racialized image of the cunning Chinaman thus reemerged in antidrug narratives, and the villain became explicitly racialized as an overt and dangerous threat from evil Asian Communists.

With this emphasis on the potential threat posed by external producers of heroin, it is not surprising that the senators were particularly interested in the nations' borders. They were especially concerned with the actual process of smuggling and how criminals could get the illicit material into North American markets. Commissioner Nicholson of the RCMP explained that the general flow of narcotics was from the United States into Canada and that traffickers were adept at smuggling large quantities of heroin across the border. He brought several exhibits for the senators, including a one-kilo tin can, a religious book with the inside cut out, a Chinese magazine cut out, a shoe with a hollow heel, and a vest with secret pockets for concealing drugs. His goal was to explain to the committee just how easy it was to smuggle in large quantities of heroin, enough to net the trafficker anywhere from $19,000 to $28,000 in one run.[60] His choice of a religious book and a Chinese magazine are telling—they reinforced both the immoral nature of the drug trade and the racialized images of Chinese Communists attempting to harm Canadian nationals. Further, all of these products could easily be smuggled in automobiles, the primary mode of cross-country transportation. This fear that smugglers were using everyday goods and tourist routes to move drugs into and across Canada encouraged the Canadian Senate committee to ultimately recommend that individuals convicted of a drug offense should have their licenses suspended as a way of hindering their movement.[61]

While the U.S.-Mexico border dominated the U.S. committee hearings, in part because Mexico was considered a primary source of heroin and marijuana in the United States, several high-ranking officials stressed the need to remain vigilant on the northern borderline. Many acknowledged the direct relationship between policing efforts at the major seaports and the drug trade across land borders: customs officials' success in policing places like New York, San Francisco, and the southern border meant that the Canadian border became a more common site of importation for traffickers. As one customs officer testified, when enforcement officials cracked down on smuggling at major seaports, the "time honored tradition of trunk smuggling from Canada" increased.[62] Enforcement officials working along the border also noticed this trend. In his interview before the Detroit session of the committee, when asked how to curb the drug problem in Detroit, Commissioner Piggins argued that one important way would be to strengthen the role of the federal government, particularly the Customs Department, so they could "stop the importation at the port of entry."[63]

Throughout the committees, senior-level officials testified to the strong working relationship between the United States and Canada, recognizing that eliminating this transnational trade required close cross-border cooperation. In his testimony before the U.S. Senate committee, Anslinger asserted that the situation between the two countries was "parallel," with both countries seeing a decline in heroin use during World War II, followed by a rapid increase with the close of the war.[64] He further explained the problems the United States had with enforcement along the Mexico border and suggested that they should seek to mirror the close relationship fostered at the U.S.-Canada border with their southern neighbor.[65] Similarly, in his description of the various agencies involved in enforcing narcotics legislation in Canada, the head of the RCMP claimed that he "would be discourteous if I did not mention as well the close link we have with the U.S. Bureau of Narcotics and the great help we get from that agency. We get the very best type of help from that Bureau."[66] McClellan of the RCMP expressed the same sentiment: "The R.C.M. Police have been most fortunate in the quality of the co-operation which we receive from the United States Bureau of Narcotics, and in particular, the Agents of that Bureau at the border points" of southern Ontario.[67]

Senior-level officials provided the senators with specific cases where this cross-border interaction facilitated drug-related busts. For example, when George Mallock, wanted by Canadian authorities for drug-related offenses, jumped the Canadian border and headed for Mexico, American authorities helped to track and arrest him. Mallock, whom officials described as a "very bad egg," was eventually tracked to Mexico City, detained, returned to Canada, and sentenced to 27½ years in prison. His brother John was not so lucky and was killed by Mexican authorities while trying to escape.[68] Similarly, Lee Won Sing, while on bail for charges laid in Washington, D.C., attempted to smuggle Chinese merchandise from Windsor through the border at Detroit. When he was searched, customs officials found a stick of opium on him and contacted the police in D.C. As a result, Sing faced not only the original charges for which he was on bail but also attempted trafficking.[69] Cases like those of the Mallock brothers and Sing were used by senior-level officials to demonstrate the effectiveness of border policing and the need for cross-border cooperation. They provided tangible results and were used as proof that, by working together, Canadian and American authorities could greatly reduce the drug traffic across both countries.

Yet, the testimonies of local officials who actually worked in the border region suggest that in reality, border policing was much more complicated. The different positions Canada and the United States held within the global illicit economy had important implications for how enforcement officers perceived the border. Though senior-level U.S. officials discussed the enforcement relationship between the two countries and provided some examples of the cross-border implications of the drug trade, the border did not dominate the senate hearings in northern cities the way it did in San Diego and El Paso. Many witnesses from border cities like Detroit failed to engage with the city's location along the national line in any great detail—they mentioned the need for more customs agents but failed to discuss the broader implications of its position along the border. This was likely due, in part, to the fact that drugs tended to flow from Detroit into Ontario rather than the other way around. It also demonstrates the divergent experiences of borderlands and the uneven relationship between the United States and Canada. Local Detroit officials seemed to find it sufficient to focus internally and to look to larger U.S. metropolises like Chicago, New York, and Cleveland as the source of supply. They were less interested in assessing how the city's location on the national border also facilitated the flow of drugs outward and into Ontario.

This was not the case for officials from southern Ontario, who were acutely aware of their position along the national line. In his testimony before the Canadian committee, McClellan of the RCMP explained in great detail the tensions of attempting to eliminate illegal smuggling without hindering formal economies, tourism, and cross-border commuters. In fact, from his initial description of the region, McClellan stressed its close proximity to the U.S. border and the steady traffic across it. He described southern Ontario as "a densely populated area containing one-quarter of the [country's] population. In addition there is a very long frontier for at least one thousand miles separated from the United States, for the most part, by the Great Lakes System but coming into contact with the United States at a number of points of dense population and heavy industrialization." He further emphasized that while Toronto had the largest population in the region, cities like Windsor and Hamilton were in close proximity to booming American cities like Detroit and Buffalo. For the RCMP in Ontario, this proximity coupled with the long border between the countries created the central enforcement problem. He explained that "there is a heavy flow of international traffic in both directions, by rail, air, and automobile. This is a very free flow of traffic in accordance with the mutual trust and understanding between the two countries. . . . [This] poses many problems for both Canadian and U.S. Immigration and Customs Officials."[70] McClellan explained that it would be completely impossible "to establish any rigid system of checking traffic without completely tying up the free movement of people and goods essential to our international commerce and tourist trade." A study of "the Ambassador Bridge and the Tunnel between Windsor and Detroit . . . would quickly indicate that any attempt to make a thorough Customs search of each vehicle would result in a complete tie-up for miles on both sides of the Border." At the time of his interview, Windsor was able to accommodate 1,000 cars per hour, and any slowing of this would be detrimental to the formal economy. For McClellan, this heavy traffic, combined with the fact that "most affluent elements of the criminal underworld on the United States side reside in areas easily accessible to the Ontario and Quebec borders," made smuggling relatively easy for traffickers and made regulation extremely difficult for enforcement officials.[71]

The veiled frustrations expressed by Canadian authorities in the 1955 committees had in fact erupted explicitly five years earlier when the Kefauver Committee passed through the city of Detroit. In many ways a precursor to the expansive 1955 investigations, the Kefauver Committee's hearings were well-publicized across Canada and raised concerns about organized crime across the U.S.-Canada border. Tensions between American and Canadian officials arose in November 1950 when a Canadian newspaper printed a story titled "Windsor Wire Service: Predict U.S. Senate Will Rap Ontario." The article claimed that the U.S. Senate was going to publicly reprimand the Ontario government's response to vice activities and suggested that the U.S. Senate would take a strong-arm approach to dealing with their Canadian neighbors. This had broader implications on illegal industries in the region, it asserted, since "the same people who are involved in the gambling rackets are mixed up with narcotics and prostitution." According to the article, "Speculation by police officials here is that the Ontario Provincial Government [OPP] will receive a severe condemnation by the U.S. Senate" and would be expected to take strong action to "clean up Windsor."[72]

The premier of Ontario, Leslie M. Frost, considered this a diplomatic affront and quickly contacted Kefauver to prevent a public lashing by the U.S. Senate committee. Frost took this one step further, though, and used it as an opportunity to suggest that it was in fact U.S. authorities who had failed to do their duty to prevent cross-border vice and smuggling. In a letter sent to Kefauver on November 23, 1950, Frost defended the work of Canadian agents, blasted the lack of cooperation he felt he received from U.S. officials, and suggested further meetings between Canadian and American police forces to deal with the problem. After providing a detailed account of the approach taken by Ontario officials over the past couple of years, which involved authorities at the municipal, provincial, and federal levels, Frost asserted that "the problem is international in nature. . . . May I draw your attention to the fact that the problems in regard to gambling and vice which we have in the Province of Ontario have their origin in the United States in nearly *all* cases. Our Forces here cannot effectively deal with the problem without the cooperation of the United States law enforcement agencies." According to the premier, if the Detroit side would give the Windsor police as much cooperation as the Ontario Provincial Police gave their American counterparts, the problem of vice in Windsor, which was "difficult if not impossible to cope with," would be very much improved. Frost closed his letter by inviting Kefauver to visit the Canadian side of the border the next time he was in the area, since it would "be a pleasure to meet him" and "to know we would get some real action."[73]

In his response to Frost on December 7, Kefauver seemed mildly annoyed by these accusations, but mainly in agreement about the need for increased cooperation between authorities on both sides of the border. Kefauver assured the premier that "any prediction that the United States Senate or this Committee will 'rap' the province of Ontario or its officials is, of course, erroneous. I assure you that the Committee has no intention of any such breach of diplomatic propriety." He also explained that the crime conditions in the United States were "sufficiently distressing as to make it entirely unnecessary to look outside the boundaries of this country for more trouble. . . . On the other hand," the senator continued, "I agree with you that the fact is that the patterns of gambling and other crime in the Detroit-Windsor area undoubtedly cross the international boundary, and in order to deal effectively with the problem law enforcement officers of each country must cooperate intimately with their counterpart officers in the other country." Kefauver noted that he was "distressed" at the accusation that American authorities were not being as cooperative as necessary and assured Frost that the committee would give special attention to this in their Detroit investigation. He then declined the invitation to visit Toronto, due to time constraints, and invited Windsor authorities to cross the border when the committee came to Detroit to provide their perspectives.[74]

Though nothing serious came from this exchange—the Kefauver Committee did not publicly "rap" Ontario enforcement officials, and Frost and Kefauver ended their correspondence on civil terms—it provides important insight into the frustrations of U.S. and Canadian authorities tasked with regulating vice in cities near the national line. Canadian and American authorities shared similar goals, and both recognized the importance of effectively policing the national border between them, but each side prioritized differently. Local authorities in Detroit were primarily concerned with the ways in which drugs were brought into their city from other large American cities like New York and Chicago, as well as from across the southern border. In contrast, Ontario officials were keenly aware of their position along the national line and the fact that it was often U.S.-run syndicates that enabled narcotics and other vice operations to operate openly in adjacent Canadian cities. As the correspondence between Frost and Kefauver suggests, Canadian officials often felt they had little chance of curtailing vice in their own cities without the help of their neighbors to the south, and this cooperation was not nearly as extensive as Canadian officials would have liked. Despite attempts to reach across the border to fight crime and vice through a cooperative effort, the realities of the global drug market and the asymmetrical relationship between bordertowns on each side of the national line sometimes undermined these objectives. Regulating borders, it turns out, was much trickier than aligning rhetoric.

Conclusion

As the 1955 committees drew to a close, the senators put forward a series of recommendations on how best to address the drug problems in their respective nations. These recommendations ultimately reflected the committees' dedication to a prohibitionist ideology that defined illegal drug use as immoral and users themselves as undesirable citizens. In the end, they both recommended increased policing, harsher sentences, and other punitive measures, such as aggressive enforcement of drug-related crimes like theft and prostitution.[75] The U.S. Senate committee's recommendations were implemented the following year in the Narcotic Control Act of 1956, which raised the minimum sentence on some drug offenses to five years and allowed a jury to impose the death penalty on anyone over the age of eighteen convicted of trafficking heroin to minors.[76] The Canadian Senate committee's recommendations were implemented in the 1961 Narcotic Control Act, which increased the maximum penalty for trafficking, possession for the purposes of trafficking, and importing and exporting from fourteen years to life. The Canadian law also enacted a mandatory minimum sentence of seven years for importing and exporting, making it the third highest minimum sentence requirement, behind only murder and treason.[77] By the end of the postwar period, blaming social ills on unwanted outsiders clearly had very real effects on men and women involved in the drug trade. Now subject to the harshest penalties enacted to date in either country, traffickers ultimately bore the brunt of the blame for North America's drug problem.

Public debates played a crucial role in creating a climate in which these decidedly harsh penalties could be enacted at the federal level. By the end of the 1950s, news stories, pop culture representations, and well-publicized federal hearings had effectively created links between transnational drug trafficking, racial minorities, and Communist subversion. By constantly depicting violent confrontations between drug traffickers and law enforcement officers, these deeply racialized images affirmed the belief that a strong enforcement presence was needed along the national line. Drug traffickers, Mafia bosses, and Communist agents had to be stopped at the border, and federal officers were just the ones to take on this job.

Since protecting the nation was a central goal in these moral narratives, border cities became key battlegrounds in the war against vice and crime. Emerging at a time when North Americans were both traveling across the borders at an unprecedented rate and increasingly fearful of subversion from the outside, bordertowns came to represent spaces of adventure and danger, intrigue and fear. The profound tension between celebrating mobility and fearing the unwanted, polluting possibilities of cross-border interaction was at the heart of postwar border rhetoric. In this way, contemporary perceptions of bordertowns as wide open were shaped in important ways by Cold War moral politics and debates over the nature of citizenship in what many North Americans saw as an increasingly global world.

Like the broader public debates, highly publicized federal hearings also helped to solidify a prohibitionist agenda that framed drug users, prostitutes, and other "deviant" individuals as dangerous to the moral fabric of the nation. By blending medical and legal discourse, the senate hearings reaffirmed the role of experts in controlling and suppressing activities deemed undesirable. They created a complex moral schema that blended ideas of physical sickness, mental weakness, and criminal behavior and simultaneously worked to define binary categories of insider-outsider, villain-victim, and good-evil. The fact that drug users came from urban neighborhoods and were, in the United States, increasingly African American and Latino, made this process even more effective. Like localized antivice rhetoric in the Detroit-Windsor region, national public debates ignored the important social and cultural roles illicit economies played in downtown neighborhoods. Instead, legal and medical authorities defined participants as marginal members of society and failed to afford them any meaningful voice in the debates over drug use and addiction. The focus on prohibition thus empowered state actors and agencies to push for increased regulation of inner-city residents, perpetuating contemporary beliefs that the "urban problem" was spiraling out of control.

The senate committees also demonstrate the difficulties inherent in regulating a boundary that was supposed to operate simultaneously as a barrier and a connecting point. American and Canadian law enforcement officials attempted to work together to create a unified front against the smuggling of illicit substances across their borders. Senior-level officials regularly praised the cooperation they received from agencies on the other side of the national line and attempted to show that they had the situation under control. The realities of policing on the ground, however, often looked much different. The tendency to blame outsiders for the nations' vice problems was sometimes reproduced among the local agencies tasked with managing the border on a daily basis. Tensions sometimes arose, as Canadians blamed their vice problem on their American counterparts' lax enforcement and as American authorities continued to put the bulk of their resources into policing their southern border. Ultimately, enforcement officials' inability to fully police the long border between them demonstrates the resilience of illicit economies and their ability to adapt to local environments. Despite the strict prohibitionist approach, heroin remained the primary drug of choice for many users, and the border continued to enable this illicit economy to flourish well into the 1960s.

CONCLUSION

Around 3:45 A.M. on July 23, 1967, Detroit police raided an after-hours club in the heart of the city's Twelfth Street community. The officers busted into the establishment, which was violating city liquor ordinances, and arrested eighty-two people. In many ways, this event in and of itself was not exceptional. Throughout the 1960s, local police had ramped up patrols and raids in black neighborhoods as part of a crackdown on crime and vice in the city.[1] On this particular morning, though, a crowd gathered to watch the officers arresting citizens in the predominantly black neighborhood. They became increasingly angry at what they saw as another example of police harassment and brutality and began to scream and throw rocks. What started as a raid on a blind pig quickly spiraled into a citywide riot, creating one of the deadliest "race riots" in American history. In the days that followed, violence between white and black residents escalated. People raided businesses and set buildings on fire. In an attempt to quell the violence, President Lyndon Johnson and Governor George Romney sent 9,200 members of the National Guard, 800 state police officers, and 4,700 paratroopers to patrol the streets of the Motor City. By the time the riot was over, forty-three people (thirty-three black and ten white) were dead, and 7,200 (mostly black) residents had been arrested.[2]

News of the violence in Detroit spread quickly to Windsor. On the evening of the 23rd, Canadians gathered on the banks of the Detroit River and watched in horror as the neighboring American metropolis burned. In the first days of the riot, some Americans—black and white—crossed into Windsor hoping to find refuge from the violence spreading across their city.[3] By July 25, though, the border itself was on lockdown, and Canadians in Detroit were barred from returning to Windsor until the chaos had subsided.[4] For many Windsor residents, the riots fundamentally changed the way they perceived the neighboring American city. A place many once saw as a close extension of their own city now seemed to be worlds apart. As a former newsman recalled, "Sixteen years ago, when I lived in Windsor, I used to enjoy visiting Detroit for its pleasant nightlife. Returning to the American city more than a decade later to report the bullet-filled hell of the 1967 riot I found Detroit like an urban Vietnam."[5] Similarly, Herb Collins, who interviewed Windsor residents about the impact of the riots on the Canadian community, explained that once the riots happened, "Windsor treated Detroit with more caution, perhaps even suspicion or fear. Residents went over [to the city], but only in company, to areas that were well-lit and policed. They knew where they were going, and went there directly without making side trips, staying too late, or deviating from their usual path."[6] Gone, it seemed, were the days of leisurely travels across the national line—neighboring Canadians were increasingly hesitant to make the short trip into the Motor City.

In the weeks that followed the violence in Detroit, Americans, too, grappled with the meaning of the riot. Although similar incidents occurred in Watts, Newark, and Chicago, the Detroit riot had the highest number of casualties. Media reports focused on everything from poverty and racial discrimination to lawlessness and violence within black communities themselves, providing a broad spectrum of speculation on the roots of this devastating event. Significantly, reports were quick to point out the role illegal economies played, emphasizing the fact that the riot began at an after-hours club where patrons were drinking well into the early hours of the morning. Some reports took this a step further, accusing pimps and prostitutes of inciting the violence. One article in the *Toledo Blade* explained that the riots began because the police took too long rounding up the customers in the bar and getting them into police wagons on the street. The commotion attracted a "rowdy" group of "pimps and prostitutes," who started to "hoot and jeer" and throw rocks at the car windows. In the looting that followed, the article claimed, men and women broke into liquor stores and pharmacies and "got drunk on gin and hopped up on drugs."[7] For many, the 1967 riot—like the Windsor "jazz riot" seven years earlier— was a blatant example of the devastating effects of illegal economies on North American cities. Fueled by criminals, drug use, and alcohol, these reports claimed, the rioting was one more example of why the nation's cities needed to be swept clean of the vice and crime that plagued city centers and threatened law-abiding citizens.

In blaming the riots on illicit economies and on the city's black communities, contemporaries failed to recognize how antivice rhetoric and other shortsighted urban reforms helped to create an environment of stark racial divides, poverty, and animosity. By the 1960s, the economic decline that began in the late 1940s had reached crisis proportions. The rioters who took to Detroit's streets were in many ways those left behind in the industrial environment—working-class residents who had long been out of work. They were also the men and women who were increasingly targeted by moral reform agendas and racialized policing practices. Residents who responded in anger and frustration to the raid on the blind pig saw it as one more example of police brutality and racialized antivice policies across increasingly depressed urban neighborhoods. As Martin Luther King Jr. tried to remind the public in the aftermath of the violence, "Revolts come out of revolting conditions."[8] By the late 1960s, it was clear that many residents, increasingly pessimistic about the future, saw few tangible solutions to the growing poverty and decay in the neighborhoods around them.

In many ways, the 1960s ushered in a new era in the Detroit-Windsor borderland, bringing to a close a period when cross-border travel was on the rise, men and women were on the move, and most were still hopeful about the future of these auto towns. Before the border cities had come to symbolize the apocalyptic future of industrial North America—an idea deeply ingrained in today's perceptions of the region—local residents grappled with the competing issues of optimism and despair, of urban growth and industrial stagnation. By focusing on illegal and informal industries—in particular, the sex and drug economies that brought countless Americans and Canadians into contact with one another—this book has refocused our attention on the women and men who were at the front lines of the region's shifting social geographies in the postwar years. Following World War II, illicit economies served multiple roles in the lives of border city residents, signaling at once the boomtown conditions that emerged in the wartime environment and the long-term economic decline that was setting into cities like Detroit and Windsor. Somewhere between mythologies of prosperity and conformity in the 1950s and the violence and urban decline associated with the 1960s lived thousands of men and women who built bustling illegal industries within the contested spaces of the urban borderland.

Illegal economies were deeply rooted in the Detroit-Windsor region, and the cities solidified their reputations as wide open during the tumultuous Prohibition years. At a time when the federal governments were trying to exact more control on cross-border travel than ever before, the rise of illegal smuggling and illicit tourism made the contradiction of the border clear: it was supposed to allow goods and people to pass through efficiently, while filtering out those deemed undesirable. The wide-open nature of Detroit and Windsor during the 1920s and early 1930s demonstrates that not only were the states unable to fully enact these objectives but also they were often at odds with the desires of local borderlanders, who had their own ideas about who should be allowed to cross the border and for what purpose.

While the economic and social climate of the 1930s reduced the size and scope of the illegal economies in Detroit and Windsor, their reputations as "sin cities" would not be forgotten. As men and women began flocking to the border cities during World War II, and as wartime industries brought unprecedented capital into the cities, conditions were ripe for the reemergence of cross-border economies based on drinking, gambling, illegal drugs, and prostitution. Within the context of a growing tourist and travel industry that made Detroit and Windsor the busiest crossing point between the two countries, illicit economies flourished, attracting men and women who wanted to discover the underbellies of the border cities. The border itself was central to this process and served an important role in signifying that one had entered a new space. In brothels, bars, jazz clubs, and dance halls and on city streets, men and women crossed racial, gender, and sexual lines, creating alternative forms of pleasure and entertainment in the bustling city centers.

While city boosters attempted to present a sanitized image of postwar travel and leisure, placing the middle-class nuclear family at the center of their marketing campaigns, the rise of illicit economies shows that a much wider range of cultural values emerged in the nations' urban centers. Drawn by the appeal of crossing the national line and purchasing goods and services in the cities' bustling leisure districts, participants in sex and drug economies challenged some of the social, moral, and racial boundaries that animated legal forms of entertainment. Building on the large number of tourists and travelers who were drawn to the region, sex workers helped to build a thriving commercial sex trade in the heart of the border cities. By marketing the appeal of nonnormative sexual interactions, which included sex across ethnic and racial lines, the commercial sex industry challenged the belief that heterosexual monogamous marriage was the only legitimate form of sexual expression. At the same time, a heroin sub-culture created an alternative economy based on consumption of pleasurable substances. Users and sellers built their own social networks, slang, and styles of dress, providing a social outlet for those unwilling or unable to engage in the conspicuous consumption touted as the bedrock of the postwar economy. By reformulating postwar definitions of consumerism, participants in vice economies created alternative social networks in which even the most marginal city residents could participate. In this way, vice economies were not anomalies in the postwar push toward leisure, consumption, and mobility—they were deeply embedded in this process.

Illicit economies also provided important forms of labor in neighborhoods struggling to adjust in the postwar environment. While the boomtown conditions initially enabled the growth of these industries on a large scale, they continued to thrive into the 1950s because they provided many local residents with a way to make money as the wartime economy leveled off. For many working-class residents, selling sex and drugs was a crucial way to supplement their often unpredictable incomes in industrial and service work. As affective forms of labor, the work cultures of the illicit economies differed in important ways from more traditional forms of labor in the region, providing some men and women with more flexible hours and a way to stay connected to a broad social community. Many often defended the work they performed in illicit economies, viewing their services as central to the working-class neighborhoods in which they lived. By participating in these alternative forms of labor, men and women thus challenged contemporary conceptions of productivity and community belonging and contributed to the cultural life of the cities' downtown neighborhoods.

Illegal economies, though, were not cure-alls for participants. The very fact that vice was deeply embedded in urban neighborhoods meant that illegal industries often mirrored the inequalities in the formal economy. Prostitution and heroin economies were segregated along race, gender, and class lines, with African Americans—especially African American women—often operating at the lowest levels. They were the most likely to be working openly in the streets, to be working for pimps, and to be arrested by local police. Since vice became concentrated in particular neighborhoods—in the increasingly rundown city center of Windsor and in the fledgling black neighborhoods of Paradise Valley, Twelfth Street, and the West Eight Mile Road in Detroit—the men and women who lived there often bore the brunt of the blame for crime and vice. They were subject to punitive housing policies, intensified policing practices, and public ridicule. In this way, though illicit economies provided important forms of income and sociability, they could also compound the social and economic struggles of women and men living in the cities' cores.

Many of the dangers that came along with vice economies were caused or exacerbated by the moral regulation aimed at eliminating them. Indeed, in response to the growing visibility of vice on the cities' streets, middle-class residents, politicians, law enforcement officials, and the media engaged in complex forms of moral regulation designed to chase out people and activities they saw as undesirable. This took place in formal and informal ways and included intensified policing strategies, vice cleanups, community group activism, and public shaming in the local media. These disparate approaches were united by the belief that vice was an infiltration from the outside that was wholly damaging to the neighborhoods in which it took place. Emerging within a Cold War environment and a correlating push to restore "traditional" gender, sexual, and familial patterns, reformers argued that vice undermined the nations' abilities to return to a sense of normalcy after the war. By the 1950s, reformers blamed some of the era's key social concerns—including urban decline, juvenile delinquency, and shifting family patterns—on vice economies.

As moral reformers increasingly associated the rise of vice with urban decline in the 1950s, efforts to eliminate these activities became explicitly racialized projects. On both sides of the border, white residents asserted that the influx of southern African Americans in particular threatened to undermine the health and welfare of the surrounding communities. Fears about interracial prostitution, heroin addiction, and "jazz riots" were central to public debates on both sides of the national line. This sense of cross-border whiteness, which allowed white Canadian and American residents to blame the cities' crime problems on the influx of racial others, helped to build cross-border connections between antivice reformers. By the time of the "race riot" of 1967, local residents had already solidified a racial narrative that blamed black residents for the cities' social ills. The closing of the border during the riots became a very tangible manifestation of what many white reformers had been attempting to do for the previous two decades: close the border to unwanted outsiders and protect their otherwise healthy communities from the violence and vice rampant in the inner city. For white residents on both sides of the border, defining the line between welcome community members and unwanted outsiders had increasingly become intertwined with the color line. The nation-building project, in short, had become an explicitly racialized undertaking by the 1960s, and it united white residents on both sides of the national line.

If debates about vice in Detroit and Windsor were shaped by the social geography of the borderland, they also had important national implications. In the postwar years, the problem of vice reached beyond the bounds of the borderland and took on mythic proportions in national debates about crime control. By the 1950s, politicians, the media, and contemporary pop culture representations in both Canada and the United States had solidified the image of bordertowns as sites of both danger and intrigue—as spaces where vice was rampant, criminals prospered, and law enforcement officials struggled to maintain peace and order. In response, federal officials organized high-profile investigations into illicit economies, like the 1955 senate committee hearings in both countries. These hearings adopted similar language, placing legal and medical experts at the center of their investigations. By weaving together the languages of addiction, disease, and danger, the American and Canadian senates were able to push for punitive policies that reinforced prohibitionist agendas at the federal level.

Adopting similar rhetoric and aligning policy, though, were two different things. In many ways, the asymmetrical relationship between Detroit and Windsor and their different positions within the global drug market provided important moments of discord. In fact, the tendency to blame vice on outsiders sometimes led local residents and law enforcement officials alike to blame their crime problems on the neighboring city. This was especially true for Windsorites, who often pointed to the large American metropolis as the source of crime and vice in their city. Canadian authorities often expressed their frustration that they did not receive nearly enough attention from their counterparts across the national line, who tended to focus their resources on policing major American cities and the U.S.-Mexico border. For Windsorites, the border was an ever-present reality in their lives; for Detroiters, the lines between the suburbs and city, the North and South, and black and white residents were often more acute. In this way, despite their efforts to provide a unified front against cross-border vice, cooperation on the ground often fell far short of public rhetoric. The "world's friendliest border," it turns out, was not without contestation, and borderlanders had to grapple with these realities on a daily basis.

Ultimately, the story of vice in the Detroit-Windsor border region—and along U.S.-Canada borderlands more generally—provides important insight into the formal and informal ways in which men and women worked to define citizenship and community belonging during the mid-twentieth century. The push and pull between state intentions and local borderlanders' desires was central to this process, for while the Canadian and American states attempted to control the borderline, the expansive nature of transnational illegal economies demonstrates the very real failures of that control. More important, we also see how everyday men and women drew on discourses of citizenship to both fight against and defend the growth of illicit economies in the border region. For many of the men and women who participated in illegal enterprises, they were important forms of work and leisure that were intimately intertwined in their local communities. In contrast, many interest groups emerged to fight the growth of these activities in *their* cities, framing vice participants as dangerous and unwanted residents reshaping their communities for the worse. Debates about illegal economies, then, were often as much about who did or did not belong in the postwar city as the particular activities themselves. These struggles to define the line separating licit from illicit activities became particularly acute in cities literally on the edges of their respective nations, and in many ways, the legacies of these debates continue to shape the way we perceive the national divide today. While discourses of security and citizenship have shifted in the post-9/11 era, the belief that bordertowns are spaces of both adventure and danger, of intrigue and infiltration, continues to resonate in public discourses about borderlands and boundary making. By tracing the roots of these ideologies in the mid-twentieth century, we can better locate the ways in which these current debates remain deeply embedded in historical struggles over who gets to define the limits of the nation and who counts as a full and welcomed citizen.

EPILOGUE

In the decades that followed the 1967 race riot, the city of Detroit—like many North American industrial cities—faced extremely difficult challenges, ones rooted in transformations that began in the early postwar years. Throughout the 1970s and 1980s, industries continued to abandon the region, crime rates soared, infrastructure crumbled, and political infighting plagued city hall.[1] If the election of the city's first black mayor, Coleman Young, provided a glimmer of hope in otherwise trying times, even Young was unable to stave off the city's massive economic and social issues. Detroit's reputation hit new lows across the nation and indeed the globe, as many came to associate the city with the apocalyptic future of America's urban centers. The city that had once been the beacon of hope and success in the industrial world now seemed to lie in ruins. For many, Detroit was no longer the Motor City; it was the "the Murder Capital of America."[2] If booming factories, fast-moving assembly lines, and Motown music once defined the city, popular culture now pictured Detroit as the American wasteland, a dire warning of what was to come for cities across the nation. Not even RoboCop, it seemed, could save the city from its dramatic and inevitable decline. Although many local residents maintained a strong sense of pride in their beloved city, the national media was much less forgiving.

In response, local politicians, business associations, and boosters struggled to remake Detroit's image in the national imagination. As in many cities across North America, they would continue to draw on urban renewal programs, proposing to build stadiums, office towers, promenades, and other attractions that would bring tourist dollars back into the city. Some of the more ambitious politicians and boosters saw Detroit's position on the border as a unique feature they could use to their advantage. In 1986, Mayor Young announced the Belle Isle International Project, a proposal that would bring as many as twelve casinos to the small island on the Detroit River. The project was designed to attract tourists and additional revenue into the struggling city.[3] The project's promoter, Patrick Meehan, claimed that such a venture would draw as many as 25 million tourists annually. If it was approved at the November city council meeting, they were set to break ground on its first 1,000-room casino hotel in January 1987. The grandiose plans called for walkways and trams to link Windsor and Detroit and for monorails to speed Belle Isle's gamblers to and from downtown Windsor. The project was a sure thing, Meehan boasted: "Casino gambling at Belle Isle is going to happen. You can absolutely be sure of that. It's on the way."[4]

To say that many Windsor residents were less enthusiastic about the plan would be an understatement. Residents openly criticized the move, arguing it would severely damage the safe and prosperous Canadian tourism industry. Already frustrated by the twelve strip clubs and open prostitution that drew Americans across the river, local residents believed that the Belle Isle International Project would greatly expand their vice problems. As one *Windsor Star* editorial explained, "The tourists that we want to come to Windsor and Essex County are those who would enjoy our riverfront, parks, and shopping. We do not need nor desire the type of tourists who want to check out the latest strip joint or to see what he can pick up on the street for a one night stand at the cheapest rate." If this project were to pass, the editorial warned, "The morality of our city will definitely be at its lowest ever and any recovery will be very long-term if possible at all."[5] Windsor did not need to foster the growth of more "Miami-style vices"; it already had more than its share.[6]

Although Young's Belle Isle International Project failed to gain city council approval, critics were not able to stave off legal gambling in the region for much longer. By the late 1990s, both Windsor and Detroit had caved in to the pragmatic needs of their cities. Despite Mayor Dennis Archer's insistence in 1993 that Detroit did not "need gambling or the problems it can bring," in 1998 he put on the table a plan to legalize gambling within the city's limits. This time, with few other prospects for economic growth, the city council approved plans to build three casinos in the city's core. That same year, Caesar's Windsor also opened for business, eager to capitalize on cross-border dollars. Though opposition was often fierce, the border cities' need to attract dollars into their cities outweighed the moral arguments against such ventures. At the turn of the twenty-first century, the Motor City was banking on the Motor City Casino, hoping it could help fill the void in tourism and industry that had long since faded with the retreat of the auto industries. In Windsor, "the old-time, blue-collar factory town adjusting to shifting economies" was similarly relying on the influx of Americans to bring tourist dollars back into their city. As one local paper explained, "Tijuana North"—a title harking back to the Prohibition days—depended on the work of men and women who kept their casinos running, their strip clubs full, and their escort services booming.[7]

The ultimate irony in the story of vice in the Detroit-Windsor region is that, despite the long history of blaming illicit industries for much of the urban decay and crime, city officials and boosters eventually turned to legalized vice as the key to their economic recovery.[8] The fact that Mayor Young became one of the most vocal proponents of legalized gambling in the city is not accidental. In fact, he ends his autobiography by criticizing the "do-gooders" who opposed his proposals to legalize gambling in the city, arguing that it would be essential for Detroit's economic recovery. His memories of the Prohibition years as the most prosperous time in the city's history clearly influenced how he viewed the region's future.[9] If illegal forms of vice had proved profitable for black communities in earlier decades, perhaps the struggling black metropolis could profit off legalized versions in the late twentieth century. He likewise insisted that Detroiters needed to work to rebuild a regional identity in concert with their Canadian neighbors; Detroiters had "been much too indifferent to [them] in the past."[10] Although Young's gambling proposals were voted down, he nonetheless had succeeded in reopening debates about the nature of city renewal projects, the practical advantages of illicit industries, and their place in working-class neighborhoods fighting to survive in the postindustrial environment.[11]

The struggle to define the borderlands relationship in the Detroit-Windsor region predated the postwar period and—as debates over legalized gambling at the end of the twentieth century indicate—also persisted well beyond it. These debates continue to take on moralizing tones that indicate the tension between fostering a cross-border community and building a barrier to stop unwanted elements from crossing between the two nations. As the controversy over legalized gambling demonstrates, debates over citizenship and belonging are still framed along the lines of licit and illicit, as Detroit and Windsor residents struggle to resuscitate their local economies and their decidedly negative international images.

Today's legalized vice industries, while bringing much-needed revenue into the local economies, also share some of the dangerous tendencies that illegal forms of vice had in the postwar years. The suburban-urban divides have become even starker in the region, and a privileging of white, suburban workers at casinos and other formerly illicit businesses continues to make it difficult for city residents to profit from these large ventures.[12] The question remains whether legalizing forms of vice will be able to solve any of the economic or social problems facing the region. The answer, as Detroit files for bankruptcy, seems decidedly negative. It is, however, clear that the deeply rooted history of cross-border vice in the region continues to shape the local economy and that illicit forms of moneymaking and leisure will continue to spark heated debates over the future of the U.S.-Canada borderlands and the meaning of citizenship for residents living on the margins of their respective nations.

Notes

INTRODUCTION

1. Anglin, "He Blew the Whistle on Windsor Vice," 62.

2. "Windsor Crackdown Fails to Prevent Vice Operations," 1; "Graver Charge Often Withdrawn States Police Official," 24; "Evidence That Attorney's Office Dictated Withdrawal of Charges"; "Ontario Fires Attorney in Vice Probe."

3. Ramirez, *Crossing the 49th Parallel*; Bukowczyk et al., *Permeable Border*; Graybill, *Policing the Great Plains*.

4. Pickering and Weber, *Borders, Mobility, and Technologies of Control*, 3.

5. Brunet-Jailly, "Special Section," 3.

6. Mason, *Rum Running and the Roaring Twenties*; Engelman, "Iron River Rum Rebellion"; Everest, *Rum across the Border*; Labadies, "Liquid Gold"; Gervais, *Rumrunners*.

7. Anzaldua, *Borderlands/la Frontera*; Lenz, "Transnational American Studies," 48–149; Martinez, *Border People*; Pratt, *Imperial Eyes*.

8. Harrison, "Now," 7.

9. Van Schendel and Abraham, *Illicit Flows and Criminal Things*, 18.

10. Bernstein, *Temporarily Yours*, 8.

11. Hickman, "'Mania Americana.'"

12. Gootenberg, "Talking Like a State," 115.

13. Canada, *Senate Special-Committee*, 28.

14. There are several notable exceptions: Boyd, *Wide Open Town*; Ross, *Burlesque West*; Sides, "Excavating the Postwar Sex District."

15. Cohen, *Consumer's Republic*; Harris, *Creeping Conformity*.

16. Sugrue, *Origins of the Urban Crisis*.

17. Thompson, "Rethinking the Politics of White Flight in the Postwar City"; Boustan, "Was Postwar Suburbanization 'White Flight'?"

18. I draw on the work of feminist scholars and sociologists who urge us to understand the ways in which informal economies are in fact embedded in larger structural forces. Cabezas, "Between Love and Money"; Preble and Casey Jr., "Taking Care of Business."

19. May, *Homeward Bound*; Adams, *Trouble with Normal*.

20. Meyerowitz, *Not June Cleaver*; Foreman, *Other Fifties*; Sugrue, "Reassessing the History of Postwar America."

21. Alan Hunt notes that there is an "umbrella effect" of moral regulation, through which specific social problems mobilize an array of "different social forces that otherwise would not only have had no contact, but might have lined up as part of opposed social blocs." In these widespread effects, moral reform is often presented as "necessary

to overcome the decline and generally has a dual thrust: a specific cure for the individual ill and an expanded or symbolic dimension." Hunt, *Governing Morals*, 9–11.

22. Gregory, *Southern Diaspora*.

23. Sugrue, *Origins of the Urban Crisis*, 23.

24. Laura McKinsey and Victor Konrad identify the Detroit-Windsor region as an *unbalanced influence zone*, where one side of the border (in this case, Detroit) has a much greater influence on the communities on the other side of the border. McKinsey and Konrad, *Borderland Reflections*, 12.

25. Laverty and Breen, "Windsor," 8.

26. I draw on Paul Gootenberg's insistence that the study of illicit activities requires both a "'structural' and 'discursive' approach, one that understands the cool hidden realities of [illicit] flows along with their overtly heated representations." Gootenberg, "Talking Like a State," 115.

CHAPTER 1

1. "Detroit River Span Dedicated to Peace," 22.

2. "Detroit Bridge Is Dedicated as New Peace Link," 22; "Nations Joint at Detroit Bridge," 13; "World's Largest Span Dedicated at Detroit," 8; "Ambassador Bridge," *Montreal Gazette*, 12; "Ambassador Bridge Open on Holiday," 1.

3. White, *Middle Ground*; Taylor, "Divided Ground"; Adelman and Aron, "From Borderlands to Borders," 818.

4. City of Detroit, "Master Plan Reports," 4.

5. Sugrue, *Origins of the Urban Crisis*, 18.

6. "Invitation to Canada," *Michigan Manufacturer and Financial Record*, March 21, 1931.

7. Poole, "Evolution of Social Services in the Border Cities," 20.

8. Border Cities Chamber of Commerce, "Your Market in Canada," 2.

9. Veres, "History of the United Automobile Workers in Windsor," 4–5.

10. Hill, "City Looks at Itself," 28.

11. Glazer, *Detroit*, 107–8.

12. U.S. Bureau of the Census, 1910, 953; U.S. Bureau of the Census, 1930, 1147.

13. Babson, *Working Detroit*, 27.

14. Smith, "Immigration and Naturalization Services (INS) at the US-Canadian Border," 128–29.

15. Zettlemoyer, "Assessment of Immigrant Needs," 1.

16. Canada, *Report on the 8th Census of Canada*, 210; Veres, "History of the United Automobile Workers in Windsor," 6.

17. "Detroit Is Back Gate," 2.

18. "Canadian House Argues Reciprocity Trends in Citizens," 16.

19. "9,200,000 Crossed the River between Detroit and Windsor," 8.

20. Poole, "Evolution of Social Services," 24–25.

21. *Canada's Most Fertile Field*, 7.

22. Border Cities Chamber of Commerce, *Canada's Southern Gateway*.

23. Ibid.

24. Stamp, *Bridging the Border*, 95.

25. Jacobson, *Barbarian Virtues*; Lee, *At America's Gates*; Brouwer, "Disgrace to 'Christian Canada.'"

26. "Smugglers in Toils," 13; "Chinese Smuggling Ring Broken," 9; "Detroit Is Back Gate," 2; Ettinger, *Imaginary Lines*, 64.

27. Lee, *Angel Island*.

28. Ngai, *Impossible Subjects*, 3.

29. Helling, "Position of Negroes, Chinese, and Italians," 47.

30. Smith, "Immigration and Naturalization Service," 129–30.

31. Klug, "Immigration and Naturalization Service," 412.

32. Hernandez, *Migra!*, 34.

33. Klug, "Immigration and Naturalization Service," 412.

34. "US Congressmen to Visit Here," 1; Smith, "Immigration and Naturalization Service," 133.

35. Klug, "Immigration and Naturalization Service," 400.

36. Unpublished versions of these cartoons are available in the Percy W. Cromwell Collection, "Clumsy," Box 2, Folder 23, Bentley Historical Library.

37. "Long Lines of Motors Crowd Detroit Ferries," 3.

38. Stamp, *Bridging the Border*, 97.

39. Ibid., 98.

40. The votes were 13,874 in favor and 8,794 against. Ibid.

41. Ibid.

42. McClintic-Marshall Co., "Ambassador Bridge," 7.

43. Ibid., 10.

44. Ibid., 46.

45. Corey, *Canadian-American Relations*, 22.

46. Farmer, *History of Detroit*, 201–2.

47. Forestell, "Bachelors, Boarding-Houses, and Blind Pigs"; Murphy, "Private Lives of Public Women."

48. Taylor, "Prostitution in Detroit," 24, 34; Schneider, *Detroit and the Problem of Order, 1830–1880*, 93–94.

49. Schneider, *Detroit and the Problem of Order*, 93–94.

50. Faires, "Poor Women, Proximate Border," 98–99.

51. The *Post* and *Detroit Evening News* quoted in Schneider, *Detroit and the Problem of Order*, 95.

52. D'Emilio and Freedmen, *Intimate Matters*, chapter 9.

53. Sangster, *Regulating Girls and Women*, 92–93.

54. Rosen, *Lost Sisterhood*, 34.

55. Mallea, *War on Drugs*, 25.

56. Marquis, "'Brewers and Distillers Paradise,'" 138.

57. Ibid.

58. Malleck, *Try to Control Yourself*, 4–6.

59. Mason, *Rum Running and the Roaring Twenties*, 19.

60. Heron, *Booze*, 248.

61. Rockaway, "Notorious Purple Gang," 116.

62. "Launch New Drive," 6; Rockaway, "Notorious Purple Gang," 117.

63. "In Windsor the Wicked," 5; "Ontario Goes Wet and the Border Seethes"; Bender, *Run for the Border*.

64. "Dominion Vice Depicted," 1.

65. "Sees Ontario Hurt by New Liquor Law."

66. Unpublished versions of these cartoons are available in the Percy W. Cromwell Collection, Box 2, Folder 24, Bentley Historical Library.

67. "Battling the Rum Runners."

68. "Ontario Goes Wet," *New York Times*.

69. Ibid.

70. "Tourist Rush Beats All Records," 1.

71. "Our Rum Capital," 121.

72. "Liquor Traffic Not Unlawful across Border," 2.

73. "Our Rum Capital," 121.

74. "Ontario Is Now Ready for Thirsty Tourists."

75. "Ontario to Be Tourist Oasis," 3.

76. "Canada Gaining Name as Refuge of Rum Runners," 3.

77. *Montreal Gazette*, 12.

78. U.S. Senate Subcommittee, *Investigation of the So-Called Rackets*, 178.

79. Moley, "The Gray Zone of Crime."

80. Wolcott, *Remaking Respectability*, 93.

81. Young, *Hard Stuff*, 17.

82. Ibid., 16–18.

83. Ibid., 20.

84. Ibid.

85. Wolcott, *Remaking Respectability*, 92.

86. Taylor, "Prostitution in Detroit," 85.

87. Ibid., 102.

88. McGowan, *Motor City Madam*, 78.

89. Taylor, "Prostitution in Detroit," 29.

90. Ibid.

91. Rose, *American Women and the Repeal of Prohibition*, 10.

92. U.S. Senate Subcommittee, *Investigation of So-Called Rackets*, 173.

93. "Detroit Hit by Crime Wave as Gunmen Arrive," 11.

94. Woodford, *This Is Detroit*, 120.

95. U.S. Senate Subcommittee, *Investigation of So-Called Rackets*, 194.

96. Association against the Prohibition Amendment, *Canadian Liquor Crossing the Border*, 10; "Payoff Man Named."

97. "Battling the Rum Runners."

98. "Absolved of Slaying of Youth in Detroit."

99. "Warns Dry Agent to Stop Shooting."

100. "Hoover Deplores Killings."

101. Woodford, *This Is Detroit*, 121.

102. Wolcott, *Remaking Respectability*, 170.

103. Poole, "Evolution of Social Services," 25.

104. Taylor, "Prostitution in Detroit," 1933.

105. Ibid., 117.

106. Ibid., 32–33.

107. Ibid., 117.

108. Ibid.

109. "Immigration Order Stirs Canada's Ire," 32.

110. "Ottawa Protests Border Ruling," 1.

111. "Detroit Executive Barred as Aliens."

112. "Immigration Order Stirs Canada's Ire," 27.

CHAPTER 2

1. "Code Section," 3. Emphasis added.

2. Hyde, *Arsenal of Democracy*, 3.

3. Ibid., 25.

4. Sugrue, *The Origins of the Urban Crisis*, 19.

5. Brown, *Illustrated History of Canada*, 464.

6. Brode, *The Slasher Killings*, 8–9.

7. Greater Windsor Industrial Commission, "Industrial Prospects are Bright in Windsor," 5.

8. Southeastern Michigan Council of Governments, "Historical Population and Employment," 7; Karibo, "Detroit's Border Brothel," 366.

9. Baulch and Zacharias, "The 1943 Detroit Race Riots."

10. Hyde, *Arsenal of Democracy*, 174.

11. Weatherford, *African American Women during World War II*, 10.

12. Hyde, *Arsenal of Democracy*, 181.

13. Teaford, *The Metropolitan Revolution*, 24.

14. Baruth-Walsh and Walsh, *Strike!*; Smith and Featherstone, *Labor in Detroit*; Babson, *Working Detroit*.

15. Baruth-Walsh and Walsh, *Strike!*

16. The average weekly earnings in Windsor were $52.50. This compared with $50.81 in St. Catharines, $49.40 in Montreal, $48.11 in Hamilton, $45.39 in Toronto, and $42.12 in Vancouver; Laverty and Breen, "Windsor: Border—Not Barrier," 56.

17. Sugrue, *The Origins of the Urban Crisis*, 109.

18. Hurley, *Diners, Bowling Alleys and Trailer Parks*, 9.

19. Cohen, *A Consumer's Republic*, 195; Harris, *Creeping Conformity*, 129–30.

20. Dubinsky, *The Second Greatest Disappointment*, 177.

21. Zinn, *Postwar America*, 94.

22. Popp, *The Holiday Makers*, 144.

23. By 1944, the restrictions on pleasure travel were lifted in both the United States and Canada, once again allowing tourism and cross-border travel to thrive. "Tourist Trade Up in Present Season," 20.

24. "Publicity Bureau Here Swamped by Tourists' Calls," 36.

25. Laverty and Breen, "Windsor: Border—Not Barrier," 56.

26. "Police Courteous to Tourists," 4; Munro, "How Canadians Can Be Distinctive," 4.

27. Laverty and Breen, "Windsor: Border—Not Barrier," 8.

28. "Canada Loses This Business," 6.

29. Heyd, "Introducing Windsor," 395.

30. Laverty and Breen, "Windsor: Border—Not Barrier," 8.

31. "Courtesy to Tourists Pays Big Dividends," 11.

32. "Urges Canadians to Cut American Flag Waving," 15.

33. Morrison, "Silver Jubilee of Opening of Ambassador Bridge," 45–46.

34. International Freedom Festival, "Souvenir Program," 1961.

35. Hill, "A City Looks at Itself," 16–17.

36. Longo, "Consuming Freedom," 120.

37. International Freedom Festival, "Souvenir Program," Part 2 (1959), 2. Bentley Historical Library.

38. Ibid., 3.

39. International Freedom Festival, "Souvenir Program" (1961), 4. Bentley Historical Library.

40. International Freedom Festival, "Souvenir Program," Parts 1 and 2 (1959), 3, 8, 20, 41. Bentley Historical Library.

41. According to the Windsor police registers, the majority of the women arrested as "inmates" and "keepers" of bawdy houses between 1940 and 1955 were born in cities other than Windsor. Their most commonly stated occupations were as follows: waitress, domestic, cashier, housewife, and factory worker. Windsor Police Department, *Annual Registers*, 1940–60.

42. "Venereal Disease," 3.

43. Windsor Police Department, *Annual Registers*, 1940–60.

44. "Say Montreal Vice Ring Nets $10,000,000 Yearly," 1; "A New Petition to Give Names in Vice Charges," 3; "Citizens Reject Sawed-Off Probe of Montreal Vice," 3; "Rooming Houses Next," 9.

45. Gregory, *The Southern Diaspora*.

46. According to Virginia Sobotka's study of women arrested for prostitution in Detroit, 41 percent of white women were from the South, 25 percent of whom moved from Kentucky and Tennessee. African American women from the South made up 53 percent of the black women arrested, 24 percent of whom came from the Deep South. Sobotka, "A Comparative Study of Prostitution," 5.

47. Joan Sangster has documented a few cases of Canadian women crossing into Detroit and other American cities for the purposes of prostitution. Sangster, *Regulating Girls and Women*, 112.

48. Babson, *Working Detroit*, 144.

49. "Mayor Reaume, 'Pleads with Married Women to Leave Jobs,'" *Windsor Daily Star*, January 23, 1946, quoted in Brode, *Unholy City*, 18.

50. Social Services, *Detroit Area Study*, "A Social Profile." This number was similar in Canada, where by 1951 more than one in four women worked as clerical workers. Philips and Philips, *Women and Work*, 36.

51. Boehm, *Making a Way Out of No Way*, 206.

52. Moon, *Untold Tales*, 299.

53. Katz, "The Sleazy, Grey World of the Call Girl," 112.

54. Windsor Police Department, *Annual Registers*, 1940–60.

55. Brophey, "Girl's Story Leads to Clean-up Drive," 3.

56. Windsor Police Department, *Annual Registers*, 1940–60.

57. "Five Charged after Raid," 3.

58. Brode, Interview with Jim Ure.

59. "Probe Heat," 6.

60. "Windsor Crackdown Fails to Prevent Vice Operations," 1.

61. Liquor License Board of Ontario, Blue Water Public House Case Files, RG-3 B335026.

62. "Code Section," 3.

63. The number of Canadians arrested for prostitution-related offenses in Detroit are as follows: 1945: 66; 1946: 42; 1947: 28; 1948: 28; 1949: 31; 1950: 57; 1951: 29; 1952: 23; 1953: 30. After 1953, the police department stopped providing the nativity of those arrested in their annual reports. See Detroit Police Department, *Annual Report*, 1945–53.

64. Whitall, "Woodward: Avenue of Escape."

65. Smith, "Detroit Wears Its Hallow a Little Crooked," 7.

66. Arrests regularly took place off Glenlodge, Wyoming, Woodside, Reimanville, and Halcott Lane, along West Eight Mile Road and the city limits. Michigan State Police Records, "Detroit Vice."

67. Citizens Committee for Equal Opportunity, "A Report by the Sub-Committee," 11.

68. Vedder, "An Analysis of the Taxi-Dance Hall," 17.

69. Ibid., 46.

70. Ibid., 35.

71. Smith, "Detroit Wears Its Hallow a Little Crooked," 7.

72. Chism, "Many Changes Seen in Night Life."

73. Detroit Urban League, *Twelfth Street*, 25.

74. According to Sobotka's study, whites went from making up 53.4 percent of prostitutes arrested in the city in the 1930s to 20.7 percent by the mid-1950s. Sobotka, "A Comparative Study," 72.

75. Ibid., 12.

76. "Probe Heat," 6.

77. Adams, *The Trouble with Normal*; Cohen, *A Consumer's Republic*; Gleason, *Normalizing the Ideal*; Valverde, "Building Anti-Delinquent Communities."

78. Sobotka, "A Comparative Study," 2.

79. Taylor, "Prostitution in Detroit," 29.

80. Ibid., 114–15.

81. McGowan, *Motor City Madam*, 73–74.

82. Ibid., 35.

83. Sugrue, *The Origins of the Urban Crisis*, 30.

84. McGowan, *Motor City Madam*, 153.

85. Ibid., 74.

86. Moon, *Untold Tales*, 299.

87. Laverty and Breen, "Windsor: Border—Not Barrier," 8.

88. "Attracted to Windsor," 3.

89. Clark, "As We See It," 2.

90. United States Army, *Instructions for American Servicemen in France*, 17. See also Roberts, *What Soldiers Do*.

91. Brode, *Unholy City*, 21. Emphasis added.

92. "Venereal Disease," 3.

93. Windsor Police Department, *Annual Reports*, 1945–60.

94. Sugrue, *The Origins of the Urban Crisis*, 23.

95. Shogan, *The Detroit Race Riot*; Langlois, "The Belle Isle Bridge Incident."

96. According to the Canadian census, there were 2,402 "Negro" residents and about 750 Chinese residents living in Windsor in 1961. Helling, *The Position of Negroes, Chinese, and Italians*, 6, 53.

97. "Minorities Lot Tough," 43; Barnett, "Canada Negroes Hit by Housing Shortage," 9.

98. Helling, *The Position of Negroes, Chinese, and Italians*.

99. Liquor Control Board of Ontario, Establishment Case Files, "St. Clair Tavern and Hotel."

100. Detroit Urban League, *A Comparative Study*, 16.

101. Lewis-Coleman, *Race against Liberalism*, 21.

102. Barnett, "Canadian Negroes Find Equality Grim Illusion," 8; "Ontario Negro Group Fearful," 1.

103. By 1959, the average white family made $7,200, and the average nonwhite family made only $4,400. United Community Services of Metropolitan Detroit, *Recent Population and Social Trends in the Detroit Area*, 12.

104. Fine, *Violence in the Model City*, 39.

105. Kornhauser, *Detroit as the People See It*, 82.

106. Detroit Urban League, *Twelfth Street*, 25.

107. Citizens Committee, "A Report by the Sub-Committee," 10.

108. Murphy, "Detroit Blues Women," 53, 65.

109. Thomas Bowles quoted in Moon, *Untold Tales*, 324.

110. Gloria Manlove quoted in Moon, *Untold Tales*, 324.

111. Betty De Ramus quoted in Langlois, "The Belle Isle Bridge Incident," 185.

CHAPTER 3

1. Mosher, "Look Out for Mary Jane," 5.

2. Carstairs, *Jailed for Possession*, 61.

3. Musto, *The American Disease*, 245.

4. Vick and Rhoades, *Drugs and Alcohol in the 21st Century*, 86.

5. U.S. Senate, *Illicit Narcotics Traffic*, 28.

6. Lansing, *Legislative Committee*, 6; U.S. Senate, *Illicit Narcotics Traffic*, 4486.

7. Canada, *Senate Special-Committee*, 314.

8. Carstairs, *Jailed for Possession*, 67.

9. U.S. Senate, *Illicit Narcotics Traffic*, 482.

10. Canada, Department of National Health and Welfare, *Annual Report*, 94.

11. Schneider, *Smack*, 43; Carstairs, *Jailed for Possession*; Courtwright, *Addicts Who Survived*.

12. Carstairs, *Jailed for Possession*, 75.

13. Lansing, *Legislative Committee*, 3.

14. Michigan State Police Records, "Detroit Vice," undercover surveillance.

15. Lansing, *Legislative Committee*, 39.

16. Moon, *Untold Tales*, 381.

17. "Probe Will Start Thursday," 3; "Man Tells Dope Story in Court," 57.

18. Lansing, *Legislative Committee*, 3.

19. Canada, *Senate Special-Committee*, 362–63. Emphasis added.

20. "Border 'Dope King' Suspect, Devlin, Held," 5.

21. Canada, *Senate Special-Committee*, 323.

22. "Reefers Not Puffed at Schools," 19.

23. U.S. Senate, *Illicit Narcotics Traffic*, Part 10, 4519.

24. Lansing, *Legislative Committee*, 48.

25. Hall, Anonymous interview, Lafayette Clinic, 7–8.

26. "Heavy Smoker Lumped with Drug Addict," 49.

27. Moyer, Interview with Gwen Hall, Lafayette Clinic. All names have been changed to maintain anonymity of interviewees.

28. Lansing, *Legislative Committee*, 30.

29. Ibid.

30. Detroit, *Report of the Mayor's Committee*, 39.

31. Canada, Department of National Health and Welfare, *Annual Report*, 78.

32. Wilson and Cohasse, *The Toast of the Town*, 156.

33. "Detroit Gets Bebop Fever," 19.

34. Clark, "Jumping Is the Theme Song in Detroit Nighteries," 19.

35. Liquor Control Board of Ontario Case Files, RG36-8; File: Arlington Public House, 893 Erie St. East, Windsor, B134022; Letter from Owner, 1959.

36. Bjorn and Gallert, *Before Motown*, 76.

37. *Michigan Chronicle*, December 6, 1947, quoted in Bjorn and Gallert, *Before Motown*, 76.

38. Canada, Department of National Health and Welfare, *Annual Report* (1949), 56; Wilber, "Reveal Crystal Beach," 13.

39. Ted Stewart, Interview with Gwen Hall, Lafayette Clinic.

40. Rodger Moyer, Interview with Gwen Hall, Lafayette Clinic.

41. Schneider, *Smack*, 43.

42. Anonymous, Interview with Gwen Hall, Lafayette Clinic.

43. McGowan, *Motor City Madam*, 79.

44. Detroit, *Report of the Mayor's Committee*, 28.

45. Mosher, "The Legal Response to Narcotic Drugs," 114.

46. News reports identified the locations of narcotics arrests in the city, which took place largely in the city's downtown core. "Marijuana Certificates Given Court," 3;

"Behind Drug Ring," 7; "Woman Waits Dope Penalty," 5; "Heroin Curb Service Told," 5–8; "Court Told How Mounties Trapped," 5.

47. Detroit, *Report of the Mayor's Committee*, 38.

48. Women were arrested and prosecuted at a much lower rate than men, though the percentage of African American women likewise rose in relation to white women. Prosecution of women in 1949: black: 5; white: 3; prosecution of women in 1958: black: 64; white: 12. Detroit Police Department, *Eighty-Fourth Annual Report* (1949), 82; Detroit Police Department, *Annual Statistical Report* (1958), 91.

49. Gardiner, *In the Mind of a Mountie*, 520.

50. Carstairs, *Jailed for Possession*, 97.

51. U.S. Senate, *Illicit Narcotics Traffic*, 4508.

52. Ibid., 4490.

53. "Hannah Concludes Detroit Rates High," A10.

54. "Detroit Officials Check Racial Bias Charges," 34A; "Detroit NAACP Charges Bias," 19.

55. Thomas, *Life for Us Is What We Make It*, 317–18.

56. High, *Industrial Sunset*.

57. Leggett, *Class, Race, and Labor*, 55; Dickinson, *Automation*; Marcson, *Automation, Alienation, and Anomie*.

58. Thomas, *Life for Us Is What We Make It*, 354.

59. Leggett, *Class, Race, and Labor*, 56–57.

60. Oliver, "The Identification of Poverty Pockets"; Heuton, "Urban Sprawl," 142. In 1945, 85 percent of the people in Essex County lived in the City of Windsor; by 1956, the city contained only 65 percent of the county population.

61. Social Services, *Detroit Area Study*, 4.

62. Anonymous, Interview with Gwen Hall, Lafayette Clinic.

63. Rodger Moyer, Interview with Gwen Hall, Lafayette Clinic.

64. Lansing, *Legislative Committee*, 39.

65. Detroit, *Report of the Mayor's Committee*, 40.

66. Canada, *Senate Special-Committee*; Lansing, *Legislative Committee*.

67. Anonymous, Interview with Gwen Hall, Lafayette Clinic.

68. John Hammond, Interview with Gwen Hall, Lafayette Clinic.

69. Lansing, *Legislative Committee*, 30.

70. Detroit, *Report of the Mayor's Committee*, 29.

71. Rodger Moyer, Interview with Gwen Hall, Lafayette Clinic.

72. Canada, *Senate Special-Committee*, 63.

73. U.S. Senate, *Illicit Narcotics Traffic*, 802.

74. Canada, *Senate Special-Committee*, 312.

75. "Trips Recalled," 1; "Return Convicted Stabber to Face Narcotics Charge," 3; "New Trial for Devlin," 39.

76. "Big Haul of Heroin Seized," 44.

77. Canada, *Senate Special-Committee*, 313.

78. White wrote an eight-page letter to U.S. Customs Officials in Washington, D.C., to bring La Prad and Dupree to their attention. Treasury Department, Bureau of

Customs, Central Files, Subject Classified Correspondence (1938–65), National Archives, Box 162, 1.

79. Ibid., 2.

80. Ibid., 4.

81. Ibid., 7.

82. Ibid., 5–6.

83. Canadian Broadcast Company Digital Archives, http://www.cbc.ca/archives /categories/society/crime-justice/pushing-past-borders-canada-international-drug -trafficking/a-growing-trade.html (June 2, 2014).

84. U.S. Senate, *Organized Crime and Illicit Traffic in Narcotics*, 409.

85. Schneider, *Iced*, 227.

86. U.S. Senate, *Organized Crime and Illicit Traffic in Narcotics*, 928.

87. Ibid., 409.

88. McGowan, *Motor City Madam*, 68.

89. U.S. Senate, *Organized Crime and Illicit Traffic in Narcotics*, 409.

90. Ibid., 400.

91. Ibid., 410.

92. Schneider, *Iced*, 229.

93. Cedilot and Noel, *Mafia, Inc.*, 2.

94. U.S. Senate, *Organized Crime and Illicit Traffic in Narcotics*, 878; Beare and Schneider, *Money Laundering in Canada*, 114.

95. Schneider, *Iced*, 231.

96. U.S. Senate, *Organized Crime and Illicit Traffic in Narcotics*, 887–88.

97. Ibid., 889.

98. Burnstein, *Motor City Mafia*, 43.

99. U.S. Senate, *Organized Crime and Illicit Traffic in Narcotics*, 413–14.

CHAPTER 4

1. "Murder Try Charged in Jazz Riot"; "50 Injured in Rioting in Canadian Jazz Show"; "Riot Erupts at Jazz Show Emancipation Fete"; "Riot Marks Jazz Show in Ontario"; "Police Quell Riot at Jazz Show"; "Big Jazz Show Spurs Rioting"; "Jazz Show Disrupted."

2. "7 Held in Rock 'N' Roll Riot," 1.

3. "Chaos Is King," 4.

4. "Toronto Hits Back," 1.

5. Cresswell, *The Tramp in America*, 15–16.

6. Owram, *Born at the Right Time*, 9.

7. Meyers, "Girls Who Leave Home for Larger Cities," 2.

8. Juvenile Delinquency Study Committee, 1c.

9. Minutes, Women's Local Council of Windsor Records, 2.

10. Ibid.

11. Ibid.

12. United Community Services, "Adolescent Girls and Services."

13. Michigan State Police Complaint, May 8, 1953, Docket # 7-54-53.

14. Letter, Robert N. Sawyer, Prosecuting Attorney to Det. Sgt. Carl W. Robinson, Racket Squad (April 1, 1954), RG 90-240, State Police—Criminal Investigations, Docket # 7-54-53, Michigan State Archives.

15. "Attracted to Windsor," 3.

16. Ibid.

17. "Local Child Said Victim," 1.

18. "Detroiters Come Here to Drink Beer," 1.

19. Ibid.

20. "Pictures Show Many Windsor Youngsters Out after Dark," 5.

21. "Attracted to Windsor," 3.

22. Sugrue, *The Origins of the Urban Crisis*, 24, 63.

23. Detroit Urban League, *Twelfth Street*, 3.

24. Weales, "Small-Town Detroit."

25. Ibid., 25.

26. Detroit Housing Commission, "Urban Renewal and Tax Revenue," 3; "Hastings-Gratiot Slum Clearance Approved," 4.

27. Fine, *Violence in the Model City*, 61.

28. Thomas, *Redevelopment and Race*, 38.

29. Fine, *Violence in the Model City*, 62.

30. City of Toronto, "Special Committee: Place of Amusement," 107.

31. Fine, *Violence in the Model City*, 62.

32. Thomas, *Redevelopment and Race*, 34.

33. Fine, *Violence in the Model City*, 62.

34. Detroit Urban League, *Twelfth Street*, 29.

35. Ibid., 18.

36. Ibid., 25. Emphasis in original.

37. Ibid., 25.

38. Ibid., 26.

39. Cohassey, "Down on Hastings Street," 87.

40. Clark, "Paradise Valley," 6.

41. Boyd, "Blind No More," 10; Stephens, "Cars Perpetuate Black and White Split," 13.

42. Faludi and Associates, *A Fifteen Year Programme for the Urban Renewal*, 7.

43. The report explained that "1,800 acres can be considered to be declining and 300 blighted. Of over 25,000 structures, 13.3 percent are vulnerable to blight; 3 percent are partly blighted and 0.7 percent completely blighted." Ibid., 1–2.

44. Ibid., 6.

45. Anglin, "He Blew the Whistle on Windsor Vice," 950.

46. Gross, "Redevelopment in Windsor to 1900," v.

47. "Call for Redevelopment Proposals," 55.

48. "Young Drifters Floating into N.Y.," 1A.

49. Glover, "Crime Wave—Hangover from War," 5.

50. Furman, "Urges New Agency on Child Welfare," 24.

51. Adams, *The Trouble with Normal*, 56–57.

52. Gleason, *Normalizing the Ideal*, 11.

53. May, *Homeward Bound*, 11.

54. Rogers, *Street Gangs in Toronto*, x. Emphasis added.

55. Mayor's Committee for Community Action for Detroit's Youth (MCCADY), 7.

56. Ibid., 8–9.

57. Ibid., 22–23.

58. "Labels Western Morals Civilization's Top Threat," 4.

59. Beattie, "Now Is the Time," 15.

60. "The Tragedy of Broken Homes," 4.

61. "M.O.H. Will Lead Drive," 3.

62. Ibid., 3. Emphasis added.

63. Detroit Public Schools, *Instructions Regarding Narcotics*, 43.

64. Ibid., 33–34.

65. "Selling Bodies to Get Dope," 1.

66. McAree, "Juvenile Junkies," 6.

67. MCCADY, "Community Action," 7.

68. Ibid., 6–14.

69. Donald S. Leonard Papers, Racial Gang Activities.

70. "Zoot-Suiters Held after Terrorized Local Youth," 3.

71. Ibid., 6.

CHAPTER 5

1. "Nation-Wide War on Dope Launched," 1.

2. Flood, "Story Protests on Sex Crimes."

3. Woodiwiss, *Organized Crime*, 248; Bernstein, *The Greatest Menace*, 9.

4. Between 1945 and 1980, there were at least five presidential and congressional commissions formed in the United States and at least six provincial or federal commissions in Canada that studied the problem of organized crime. Schneider, *Iced*, 227.

5. Woodiwiss, *Organized Crime*, 244; Moore, *The Kefauver Committee and the Politics of Crime*. On the impact of the Kefauver Committee in Canada, see Morton, *At Odds*, 147.

6. Bernstein, "What Did Apalachin Prove?," 10–11.

7. Woodiwiss, *Organized Crime*, 244–45.

8. Phillips, "The Case of the Drug Peddling Priest," 15.

9. Pearson, "Fifty Members of the Mafia," 6. For reprints of the article, see "The Merry-Go Round," 4; "Mafia Hold in US Bared," 3; "The Washington Merry-Go-Round"; "Drew Pearson's Washington Merry-Go-Round," 4.

10. "Says Mafia Is Just One Big Family," 11.

11. Schatzberg and Kelly, *African American Organized Crime*, 108.

12. "US Agents Smash Big Narcotics Ring," 26.

13. "San Francisco Agents Seize Narcotics from China," 9.

14. "Vancouver Police Break Up Canada-Wide Lottery," 3.

15. Winchell, "Áu Revoir!," 20.

16. Wilber, "Reveal Crystal Beach Teen-Age Dope Plot"; Wilber, "It Can Happen Here."

17. *Johnny Stool Pigeon*, 1949.

18. http://www.episodeworld.com/show/Border_Patrol/season=all/english/plotguide (March 14, 2015).

19. Bernstein, "What Did Apalachin Prove?," 13–14.

20. This included Vancouver, Winnipeg, Toronto, Ottawa, and Montreal.

21. The cities included were Detroit, Washington, D.C., Philadelphia, New York, Austin, Dallas, Fort Worth, Houston, San Antonio, San Francisco, Los Angeles, Chicago, and Cleveland.

22. U.S. Senate, *Illicit Narcotics Traffic*, 2.

23. Ibid., 4.

24. Canada, *Senate Special-Committee*, ix.

25. U.S. Senate, *Illicit Narcotics Traffic*, 2.

26. Of the twenty-three witnesses interviewed by the Canadian Senate Committee in Vancouver, ten, or 43 percent, were law enforcement officials. Physicians and psychiatrists represented about 30 percent of the witness list. The remainder was a miscellaneous group of provincial legislators, members of social organizations, clergy, and laypeople. The breakdown for the U.S. Senate Committee was likewise centered on experts, with law enforcement officials making up more than 63 percent of those interviewed in the opening hearing, and the remaining witnesses were medical workers.

27. Musto, *The American Disease*, 241.

28. Gleason, "Psychology and the Construction of the Normal Family," 446–47.

29. U.S. Senate, *Illicit Narcotics Traffic*, 38–39. Emphasis added.

30. Canada, *Senate Special-Committee*, 28.

31. Ibid., 209.

32. Ibid., 34.

33. Ibid., 4480.

34. U.S. Senate, *Illicit Narcotics Traffic*, 161.

35. Canada, *Senate Special-Committee*, 24.

36. U.S. Senate, *Illicit Narcotics Traffic*, 718.

37. Ibid., 783.

38. Ibid., 548.

39. Ibid., 3890.

40. Ibid., 3893, 4698, 4234.

41. Ibid., 4514–15.

42. Canada, *Senate Special-Committee*, 317, 322.

43. Ibid., 284.

44. Ibid., 295.

45. Ibid., 328, 296.

46. Ibid., 815.

47. Ibid., 972.

48. Ibid., 4522.

49. Ibid., 4605.

50. Ibid., 104.

51. Freedman, "The Prison Lesbian," 404–5.

52. Canada, *Senate Special-Committee*, 63.

53. U.S. Senate, *Illicit Narcotics Traffic*, 4492.

54. Moore, *The Kefauver Committee*.

55. Musto, *The American Disease*, 231.

56. U.S. Senate, *Illicit Narcotics Traffic*, 205.

57. Marchetti, *Romance and the "Yellow Peril,"* 38.

58. Klein, *Cold War Orientalism*, 39–40.

59. Anderson, *Vancouver's Chinatown*.

60. Canada, *Senate Special-Committee*, 22–23.

61. Ibid., xix.

62. U.S. Senate, *Illicit Narcotics Traffic*, 802.

63. Ibid., 4483.

64. Ibid., 26.

65. Ibid., 107.

66. Canada, *Senate Special-Committee*, 21.

67. Ibid., 314.

68. U.S. Senate, *Illicit Narcotics Traffic*, 707–8.

69. Ibid., 824–25.

70. Canada, *Senate Special-Committee*, 313.

71. Ibid., 312.

72. "Windsor Wire Service," 3.

73. Letter from Frost to Kefauver. Emphasis added.

74. Letter from Kefauver to Frost.

75. Solomon and Green, "The First Century," 104.

76. Musto, *The American Disease*, 231.

77. Solomon and Green, "The First Century," 105.

CONCLUSION

1. Doody, *Detroit's Cold War*, 67–68.

2. Burns, "Waging Cold War in a Model City," 10; Darden et al., *Detroit*; Fine, *Violence in the Model City*.

3. "Border Closed," 2.

4. "Border Officials Lift Ban," 35.

5. Kidd, "Detroit Is Known as 'Murder City, USA,'" 9.

6. Colling, *Turning Points*, 5.

7. Pearson, "Reasons for Detroit Riots Are Listed," 7.

8. "Detroit Quieter, But Toll of Dead Stands at 24," 43.

EPILOGUE

1. By the 1980s, Detroit's economy was so depressed that its assessed valuation was lower than it had been in 1960. Darden et al., *Detroit*, 22.

2. Greenberg, *Don't Go There!*, 214–15.

3. "Creation of Gambling Resort on Belle Isle Reportedly Proposed," 5.

4. "Casino Would Bring Miami-Style Vices," 1.

5. Reaume, "No Dice on Detroit's Plan," 13.

6. "Casino Would Bring Miami-Style Vices," 1.

7. Lyke, "In Windsor, Culture and Sin Go Hand in Hand."

8. Detroit and Windsor were not alone in their turn to casinos and other forms of formerly illicit entertainment. Throughout the 1990s, cities across North America contemplated plans to renew rundown industrial neighborhoods by building casinos and related industries. Judd, "Promoting Tourism in US Cities," 294.

9. Young, *Hard Stuff*, 18–25.

10. Ibid., 314.

11. Rich, *Coleman Young and Detroit Politics*, 121.

12. "Workers' Suit Accuses Detroit Casino of Bias," 4.

Bibliography

GOVERNMENT PUBLICATIONS

Canada. Department of National Health and Welfare. *Annual Report*. Ottawa: Queen's Printer, 1959.

Canada. Dominion Bureau of Statistics. *Report on the 8th Census of Canada, 1941, VII Gainfully Occupied by Occupations, Industries, etc*. Ottawa: Edmond Cloutier, 1946.

Canada. Senate. *Proceedings and Report of Canada Parliament Senate Special-Committee on the Traffic in Narcotic Drugs in Canada*. Ottawa: Queen's Printer, 1955.

City of Detroit. "Master Plan Reports: Economic Base of Detroit." Detroit: City Plan Commission, 1944.

City of Toronto. "Special Committee: Place of Amusement—Report and Recommendations." Toronto: City of Toronto, 1977.

Detroit. *Report of the Mayor's Committee for the Rehabilitation of Narcotic Addict*. Detroit: City of Detroit, 1953.

Detroit Housing Commission. "Urban Renewal and Tax Revenue." Detroit: Detroit Housing Commission, 1965.

Greater Windsor Industrial Commission. "Industrial Prospects Are Bright in Windsor." Windsor: Dominion Bureau of Statistics, 1957.

Helling, Rudolf A. *The Position of Negroes, Chinese, and Italians in the Social Structure of Windsor, Ontario*. Ottawa: Ontario Human Rights Commission, 1965.

Juvenile Delinquency Study Committee. September 24, 1943. Library of Michigan, p. 1c. Reprinted from Federal Security Agency. "Techniques of Law Enforcement against Prostitution." Washington, D.C.: Government Printing Office, 1943.

Lansing. *Minutes of the Legislative Committee to Study the Narcotic Problem in Michigan*. August 22, 1951. Legislative Records of the House and Senate Study. Box 6. Archives of Michigan.

Mayor's Committee for Community Action for Detroit's Youth. "Community Action for Detroit Youth: A Request for a Planning Grant for a Major Demonstration Project under the Federal Juvenile Delinquency Act." Detroit: Mayor's Committee, 1962.

Southeastern Michigan Council of Governments. "Historical Population and Employment by Minor Civil Divisions." Detroit: Information Services, 2002.

United States. "Customs Hints." Pamphlet. November 5, 1954. RG 287, Box T454. National Archives, Washington, D.C.

United States Army. *Instructions for American Servicemen in France during World War II*. Chicago: University of Chicago Press, 2008.

U.S. Bureau of Census. *Fourteenth Census of the United States, 1920.* Vol. 3, *Population.* Washington, D.C.: Government Printing Office, 1931.

———. *Thirteenth Census of the United States, 1910.* Vol. 3, *Population.* Washington, D.C.: Government Printing Office, 1913.

United States Senate. Committee on Government Operations, Permanent Subcommittee on Investigations. *Organized Crime and Illicit Traffic in Narcotics: Hearings . . . Eighty-eighth Congress, First Session Pursuant to Senate Resolution 17, 88th Congress.* Washington, D.C.: Government Printing Office, 1963–65.

United States Senate. *Illicit Narcotics Traffic: Hearings before the Subcommittee on Improvements in the Federal Criminal Code of the Committee on the Judiciary, United States Senate, Eighty-fourth Congress, First session, Pursuant to S. Res. 67.* Washington, D.C.: Government Printing Office, 1955.

U.S. Senate Subcommittee. *Investigation of the So-Called "Rackets"; Hearings before a Subcommittee of the Committee on Commerce.* S. Res. 74, Vol. 1, Part 3. Washington, D.C.: Government Printing Office, 1934.

PRIMARY SOURCES

"Absolved of Slaying of Youth in Detroit." *New York Times*, June 13, 1929.

"The Ambassador Bridge." *Montreal Gazette*, November 13, 1929, 12.

"Ambassador Bridge Open on Holiday: Immense New Link between Canada and US Ready at Windsor." *Calgary Herald*, November 9, 1929, 1.

Anglin, Gerald. "He Blew the Whistle on Windsor Vice." *Maclean's*, May 1, 1950.

Association against the Prohibition Amendment. *Canadian Liquor Crossing the Border.* Washington, D.C.: National Press Building, 1929.

"Attracted to Windsor." *Windsor Daily Star*, May 25, 1943, 3.

Barnett, Albert G. "Canada Negroes Hit by Housing Shortage." *Chicago Defender*, December 15, 1945, 9.

———. "Canadian Negroes Find Equality Grim Illusion." *Chicago Defender*, November 17, 1945, 8.

"Battling the Rum Runners in Prohibition's No Man's Land." *New York Times*, July 29, 1923.

Beattie, Helen. "Now Is the Time to Fight Juvenile Delinquency." *Globe and Mail*, January 7, 1946.

"Behind Drug Ring." *Saskatoon Star*, April 11, 1946, 7.

"Big Haul of Heroin Seized on Traveler." *New York Times*, February 10, 1956, 44.

"Big Jazz Show Spurs Rioting." *Spokane Daily Chronicle*, August 2, 1960.

"Big Narcotics Haul Made in Montreal." *New York Times*, July 10, 1959, 8.

Board of Education of the City of Detroit. *Instructions Regarding Narcotics.* Detroit: Detroit Public Schools, 1952.

"Bob-Lo Trip 'Illegal' for Canadians." *Windsor Star*, June 21, 1943, 5.

Border Cities Chamber of Commerce. *Canada's Southern Gateway: The Gate Stands Always Open for Our Southern Friends.* Windsor: Border Cities Chamber of Commerce, c. 1928.

——. *Your Market in Canada: An Analysis of Canada's Buying Power, Commodity Requirements, Market Expansion, Trading Facilities, and American Establishments*. Windsor: Border City Chamber of Commerce, c. 1930.

"Border Closed." *Regina Leader-Post*, July 29, 1967, 2.

"Border 'Dope King' Suspect, Devlin, Held on $25,000 Bail." *Windsor Daily Star*, March 27, 1956, 5.

"Border Officials Lift Ban." *Regina Leader-Post*, 24 July 1967, 35.

"Bower Tells Bridge Plan." *Border Cities Star*, July 9, 1925, 5.

Boyd, Malcolm. "Blind No More." *Pittsburgh Courier*, February 2, 1963, 10.

Brode, Patrick. Interview with Jim Ure. January 20, 2006. Unpublished.

Brophey, Tom. "Girl's Story Leads to Clean-up Drive." *Windsor Daily Star*, July 27, 1946, 3.

"Call for Redevelopment Proposals." *New York Times*, September 30, 1963, 55.

"Canada Gaining Name as Refuge of Rum Runners." *Ottawa Citizen*, June 15, 1929, 3.

"Canada Loses This Business." *Financial Post*, October 6, 1951, 6.

Canada's Most Fertile Field for Advertising. Windsor: Border Cities Star, 1928.

Canadian Broadcast Company Digital Archives. http://www.cbc.ca/archives /categories/society/crime-justice/pushing-past-border. June 2, 2014.

"Canadian House Argues Reciprocity Trends in Citizens." *Christian Science Monitor*, May 5, 1911, 16.

"Canadians Said Part Drug Ring." *Saskatoon Star*, August 12, 1963, 18.

"Casino Would Bring Miami-Style Vices, Many Fear." *Windsor Star*, July 19, 1986, 1.

"Chaos Is King." *Florence Times Daily* (AL), August 6, 1960, 4.

"Chinese Smuggling Ring Broken." *Boston Evening Transcript*, October 14, 1904, 9.

Chism, Larry. "Many Changes Seen in Night Life during Past 10 Years." *Michigan Chronicle*, April 13, 1946.

Citizens Committee for Equal Opportunity. "A Report by the Sub-Committee on Police-Community Relations: The Police, Law Enforcement, and the Detroit Community." Detroit: Citizens Committee for Equal Opportunity, 1965.

"Citizens Reject Sawed-Off Probe of Montreal Vice." *Globe and Mail*, October 23, 1946, 3.

Clark, Dave. "Jumping Is the Theme Song in Detroit Nighteries." *Chicago Defender*, August 15, 1953, 19.

——. "Paradise Valley." *Atlanta Daily World*, May 27, 1953, 6.

Clark, W. L. "As We See It." *Windsor Daily Star*, October 2, 1946, 2.

"Code Section." *Windsor Daily Star*, July 26, 1946, 3.

"Courtesy to Tourists Pays Big Dividends." *Windsor Star*, May 26, 1951, 11.

"Court Told How Mounties Trapped Alleged Local Drug Ring." *Windsor Daily Star*, August 2, 1951, 5.

"Crackdown on Negro Rioters." *Windsor Star*, August 13, 1964, 1.

"Creation of Gambling Resort on Belle Isle Reportedly Proposed." *Toledo Blade*, April 10, 1985, 5.

"Crime in Toronto and Montreal." *Windsor Daily Star*, June 1, 1950, 3.

"Crime Probe Nears." *Windsor Star*, March 13, 1962, 49.

"Detroit Bridge Is Dedicated as New Peace Link." *Chicago Tribune*, November 12, 1929, 22.

"Detroiters Come Here to Drink Beer." *Windsor Daily Star*, June 24, 1943, 1.

"Detroit Executive Barred as Aliens." *New York Times*, January 21, 1931.

"Detroit Gets Bebop Fever at El Sino Club." *Chicago Defender*, June 7, 1947, 19.

"Detroit Hit by Crime Wave as Gunmen Arrive." *Pittsburgh Press*, February 16, 1930, 11.

"Detroit Is Back Gate." *Milwaukee Journal*, March 4, 1929, 2.

"Detroit NAACP Charges Bias; Pastor Raps Wealthy Negroes." *Pittsburgh Courier*, January 7, 1961, 19.

"Detroit Officials Check Racial Bias Charges." *Hartford Courant*, December 18, 1960, 34A.

Detroit Police Department. *Annual Report*. Detroit: The Department, 1920–60.

Detroit Public Schools. *Instructions Regarding Narcotics*. Detroit: Detroit Public Schools, 1952.

"Detroit Quieter, but Toll of Dead Stands at 24." *Windsor Star*, July 2, 1967, 43.

"Detroit River Span Dedicated to Peace." *New York Times*, November 12, 1929, 22.

Detroit Urban League. *A Comparative Study of Life Styles and Social Attitudes of Middle Income Status Whites and Negroes in Detroit*. Detroit: Detroit Urban League, 1968.

———. *Twelfth Street: An Analysis of a Changed Community*. Detroit: Detroit Community Services Department, 1961.

Deutsch, Albert. *Sex Habits of American Men: A Symposium on the Kinsey Reports*. New York: Prentice-Hall, 1948.

Dixon, Ray S. "The History of Social Hygiene Activities in Detroit." M.A. thesis, Wayne State University, 1936.

"Dominion Vice Depicted." *New York Times*, April 17, 1926, 1.

Donald S. Leonard Papers. Box 20, Folder 2. Racial Gang Activities (2). Bentley Historical Library.

"Drew Pearson's Washington Merry-Go-Round." *Warsaw [Ind.] Times-Union*, October 10, 1950, 4.

"Evidence That Attorney's Office Dictated Withdrawal of Charges." *Saskatoon Star-Phoenix*, October 6, 1950.

"Ex-Health Official Raps View Drug Addicts Can't Be Cured." *Vancouver Sun*, September 24, 1955, 1.

Faludi, E. G., and Associates. *A Fifteen Year Programme for the Urban Renewal of the City of Windsor and Its Metropolitan Area*. Toronto: Faludi and Associates, 1959.

"50 Injured in Rioting in Canadian Jazz Show." *Chicago Tribune*, August 3, 1960.

"Five Charged after Raid." *Windsor Daily Star*, October 4, 1948, 3.

Francis, Robert. "Hopheads." *Maclean's*, February 15, 1947, 50.

Furman, Bess. "Urges New Agency on Child Welfare: Federal Courts Probation Chief Tells Senators Delinquency Will Be a Post-War Problem." *New York Times*, December 2, 1943, 24.

Glazer, Sidney. *Detroit: A Study in Urban Development*. New York: Bookman Associates, 1965.

Glover, Bill. "Crime Wave—Hangover from War." *Hartford Courant*, December 16, 1945, 5.

"Graver Charge Often Withdrawn States Police Official." *Montreal Gazette*, October 6, 1950, 24.

Gray, James H. "A Tourist Talks Back." *Maclean's*, June 1, 1948, 50–54.

Hall, Gwen. Interviews. Lafayette Clinic. Methadone Treatment for Heroin Addiction Collection. Box 70-U, Folder: Oral History Partial Transcript #1, Bentley Historical Library.

"Hannah Concludes Detroit Rates High in Race Relations Progress." *Washington Post, Times Herald*, December 17, 1960, A10.

Harrison, R. M. "Now." *Windsor Daily Star*, July 5, 1946, 7.

"Hastings-Gratiot Slum Clearance Approved." *Michigan Chronicle*, November 30, 1946, 4.

"Heavy Smoker Lumped with Drug Addict." *Calgary Herald*, May 11, 1962, 49.

"Heroin Curb Service Told." *Windsor Daily Star*, September 12, 1951, 5–8.

Heyd, Ruth. "Introducing Windsor." *ALA Bulletin*. Detroit Conference Issue. May 1965, 395.

Hill, O. Mary. "A City Looks at Itself." *Canadian Business*, April 1952, 16–17.

"Hoover Deplores Killings, but Asks Border Citizens to Help Enforce Dry Law." *New York Times*, June 19, 1929.

Houseman Spitzley Corporation. "Plan to Profit through Present Prosperity: This Message Will Show You How." Detroit: Joseph Mack, c. 1926. Bentley Historical Library, William C. Weber Papers, Box 20.

"Immigration Order Stirs Canada's Ire." *Miami News*, May 15, 1927, 32.

International Freedom Festival. "Souvenir Program." 1961. Bentley Historical Library.

———. "Souvenir Program." Part 2. 1959. Bentley Historical Library.

"The Invitation to Canada." *Michigan Manufacturer and Financial Record*, March 21, 1931.

"In Windsor the Wicked." *Lethbridge Daily Herald*, May 14, 1921, 5.

"Jazz Show Disrupted." *Vancouver Sun*, August 3, 1960.

Johnny Stool Pigeon. DVD. Directed by William Castle, Universal International Pictures, University City, Calif., 1949.

Katz, Sidney. "The Sleazy, Grey World of the Call Girl." *Maclean's*, April 1959, 15–24.

"Kefauver Sponsors Laws to Aid Rehabilitation of Juveniles." *Reading Eagle*, February 5, 1955.

Kidd, Paul. "Detroit Is Known as 'Murder City, USA.'" *Calgary Herald*, November 15, 1971, 9.

Kornhauser, Arthur. *Detroit as the People See It: A Survey of Attitudes in an Industrial City*. Detroit: Wayne University Press, 1952.

"Labels Western Morals Civilization's Top Threat." *Globe and Mail*, February 27, 1952, 4.

"Lack of Vice, Narcotics Curbs in Mexico Hit." *Los Angeles Times*, August 2, 1956, B11.

"Launch New Drive on US-Canadian Boundary to Halt Flow of Liquor." *Danville Bee*, July 19, 1927, 6.

Laverty, Ewing, and Melwyn Breen. "Windsor: Border—Not Barrier." *Saturday Night*, April 25, 1950, 8–10, 56.

"Leader of Narcotics Ring Faces 40 Years in Prison." *Nashua Telegraph*, September 22, 1965, 2.

Letter from Frost to Kefauver. November 23, 1959. RG 3-23, Box 213. Windsor Police Commission, File 313 G, B292181, Archives of Ontario.

Letter from Kefauver to Frost. December 7, 1950. RG 3-23, Box 213. Windsor Police Commission, File 313 G, B292181, Archives of Ontario.

Liquor Control Board of Ontario. Blue Water Hotel, Windsor [between 1927 and 1961]. Archives of Ontario. RG 36-8, barcode B335026.

———. Establishment Case Files. RG-36-8, Archives of Ontario.

———. "St. Clair Tavern and Hotel." Letter to the LLBO. Archives of Ontario. RG 36-8, Box 345/B 401274.

"Liquor Traffic Not Unlawful across Border." *Stevens Point Daily Journal*, July 1, 1929, 2.

"Local Child Said Victim." *Windsor Daily Star*, September 22, 1941, 1.

"Long Lines of Motors Crowd Detroit Ferries." *Border Cities Star*, May 31, 1922, 3.

"Mafia Hold in US Bared." *Tuscaloosa News*, October 10, 1950, 3.

"Man Tells Dope Story in Court." *Windsor Daily Star*, June 10, 1964, 57.

"Marijuana Certificates Given Court." *Windsor Daily Star*, July 19, 1943, 3.

Mayo, Elton. *The Social Problem of an Industrial Civilization*. Cambridge: Harvard University Press, 1945.

"Mayor Reaume 'Pleads with Married Women to Leave Jobs.'" *Windsor Daily Star*, January 23, 1946.

McAree, J. V. "Juvenile Junkies." *Globe and Mail*, November 23, 1951, 6.

McClintic-Marshall Co. "Ambassador Bridge." Pittsburgh: McClintic-Marshall Co., c. 1930.

McGowan, Helen. *Motor City Madam*. New York: Pageant Press, 1964.

"The Merry-Go Round." *Palm Beach Post*, October 10, 1950, 4.

Meyers, G. C. "Girls Who Leave Home for Larger Cities Face Dangers, Don't Fare So Well Away from Families." *Windsor Daily Star*, November 30, 1944, 2.

Michigan State Police Complaint. May 8, 1953. RG 90-240, State Police—Criminal Investigations, Docket # 7-54-53. Michigan State Archives.

Michigan State Police Records. Royal Oak Township. "Detroit Vice." RG 90. Michigan State Archives.

"Minorities Lot Tough: Having Trouble Finding Jobs." *Windsor Star*, April 27, 1964, 43.

"M. O. H. Will Lead Drive." *Windsor Star*, January 18, 1945, 3.

Moley, Raymond. "The Grey Zone of Crime." *New York Times*, January 11, 1931.

Montreal Gazette, October 10, 1927, 12.

Morrison, N. F. "Silver Jubilee of Opening of Ambassador Bridge." In Essex County Historical Association. *Radio Sketches of Periods-Events-Personalities from the*

History of the Essex County–Detroit Area. Windsor: Essex County Historical Association, 1963.

Mosher, Jack. "Look Out for Mary Jane." *Maclean's*, June 15, 1938.

Munro, Angus. "How Canadians Can Be Distinctive." *Windsor Daily Star*, August 4, 1950, 4.

"Murder Try Charged in Jazz Riot." *Boston Globe*, August 3, 1960.

"Narcotics Agents Seize 16 in Buffalo Smuggling Setup." *Chicago Daily Tribune*, February 11, 1960, 14.

"Narcotics Users Put at 60,000." *New York Times*, June 3, 1955, 25.

"Nations Joint at Detroit Bridge." *Los Angeles Times*, November 12, 1929, 13.

"Nation-Wide War on Dope Launched by Authorities." *Washington Post*, January 5, 1952, 1.

"Negro Marauders Attack Whites." *Windsor Star*, June 1, 1964, 30.

"A New Petition to Give Names in Vice Charges." *Globe and Mail*, January 4, 1946, 3.

"New Trial for Devlin: Jury Locked in Dope Case." *Windsor Star*, June 22, 1964, 39.

"9,200,000 Crossed the River between Detroit and Windsor Last Year." *Evening Record*, November 27, 1913, 8.

Oliver, L. H. T. "The Identification of Poverty Pockets in the City of Windsor." M.A. thesis, University of Windsor, 1971.

Ontario. *Report of the Ontario Police Commission on Organized Crime*. Toronto: The Commission, 1964.

"Ontario Fires Attorney in Vice Probe." *Los Angeles Times*, September 15, 1950, 21.

"Ontario Goes Wet and the Border Seethes." *New York Times*, May 15, 1927.

"Ontario Is Now Ready for Thirsty Tourists." *New York Times*, July 3, 1927.

"Ontario Negro Group Fearful." *Ottawa Citizen*, August 11, 1965, 1.

"Ontario to Be Tourist Oasis." *Milwaukee Journal*, March 10, 1927, 3.

"Ottawa Protests Border Ruling." *Border Cities Star*, June 8, 1927, 1.

"Our Rum Capital: An Amazing Picture." *New York Times*, May 27, 1928, 121.

"Payoff Man Named in Detroit Rum Graft." *New York Times*, December 2, 1928.

Pearson, Drew. "Dope Smuggling Probe May Bring Law Change." *Spokane Daily Chronicle*, December 20, 1955, 28.

———. "Fifty Members of the Mafia Control Big Rackets in United States." *St. Petersburg Times*, October 10, 1950, 6.

———. "Reasons for Detroit Riots Are Listed." *Toledo Blade*, July 28, 1967, 7.

———. "Sen. Daniel's Inquiry into Narcotics Praised." *Washington Post and Times Herald*, December 20, 1955, 31.

Percy W. Cromwell Collection. Box 2, Folder 24, The Bentley Historical Library.

Phillips, Alan. "The Case of the Drug Peddling Priest." *Maclean's*, August 1, 1954, 15.

"Pictures Show Many Windsor Youngsters Out after Dark Despite Warning by Police and Parents." *Windsor Star*, July 30, 1946, 5.

"Police Courteous to Tourists." *Windsor Daily Star*, May 27, 1950, 4.

"Police Deny Charges of Drugs, Prostitution." *Globe and Mail*, February 26, 1959, 5.

"Police Keep Pressure on 'Hot Spot.'" *Windsor Daily Star*, August 14, 1950, 5.

"Police Quell Riot at Jazz Show. One Critically Stabbed." *Saskatoon Star–Phoenix*, August 2, 1960.
"Probe Heat Hasn't Cooled Off Joints." *Windsor Daily Star*, March 14, 1950, 6.
"Probe Will Start Thursday: Will Investigate Charges of Laxity against Police Department." *Windsor Daily Star*, March 14, 1950, 3.
"Publicity Bureau Here Swamped by Tourists' Calls." *Ottawa Citizen*, July 4, 1947, 36.
"RCMP Reviews Careers of Canada's Crime Kings." *Winnipeg Free Press*, January 6, 1955, 22.
Reaume, Dan. "No Dice on Detroit's Plan for Legalized Gambling." *Windsor Star*, July 22, 1986, 13.
"Reefers Not Puffed at Schools: Ontario Musicians, Beatniks, Criminal Drug Addicts." *Windsor Star*, May 12, 1960, 19.
"Return Convicted Stabber to Face Narcotics Charge." *Windsor Star*, March 29, 1956, 3.
"Riot Erupts at Jazz Show Emancipation Fete." *Milwaukee Journal*, August 2, 1960.
"Riot Marks Jazz Show in Ontario." *Hartford Courant*, August 2, 1960.
Robert, Robert N. Letter. Prosecuting Attorney to Detroit Sgt. Carl W. Robinson, Racket Squad. April 1, 1954. RG 90-240, State Police—Criminal Investigations, Docket # 7-54-53, Michigan State Archives.
Rogers, Kenneth H. *Street Gangs in Toronto: A Study of the Forgotten Boy*. Toronto: Ryerson Press, 1945.
"Rooming Houses Next in Montreal Anti-Vice Drive." *Globe and Mail*, February 18, 1947, 9.
"San Francisco Agents Seize Narcotics from China." *Spokane Daily Chronicle*, December 6, 1955, 9.
"Say Montreal Vice Ring Nets $10,000,000 Yearly; Citizens Accuse Police." *Globe and Mail*, December 15, 1945, 1.
"Says Mafia Is Just One Big Family." *Chicago Defender*, July 19, 1958, 11.
"Sees Ontario Hurt by New Liquor Law." *New York Times*, October 18, 1927.
"Selling Bodies to Get Dope." *Afro-American*, July 7, 1951, 1.
"Senate Report on Child Crime Discards Traditional 'Causes.'" *New York Times*, May 6, 1957, 1.
"Senate Takes Aim at Youth Crime." *Christian Science Monitor*, May 6, 1957, 1.
"Senate Warns of Growth of Juvenile Delinquency." *Pittsburgh Post-Gazette*, May 6, 1957, 2.
"7 Held in Rock 'N' Roll Riot." *Windsor Daily Star*, August 2, 1960, 1.
"60,000 Addicts in Nation, US Experts Claim." *Chicago Tribune*, June 3, 1955, 11.
"60,000 Use Narcotics in Country." *Hartford Courant*, June 3, 1955, 31.
Smith, Harold. "Detroit Wears Its Hallow a Little Crooked." *Chicago Tribune*, December 27, 1948, 7.
"Smugglers in Toils: Finding of Frozen Chinaman in Refrigerator Car Leads to Discovery." *Youngstown Vindicator*, April 1, 1904, 13.
Sobotka, Virginia. "A Comparative Study of Prostitution: Trends in the Social Characteristics of the 'Street-Walking' Prostitute from 1935 to 1957." M.A. thesis, Wayne State University, 1961.

Social Services. *Detroit Area Study.* 1956. Archives of Michigan, RG 69-68.

"Solons Hear Warning on Narcotics." *New London Day,* June 2, 1955, 1.

Stephens, Robert. "Cars Perpetuate Black and White Split." *Observer* (London), January 19, 1964, 13.

Taylor, Glen Seymour. "Prostitution in Detroit." Ph.D. diss., University of Michigan, 1933.

"3 Extradited on Charges of Smuggling." *Calgary Herald,* June 10, 1961, 53.

"Toronto Hits Back, Claims to Be 'Good.'" *Calgary Herald,* October 19, 1950, 1.

Touch of Evil. DVD. Directed by Orson Welles, Universal International Pictures, University City, Calif., 1959.

"Tourist Industry Regaining Ground." *Windsor Daily Star,* August 10, 1940, 3.

"Tourist Rush Beats All Records." *Border Cities Star,* July 5, 1927, 1.

"Tourist Trade Up in Present Season: Canadian Official Reports More Travel from the United States." *Montreal Gazette,* August 26, 1944, 20.

"The Tragedy of Broken Homes." *Toronto Daily Star,* April 21, 1954, 4.

Treasury Department. Bureau of Customs. Central Files. Subject Classified Correspondence. 1938–65. Box 162. National Archives, Washington, D.C.

"Trips Recalled: Fox Remembers Going with Devlin." *Windsor Star,* June 13, 1964, 1.

"25 Arrested in 2 Raids: Prostitution Charged by Morality Officers." *Windsor Daily Star,* June 21, 1948, 3.

"Two Hanged in Canada." *St. Joseph News-Press,* December 11, 1962, 9.

United Community Services of Metropolitan Detroit. "Adolescent Girls and Services." UCSD Papers. Studies and Reports, Box #1, [c. 1959], Walter P. Reuther Library.

——. *Prostitution, Venereal Diseases, and Sex Education: An Assessment of Social Health Problems in Metropolitan Detroit.* Detroit: United Community Services of Metropolitan Detroit, 1968.

——. *Recent Population and Social Trends in the Detroit Area.* Detroit: United Community Services of Metropolitan Detroit, 1964.

"US Agents Smash Big Narcotics Ring." *New York Times,* April 6, 1954, 26.

"US Congressmen to Visit Here, Study Immigration Effects." *Border Cities Star,* June 8, 1927, 1.

"Urges Canadians to Cut American Flag Waving." *Windsor Star,* September 13, 1951, 15.

"Vancouver Police Break Up Canada-Wide Lottery, Smuggling, Dope Ring in Chinatown." *Saskatoon Star-Phoenix,* June 22, 1946, 23.

Vedder, Clyde Bennett. "An Analysis of the Taxi-Dance Hall as a Social Institution with Special Reference to Los Angeles and Detroit." Ph.D. diss., University of Southern California, 1947.

"Venereal Disease: A Challenge to Leadership." *Windsor Daily Star,* November, 30, 1944, 3.

Veres, Joseph Louis. "History of the United Automobile Workers in Windsor, 1936–1956." M.A. thesis, University of Western Ontario, 1956.

"Warns Dry Agent to Stop Shooting." *New York Times,* May 12, 1928.

"The Washington Merry-Go-Round." *Spokane Daily Chronicle,* October 10, 1950.

Weales, Gerald. "Small-Town Detroit: Motor City on the Move." *Commentary*,
September 1, 1956. http://www.commentarymagazine.com/article/small-town
-detroitmotor-city-on-the-move/. June 23, 2014.

Wilber, Carey. "It Can Happen Here." *Globe and Mail*, June 30, 1951, 13.

———. "Reveal Crystal Beach Teen-Age Dope Plot." *Globe and Mail*, June 27, 1951, 1.

Winchell, Walter. "Áu Revoir!" *Star-News*, September 12, 1951, 20.

"Windsor Crackdown Fails to Prevent Vice Operations." *Detroit Free Press*, April 9,
1950, 1.

Windsor Police Department. *Annual Registers*, 1940–60. RG 8. Windsor Public
Library.

"Windsor Wire Service: Predict US Senate Will Rap Ontario." *Globe and Mail*,
November 23, 1950, 3.

Women's Local Council of Windsor Records. Minutes. Windsor Municipal Archives,
MS 19 I-1/3. September 30, 1946.

"Woman Waits Dope Penalty." *Windsor Daily Star*, November 20, 1951, 5.

"Won't Allow Vice Chief to Resign: Must Fact Action by Police Officials." *Windsor
Daily Star*, July 31, 1946, 1.

"Workers' Suit Accuses Detroit Casino of Bias." *Toledo Blade*, November 19, 2001, 4.

"World's Largest Span Dedicated at Detroit." *Hartford Courant*, November 12,
1929, 8.

Young, Coleman. *Hard Stuff: The Autobiography of Coleman Young*. New York:
Viking, 1994.

"Young Drifters Floating into N.Y. Up Delinquency Figures." *New York Amsterdam
News*, July 1, 1944, 1A.

Zettlemoyer, Nancy E. "An Assessment of Immigrant Needs and Their Fulfillment
in Metropolitan Windsor." Windsor: Windsor Citizenship Committee, 1961.

"Zoot-Suiters Duck Police Chief's Son." *Montreal Gazette*, July 12, 1943, 6.

"Zoot-Suiters Held after Terrorized Local Youth." *Windsor Daily Star*, July 10,
1943, 3.

SECONDARY SOURCES

Acker, Carline Jean. "Portrait of an Addicted Family: Dynamics of Opiate Addiction
in the Early Twentieth Century." In *Altering American Consciousness: The
History of Alcohol and Drug Use in the United States, 1800-2000*, edited by
Carline Jean Acker, 165–81. Boston: University of Massachusetts Press, 2004.

Adams, Mary Louise. *The Trouble with Normal: Postwar Youth and the Making of
Heterosexuality*. Toronto: University of Toronto Press, 1997.

Adelman, Jeremy, and Stephen Aron. "From Borderlands to Borders: Empires,
Nation-States, and the Peoples in Between in North American History."
American Historical Review 104, no. 3 (June 1999): 814–41.

Anderson, Eric. "Prostitution and Social Justice: Chicago 1910–1915," *Social Service
Review* 48, no. 2 (1974): 203–28.

Anderson, Kay. *Vancouver's Chinatown: Racial Discourse in Canada, 1875–1980*.
Montreal: McGill–Queen's University Press, 1991.

Anzaldua, Gloria. *Borderlands/la Frontera: The New Mestiza*. San Francisco: Aunt
 Lute Books, 1999.
Auerbach, Jonathan. *Dark Borders: Film Noir and American Citizenship*.
 Durham, N.C.: Duke University Press, 2011.
Avery, Donald. *Reluctant Hosts: Canada Response to Immigrant Workers,
 1896–1994*. Toronto: McClelland & Stewart, 1995.
Avila, Eric. *Popular Culture in the Age of White Flight: Fear and Fantasy in
 Suburban Los Angeles*. Berkeley: University of California Press, 2004.
Babson, Steve. *Working Detroit: The Making of a Union Town*. Detroit: Wayne State
 University Press, 1986.
Backhouse, Constance. *Colour Coded: A Legal History of Racism in Canada,
 1900–1950*. Toronto: University of Toronto Press, 1999.
Baldwin, Davarian. *Chicago's New Negroes: Modernity, Great Migration, and Black
 Urban Life*. Chapel Hill: University of North Carolina Press, 2007.
Baruth-Walsh, Mary E., and Gregory Mark Walsh. *Strike! 99 Days on the Line:
 The Worker's Own Story of the 1945 Windsor Ford Strike*. New Castle, Ontario:
 Penumbra Press, 1995.
Baulch, Vivian M., and Patricia Zacharias. "The 1943 Detroit Race Riots." *Detroit
 News*. https://www.mtholyoke.edu/courses/rschwart/clio/detroit_riot
 /DetroitNewsRiots1943.htm. January 1, 2015.
Beare, Margaret E., and Stephen Schneider. *Money Laundering in Canada: Chasing
 Dirty and Dangerous Money*. Toronto: University of Toronto Press, 2007.
Bedford, Judy. "Prostitution in Calgary, 1905–1914." *Alberta History* 29, no. 2
 (Spring 1981): 1–11.
Bell, Robert R. *Social Deviance: A Substantive Analysis*. Homewood, Ill.: Dorsey
 Press, 1971.
Bender, Thomas. *Run for the Border: Vice and Virtue in US-Mexico Border
 Crossings*. New York: New York University Press, 2012.
Ben-Yehuda, Nachman. *Deviance and Moral Boundaries: Witchcraft, the Occult,
 Science Fiction, Deviant Sciences, and Scientists*. Chicago: University of Chicago
 Press, 1985.
Bernstein, Elizabeth. *Temporarily Yours: Intimacy, Authenticity, and the
 Commerce of Sex*. Chicago: University of Chicago Press, 2010.
Bernstein, Lee. *The Greatest Menace: Organized Crime in Cold War America*.
 Amherst: University of Massachusetts Press, 2002.
———. "What Did Apalachin Prove? Mafia Skepticism in Cold War Politics and
 Culture." *Trends in Organized Crime* 10, no. 4 (December 2007): 3–15.
Best, Joel. *Controlling Vice: Regulating Brothel Prostitution in St. Paul, 1865–1883*.
 Columbus: Ohio State University Press, 1998.
Bjorn, Lars, and Jim Gallert. *Before Motown: The History of Jazz in Detroit,
 1920–1960*. Ann Arbor: University of Michigan Press, 2001.
Boehm, Lisa Krissoff. *Making a Way Out of No Way: African American Women and
 the Second Great Migration*. Jackson: University Press of Mississippi, 2009.
Boustan, Leah Platt. "Was Postwar Suburbanization 'White Flight'? Evidence from the
 Black Migration." *Quarterly Journal of Economics* 125, no. 1 (February 2010): 417–43.

Bow, Brian. *The Politics of Linkage: Power, Interdependence, and Ideas in Canada-US Relation*. Toronto: University of Toronto Press, 2009.

Boyd, Nan Alamilla. *Wide Open Town: A History of Queer San Francisco to 1965*. Berkeley: University of California Press, 1993.

Boyer, Paul. *Urban Masses and Moral Order in America, 1820–1920*. Cambridge, Mass.: Harvard University Press, 1978.

Boyle, Kevin. *The UAW and the Heyday of American Liberalism, 1945–1968*. Ithaca, N.Y.: Cornell University Press, 1995.

Brandt, Allan M. *No Magic Bullet: A Social History of Venereal Disease in the United States since 1880*. New York: Oxford University Press, 1987.

Brandt, Allan M., and Paul Rozin, eds. *Morality and Health*. New York: Routledge, 1997.

Brennan, Denise. "Selling Sex for Visas: Sex Tourism as a Stepping-Stone to International Migration." In *Global Woman: Nannies, Maids, and Sex Workers in the New Economy*, edited by Barbara Ehrenreich and Arlie Russell Hochschild, 154–68. New York: Metropolitan Books, 2002.

Bristow, Nancy K. "Victory Girls, Khaki-Whakis, and Patriotutes: The Regulation of Female Sexuality during World War II." *Journal of the History of Childhood and Youth* 4, no. 2 (2011): 349–51.

Brode, Patrick. *The Slasher Killings: A Canadian Sex-Crime Panic, 1945–1946*. Detroit: Wayne State University Press, 2009.

———. *Unholy City: Vice in Windsor, Ontario, 1950*. Windsor: Essex County Historical Society, 2012.

Brouwer, Ruth Compton. "A Disgrace to 'Christian Canada': Protestant Foreign Missionary Concerns about the Treatment of South Asians in Canada, 1907–1920." In *A Nation of Immigrants: Women, Workers, and Communities in Canadian History, 1840s–1960s*, edited by Franca Iacovetta, Paula Draper, and Robert Ventresca. Toronto: University of Toronto Press, 1998.

Brown, Craig, ed. *The Illustrated History of Canada*. Montreal: McGill–Queen's University Press, 2012.

Brown, Leslie. *Upbuilding Black Durham: Gender, Class, and Black Community Development in the Jim Crow South*. Chapel Hill: University of North Carolina Press, 2008.

Brownstein, Henry H. *The Rise and Fall of a Violent Crime Wave: Crack Cocaine and the Social Construction of a Crime Problem*. Monsey, N.Y.: Criminal Justice Press, 1996.

Brunet-Jailly, Emmanuel. "Special Section: Borders, Borderlands, and Theory." *Geopolitics* 16, no. 6 (2011): 1–6.

———, ed. *Borderlands: Comparing Border Security in North America and Europe*. Ottawa: University of Ottawa Press, 2007.

Bukowczyk, John, Nora Faires, David R. Smith, and Randy William Widdis, eds. *Permeable Border: The Great Lakes Region as Transnational Basin*. Pittsburgh: University of Pittsburgh Press, 2005.

Burnham, John C. "The Progressive Era Revolution in American Attitudes Towards Sex." *Journal of American History* 59 (1973): 885–907.

Burns, Andrea. "Waging Cold War in a Model City: The Investigation of 'Subversive' Influences in the 1967 Detroit Riot." *Michigan Historical Review* 30, no. 1 (Spring 2004): 3–30.

Burnstein, Scott M. *Motor City Mafia: A Century of Organized Crime in Detroit.* Charleston, S.C.: Arcadia, 2006.

Butler, Anne. *Daughters of Joy, Sisters of Misery: Prostitutes in the American West, 1865–90.* Urbana: University of Illinois Press, 1985.

Cabezas, Amalia. "Between Love and Money: Sex, Tourism, and Citizenship in Cuba and the Dominican Republic." *Signs: Journal of Women and Culture* 29, no. 4 (2004): 987–1015.

Calavita, Kitty. *US Immigration Law and the Control of Labor, 1820–1924.* London: Academic Press, 1984.

Campbell, Bruce, and Ed Finn, eds. *Living with Uncle: Canada-US Relations in an Age of Empire.* Toronto: Lorimer, 2006.

Canaday, Margot. *The Straight State: Sexuality and Citizenship in Twentieth-Century America.* Princeton, N.J.: Princeton University Press, 2009.

Carstairs, Catherine. "Becoming a Hype: Heroin Consumption, Subcultural Formation, and Resistance in Canada, 1945–1965." *Contemporary Drug Problems* 29 (2002): 91–115.

——. *Jailed for Possession: Illegal Drug Use, Regulation, and Power in Canada, 1920–1961.* Toronto: University of Toronto Press, 2006.

Cedilot, Andre, and Andre Noel. *Mafia, Inc.: The Long, Bloody Reign of Canada's Sicilian Clan.* Montreal: Quebecor Media, 2012.

Chopra-Gant, Mike. *Hollywood Genres and Postwar America: Masculinity, Family, and Nation in Popular Movies and Film Noire.* New York: I. B. Tauris, 2006.

Chunn, Dorothy E., Robert J. Menzies, and Robert L. Adamoski, eds. *Contesting Canadian Citizenship: Historical Readings.* Peterborough, Ontario: Broadview Press, 2002.

Clarke, Stephen F., et al. *Canada-US Relations in Focus.* New York: Nova Science, 2008.

Cohassey, John Frederick. "Down on Hastings Street: A Study of Social and Cultural Change in a Detroit Community." M.A. thesis, Wayne State University, 1993.

Cohen, Lizabeth. *A Consumer's Republic: The Politics of Mass Consumption in Postwar America.* New York: Vintage, 2003.

Colling, Herb. *Turning Points: The Detroit Race Riot of 1967, a Canadian Perspective.* Toronto: Natural Heritage, 2003.

Connelly, Mark T. *The Response to Prostitution in the Progressive Era.* Chapel Hill: University of North Carolina Press, 1980.

Corber, Robert J. *Homosexuality in Cold War America: Resistance and the Crisis of Masculinity.* Durham, N.C.: Duke University Press, 1997.

Corey, Albert Bickmore. *Canadian-American Relations along the Detroit River.* Detroit: Detroit Historical Society, 1957.

Cosgrove, Stuart. "The Zoot-Suit and Style Warfare." *History Workshop Journal* 18 (1984): 77–91.

Courtwright, David T. *Addicts Who Survived: An Oral History of Narcotics Use in America, 1923-1965*. Knoxville: University of Tennessee Press, 1989.

——. *Dark Paradise: Opiate Addiction in America before 1940*. Cambridge, Mass.: Harvard University Press, 1982.

Cresswell, Tim. *The Tramp in America*. London: Reaktion Books, 2001.

Daniels, Roger. *Not Like US: Immigrants and Minorities in America, 1890-1924*. Chicago: Ivan R. Dee, 1997.

Darden, Joe T., et al. *Detroit: Race and Uneven Development*. Philadelphia: Temple University Press, 1987.

Davis, Donald Finlay. *Conspicuous Production: Automobiles and Elites in Detroit, 1899-1933*. Philadelphia: Temple University Press, 1988.

Delmont, Mathew F. "American Bandstand and School Segregation." Ph.D. diss., Brown University, 2008.

D'Emilio, John, and Estelle B. Freedman. *Intimate Matters: A History of Sexuality in America*. Chicago: University of Chicago Press, 1988.

Dickinson, D. *Automation: The Advent of the Automatic Factory*. New York: Van Nostrand, 1952.

Dixon Vuic, Kara. "I Have Worn Out Another Pair of Shoes for My Country: Gender Sexuality and World War II." *Reviews in American History* 38, no. 1 (2010): 127–32.

Doherty, Thomas. *Teenagers and Teenpics: The Juvenilization of American Movies in the 1950s*. Boston: Unwin Hyman, 1988.

Donnan, Hastings, and Thomas M. Wilson. *Borders: Frontiers of Identity, Nation and State*. Oxford: Berg, 2001.

Doody, Colleen. *Detroit's Cold War: The Origins of Postwar Conservatism*. Champaign: University of Illinois Press, 2013.

Doray, Bernard. *From Taylorism to Fordism: A Rational Madness*. London: Free Association, 1988.

Draus, Paul, Juliette Roddy, and Mark Greenwald. "'I Always Kept a Job': Income Generation, Heroin Use, and Economic Uncertainty in 21st Century Detroit." *Journal of Drug Issues* 40, no. 4 (October 2010): 841–69.

Dubinsky, Karen. *The Second Greatest Disappointment: Honeymooners, Heterosexuality, and the Tourist Industry in Niagara Falls*. New Brunswick, N.J.: Rutgers University Press, 1999.

Duffy, John. *The Sanitarians: A History of American Public Health*. Champaign: University of Illinois Press, 1992.

Dunae, Patrick. "Geographies of Sexual Commerce and the Production of Prostitutional Space: Victoria, British Columbia, 1860–1914." *Journal of the Canadian Historical Association* 19, no. 1 (2008): 115–42.

Dyer-Witheford, Nick, and Greig de Peuter. *Games of Empire: Global Capitalism and Video Games*. Minneapolis: Regents of the University of Minnesota, 2001.

Engelman, Larry. "The Iron River Rum Rebellion." *Mid America* 55 (January 1973): 37–53.

Enstad, Nan. *Ladies of Labor, Girls of Adventure: Working Women, Popular Culture, and Labor Politics at the Turn of the Twentieth Century*. New York: Columbia University Press, 1999.

Ettinger, Patrick. *Imaginary Lines: Border Enforcement and the Origins of Undocumented Immigration 1883-1930*. Austin: University of Texas Press, 2009.

Everest, Allan S. *Rum across the Border: The Prohibition Era in Northern New York*. Syracuse, N.Y.: Syracuse University Press, 1978.

Fahrni, Magda, and Robert Rutherdale, eds. *Creating Postwar Canada: Community, Diversity, and Dissent, 1945-1975*. Vancouver, British Columbia: UBC Press, 2008.

Faires, Nora. "Poor Women, Proximate Border: Migrants from Ontario to Detroit in the Late-Nineteenth Century." *Journal of American Ethnic History* 20, no. 3 (Spring 2001): 88-109.

Farley, Reynolds, Sheldon Danziger, and Harry J. Holzer. *Detroit Divided*. New York: Russell Sage Foundation, 2000.

Farmer, Silas. *History of Detroit and Wayne County and Early Michigan: A Chronological Cyclopedia of the Past and Present*. Detroit: Silas Farmer, 1890.

Feldman, Egal. "Prostitution, the Alien Woman, and the Progressive Imagination, 1910-1915." *American Quarterly* 19 (1967): 192-206.

Fine, Sidney. *Violence in the Model City: The Cavanaugh Administration, Race Relations, and the Detroit Riot of 1967*. Ann Arbor: University of Michigan Press, 1989.

Flood, Dawn Rae. "Story Protests on Sex Crimes: Local Debates about Race and Rep in Postwar Chicagoland." *Journal of the Illinois State Historical Society* 102 (1998): 429-58.

Foreman, Joel, ed. *The Other Fifties: Interrogating Midcentury Icons*. Urbana: University of Illinois Press, 1997.

Forestell, Nancy M. "Bachelors, Boarding-Houses, and Blind Pigs: Gender Construction in a Multi-Ethnic Mining Camp, 1909-1920." In *A Nation of Immigrants: Women, Workers, and Communities in Canadian History, 1840s-1960s*, edited by Franca Iacovetta, Paula Draper, and Robert Ventresca, 251-90. Toronto: University of Toronto Press, 1998.

Freedman, Estelle B. "The Prison Lesbian: Race, Class, and the Construction of the Aggressive Female Homosexual, 1915-1965." *Feminist Studies* 22, no. 2 (Summer 1996): 397-423.

Freund, David M. P. *Colored Property: State Policy and White Racial Politics in Suburban America*. Chicago: University of Chicago Press, 2007.

Fujita, Kuniko. *Black Worker's Struggles in Detroit's Auto Industry, 1935-1975*. Saratoga, Calif.: Century Twenty One Publishing, 1980.

Gardiner, T. M. *In the Mind of a Mountie*. Victoria, British Columbia: Agio, 2010.

Gervais, C. H. *The Rumrunners: A Prohibition Scrapbook*. Thornhill, Ontario: Firefly Books, 1980.

Gilfoyle, Timothy. *City of Eros: New York City, Prostitution, and the Commercialization of Sex, 1790-1920*. New York: W. W. Norton, 1992.

Glasbeek, Amanda, ed. *Moral Regulation and Governance in Canada: History, Context, and Critical Issues*. Toronto: Canadian Scholars' Press, 2006.

Gleason, Mona. *Normalizing the Ideal: Psychology, Schooling, and the Family in Postwar Canada*. Toronto: University of Toronto Press, 1999.

——. "Psychology and the Construction of the Normal Family in Postwar Canada." *Canadian Historical Review* 78, no. 3 (September 1997): 442–77.

Glenn, Evelyn Nakano. *Unequal Freedom: How Race and Gender Shaped American Citizenship and Labor*. Cambridge, Mass.: Harvard University Press, 1992.

Gootenberg, Paul. "Talking Like a State: Drugs, Borders, and the Language of Control." In *Illicit Flows and Criminal Things: States, Borders, and the Other Side of Globalization*, edited by Willem van Schendel and Itty Abraham. Bloomington: Indiana University Press, 2005.

Graebner, William. "Coming of Age in Buffalo: The Ideology of Maturity in Post-War America." *Radical History Review* 34 (1986): 54–74.

——. *Coming of Age in Buffalo: Youth and Authority in the Postwar Years*. Philadelphia: Temple University Press, 1990.

Grason, Kyle. *Chasing Dragons: Security, Identity, and Illicit Drugs in Canada*. Toronto: University of Toronto Press, 2008.

Gray, James H. *Red Lights on the Prairies*. Saskatoon, Saskatchewan: Fifth House, 1995.

Graybill, Andrew. *Policing the Great Plains: Rangers, Mounties, and the North American Frontier*. Lincoln: University of Nebraska Press, 2007.

Greenberg, Peter. *Don't Go There! The Travel Detective's Essential Guide to the Must-Miss Places of the World*. New York: Rodale, 2009.

Gregory, James M. *The Southern Diaspora: How the Great Migrations of Black and White Southerners Transformed America*. Chapel Hill: University of North Carolina Press, 2005.

Gross, William. "Redevelopment in Windsor to 1900." M.A. thesis, University of Windsor, 1961.

Hallowell, Gerald A. *Prohibition in Ontario, 1919–1923*. Ottawa: Ontario Historical Society, 1972.

Harris, Richard. *Creeping Conformity: How Canada Became Suburban, 1900–1960*. Toronto: University of Toronto Press, 2004.

Hernandez, Kelly Lytel. *Migra! A History of the US Border Patrol*. Berkeley: University of California Press, 2010.

Heron, Craig. *Booze: A Distilled History*. Toronto: Between the Lines, 2003.

——. "The Boys and Their Booze: Masculinities and Public Drinking in Working-Class Hamilton, 1890–1946." *Canadian Historical Review* 86, no. 3 (September 2005): 411–52.

Heuton, Robert A. "Urban Sprawl: A Comparative Study of the Detroit-Windsor Region." Ph.D. diss., Wayne State University, 2005.

Hickman, Timothy A. "'Mania Americana': Narcotic Addiction and Modernity in the United States, 1870–1920." *Journal of American History* 90, no. 4 (March 2004): 1269–94.

High, Steven. *Industrial Sunset: The Making of North America's Rustbelt, 1969–1984*. Toronto: University of Toronto Press, 2003.

Hobson, Barbara Meil. *Uneasy Virtue: The Politics of Prostitution and the American Moral Reform Tradition*. New York: Basic Books, 1987.

Hubbard, Philip. *Sex and the City: Geographies of Prostitution in the Urban West*. Brookfield, Vt.: Ashgate, 1999.

Hunt, Alan. *Governing Morals: A Social History of Moral Regulation*. Cambridge: Cambridge University Press, 1999.

Hurley, Andrew, *Diners, Bowling Alleys and Trailer Parks: Chasing the American Dream in Postwar Consumer Culture*. New York: Basic Books, 2001.

Hyde, Charles K. *Arsenal of Democracy: The American Automobile Industry in World War II*. Detroit: Wayne State University Press, 2013.

Iacovetta, Franca. "Gossip, Contest, and Power in the Making of Suburban Bad Girls: Toronto, 1945–60." *Canadian Historical Review* 80, no. 1 (December 1999): 585–624.

Jacobson, Mathew Frye. *Barbarian Virtues: The United States Encounters Foreign Peoples at Home and Abroad, 1876–1917*. New York: Hill and Wang, 2000.

Jamieson, Patrick, and Daniel Romer. *The Changing Portrayal of Adolescents in the Media since 1950*. Oxford: Oxford University Press, 2008.

Johnson, David. *The Lavender Scare: The Cold War Persecution of Gays and Lesbians in the Federal Government*. Chicago: University of Chicago Press, 2004.

Judd, Dennis R. "Promoting Tourism in US Cities." In *Readings in Urban History*, edited by Susan Fainstein and Scott Campbell. Oxford: Blackwell, 2002.

Karibo, Holly. "Detroit's Border Brothel: Sex Tourism in Windsor, Ontario 1945–1960." *American Review of Canadian Studies* 40, no. 3 (September 2010): 362–78.

Katz, Donald. *Home Fires: An Intimate Portrait of One Middle-Class Family in Postwar America*. New York: Aaron Asher Books, 1992.

Kelley, Robin D. G. *Race Rebels: Culture, Politics, and the Black Working Class*. New York: Free Press, 1994.

Kennedy, Elizabeth Lapovsky, and Madeline Davis. *Boots of Leather, Slippers of Gold: The History of a Lesbian Community*. New York: Penguin, 1994.

Keshen, Jeffrey A. *Saints, Sinners, and Soldiers: Canada's Second World War*. Vancouver, British Columbia: UBC Press, 2004.

Kessler Harris, Alice. *Out to Work: A History of Wage-Earning Women in the United States*. Oxford: Oxford University Press, 2003.

Kinsman, Gary. *The Regulation of Desire: Sexuality in Canada*. Montreal: Black Rose Press, 1987.

Klein, Christina. *Cold War Orientalism: Asia in the Middlebrow Imagination, 1945–1961*. Berkeley: University of California Press, 2003.

Klug, Thomas. "The Immigration and Naturalization Service (INS) and the Making of a Border-Crossing Culture on the US-Canada Border, 1891-1941." *American Review of Canadian Studies* 40, no. 3 (September 2010): 395–415.

Knotter, Ad. "The Border Paradox. Uneven Development, Cross-Border Mobility and the Comparative History of the Euregio Meuse-Rhine." *Fédéralisme Régionalisme* 3 (2002–3).

Knowles, Valerie. *Strangers at Our Gates: Canadian Immigration and Immigration Policy, 1540–1997*. Toronto: Dundrun Press, 1997.

Konrad, Victor, and Heather N. Nicol. "Border Culture, the Boundary between Canada and the United States, and the Advancement of Borderlands Theory." *Goepolitics* 16 (2011): 70–90.

Kozol, Wendy. *Life's America: Family and Nation in Postwar Photojournalism.* Philadelphia: University of Pennsylvania Press, 1994.

Krasnick, Cheryl. "The Aristocratic Vice: The Medical Treatment of Drug Addicts at the Homewood Retreat, 1883–1900." *Ontario History* 74 (1983): 138–84.

Labadies, Paul. "Liquid Gold." *Michigan History* 78 (September–October 1994): 25–26.

Langlois, Janet. "The Belle Isle Bridge Incident: Legend, Dialectic and Semiotic System in the 1943 Detroit Race Riots." *Journal of American Folklore* 96 (1983): 183–99.

Laxer, James. *The Border: Canada, the US, and Dispatches from the 49th Parallel.* Toronto: Anchor Canada, 2004.

Leavitt, Judith Walzer, and Ronald L. Numbers, eds. *Sickness and Health: Readings in the History of Medicine and Public Health.* Madison: University of Wisconsin Press, 1978.

Le Camp, Lorraine. "Racial Considerations of Minstrel Shows and Related Images in Canada." Ph.D. thesis, University of Toronto, 2005.

Lee, Alfred McClung, and Norman Daymond Humphrey. *Race Riot, Detroit 1943.* New York: Octagon Books, 1968.

Lee, Erika. *Angel Island: Immigrant Gateway to America.* Oxford: Oxford University Press, 2010.

——. *At America's Gates: Chinese Immigration during the Exclusion Era, 1882–1943.* Chapel Hill: University of North Carolina Press, 2003.

Leggett, John C. *Class, Race, and Labor: Working-Class Consciousness in Detroit.* New York: Oxford University Press, 1968.

LeMay, Michael C. *From Open Door to Dutch Door: An Analysis of U.S. Immigration Policy since 1820.* New York: Praeger, 1987.

Lenz, Gunter H. "Transnational American Studies: Negotiation Cultures of Difference–Multicultural Identities, Communities, and Border Discourses." In *Multiculturalism in Transit: A German-American Exchange*, edited by Klaus J. Milich and Jeffrey M. Peck, 129–66. New York: Berghahn Books, 1998.

Leonard, Kevin Allen. "Containing 'Perversion': African Americans and Same-Sex Desire in Cold War Los Angeles." *Journal of the History of Sexuality* 20, no. 3 (2011): 545–67.

Leung, Carianne K. Y. "Usable Pasts, Staged Belongings: A Critique of a Heritage of Multiculturalism Discourse." Ph.D. thesis, University of Toronto, 2007.

Lewis, Robert D. *Manufacturing Suburbs: Building Work and Home on the Metropolitan Fringe.* Philadelphia: Temple University Press, 2004.

Lewis-Coleman, David M. *Race against Liberalism: Black Workers and the UAW in Detroit.* Urbana: University of Illinois Press, 2008.

Lidz, Charles, and Andrew Walker. *Heroin, Deviance, and Morality.* London: Sage, 1980.

Littauer, Amanda H. "The B-Girl Evil: Bureaucracy, Sexuality, and the Menace of Barroom Vice in Postwar California." *Journal of the History of Sexuality* 12, no. 2 (2003): 171–204.

Longo, Julie. "Consuming Freedom: The International Freedom Festival as Transnational Tourism Strategy on the Windsor-Detroit Border, 1959–1976." *Michigan Historical Review* 34, no. 2 (Fall 2008): 119–37.

Luibheid, Eithne. *Entry Denied: Controlling Sexuality at the Border*. Minneapolis: University of Minnesota Press, 2002.

Lumley, Darwyn. *Breaking the Banks in the Motor City: The Auto Industry, the 1933 Detroit Banking Crisis, and the Start of the New Deal*. Jefferson, N.C.: McFarland, 2009.

Lyke, M. L. "In Windsor, Culture and Sin Go Hand in Hand." *Seattle P.I.*, February 2, 2006.

Mallea, Paula. *The War on Drugs: A Failed Experiment*. Toronto: Dundurm, 2014.

Malleck, Dan. "An Innovation from across the Line: The American Drinker and Liquor Regulation in Two Ontario Border Communities, 1927–1944." *Journal of Canadian Studies* 41, no. 1 (Winter 2007): 151–71.

———. *Try to Control Yourself: The Regulation of Public Drinking in Post-Prohibition Ontario, 1927–1944*. Vancouver, British Columbia: UBC Press, 2012.

Marchetti, Gina. *Romance and the "Yellow Peril": Race, Sex, and Discursive Strategies in Hollywood Fiction*. Berkeley: University of California Press, 1993.

Marcson, Simon, ed. *Automation, Alienation, and Anomie*. New York: Harper & Row, 1970.

Marquis, Greg. "'Brewers and Distillers Paradise': American Views of Canadian Alcohol Policies, 1919–1935." *Canadian Review of American Studies* 34, no. 2 (2004): 135–66.

Martinez, Oscar J. *Border People: Life and Society in the US-Mexico Borderlands*. Tucson: University of Arizona Press, 1994.

Mason, Philip P. *Rum Running and the Roaring Twenties: Prohibition on the Ontario-Michigan Waterway*. Detroit: Wayne State University Press, 1995.

May, Elaine Tyler. *Homeward Bound: American Families in the Cold War Era*. New York: Basic Books, 1988.

McDougall, John. *Drifting Together: The Political Economy of Canada-US Integration*. Toronto: University of Toronto Press, 2006.

McKinsey, Laura, and Victor Konrad. *Borderland Reflections: The United States and Canada*. Borderlands Monograph Series, no. 1. Orono, Maine: Canadian-American Center, University of Maine at Orono, 1989.

Meijer, Kenneth. *The Politics of Sin: Drugs, Alcohol, and Public Policy*. London: M. E. Sharpe, 1994.

Meiklejohn, Susan Turner. *Wages, Race, Skills, and Space: Lessons from Employers in Detroit's Auto Industry*. New York: Garland, 2000.

Meyerowitz, Joanne, ed. *Not June Cleaver: Women and Gender in Postwar America*. Philadelphia: Temple University Press, 1994.

Mohi, Raymond A. "Race and Housing in the Postwar City: An Explosive History." *Journal of the Illinois State Historical Society* 94, no. 1 (Spring 2001): 8–30.

Moon, Elaine Latzman. *Untold Tales, Unsung Heroes: An Oral History of Detroit's African American Community, 1918-1967.* Detroit: Wayne State University Press, 1994.

Moore, William Howard. *The Kefauver Committee and the Politics of Crime, 1950-1952.* Columbia: University of Missouri Press, 1974.

Morton, Suzanne. *At Odds: Gambling and Canadians, 1919-1969.* Toronto: University of Toronto Press, 2003.

Mosher, Clayton. "The Legal Response to Narcotic Drugs in Five Ontario Cities, 1908-1961." Ph.D. diss., University of Toronto, 1992.

Mumford, Kevin. *Interzones: Black/White Sex Districts in Chicago and New York in the Early Twentieth Century.* New York: Columbia University Press, 1997.

Murphy, Heather A. *Not in This Family: Gays and the Meaning of Kinship in Postwar North America.* Philadelphia: University of Pennsylvania Press, 2010.

Murphy, Mary. "The Private Lives of Public Women: Prostitution in Butte, Montana 1878-1917." *Frontiers* 7, no. 3 (1984): 31-35.

Murphy, Michael Duggan. "Detroit Blues Women." Ph.D. diss., Wayne State University, 2011.

Musto, David. *The American Disease: Origins of Narcotic Control.* 3rd ed. Oxford: Oxford University Press, 1999.

Nestle, Joan. *A Restricted Country.* Ithaca, N.Y.: Firebrand Books, 1987.

Ngai, Mai. *Impossible Subjects: Illegal Aliens and the Making of Modern America.* Princeton, N.J.: Princeton University Press, 2005.

Nicol, Heather N., and Rupert Dobbin. "Planning at the Edge: Evaluating Ontario's Planning Legislation since World War II." In *(Re)Development at the Urban Edges: Reflections on the Canadian Experience*, edited by Heather Nicol and Greg Halseth. Waterloo, Ontario: University of Waterloo, 2000.

Nicolaides, Becky M. *My Blue Heaven: Life and Politics in the Working-Class Suburbs of Los Angeles, 1920-1965.* Chicago: University of Chicago Press, 2002.

Nilson, Deborah. "The Social Evil: Prostitution in Vancouver 1900-1920." In *In Her Own Right: Selected Essays in Women's History in B.C.*, edited by Barbara Latham and Cathy Kess. Victoria, British Columbia: Camosun College, 1980.

Owram, Doug. *Born at the Right Time: A History of the Baby Boom Generation.* Toronto: University of Toronto Press, 1996.

Pagan, Eduardo. *Murder at the Sleepy Lagoon: Zoot Suits, Race, and Riot in Wartime Los Angeles.* Chapel Hill: University of North Carolina Press, 2003.

Parascandola, John. "Quarantining Women: Venereal Disease Rapid Treatment Centers in World War II America." *Bulletin of the History of Medicine* 83, no. 3 (2009): 431-59.

Parr, Joy. *Domestic Goods: The Material, the Moral, and the Economic in Postwar Canada.* Toronto: University of Toronto Press, 1999.

Philips, Paul, and Erin Philips. *Women and Work: Inequality in the Canadian Labor Market.* Toronto: James Lorimer, 2000.

Pickering, Sharon, and Leanne Weber, eds. *Borders, Mobility, and Technologies of Control.* Dordrecht, Netherlands: Springer, 2006.

Pierson, Ruth. "The History of Women's Paid Work." In *Women's Paid and Unpaid Work: Historical and Contemporary Perspectives*, edited by Paula Bourne, 17–34. Toronto: New Hogtown Press, 1985.

Pittenger, W. Norman. *The Christian View of Sexual Behavior: A Reaction to the Kinsey Report*. Greenwich, Conn.: Seabury Press, 1954.

Pivar, David J. "Cleansing the Nation: The War on Prostitution, 1917–1921." *Prologue* 12 (1980): 29–40.

Poole, Joan. "The Evolution of Social Services in the Border Cities during the Great Depression." Ph.D. diss., University of Windsor, 1990.

Popp, Richard K. *The Holiday Makers: Magazines, Advertising, and Mass Tourism in Postwar America*. Baton Rouge: Louisiana State University Press, 2012.

Poy, Vivienne. *Calling Canada Home: Canadian Law and Immigrant Chinese Women from South China and Hong Kong, 1860–1990*. Toronto: University of Toronto Press, 2003.

Pratt, John. "The Rise and Fall of Homophobia and Sexual Psychopath Legislation in Postwar Society." *Psychology, Public Policy, and Law* 4 (March 1998): 25–49.

Pratt, Mary Louise. *Imperial Eyes: Travel Writing and Transculturation*. New York: Routledge, 1992.

Preble, Edward A., and John J. Casey Jr. "Taking Care of Business—The Heroin User's Life on the Street." *International Journal of the Addictions* 4 (March 1969): 1–24.

Race, Kane. "Recreational States: Drugs and the Sovereignty of Consumption." *Culture Machine* 7 (2005). http://www.culturemachine.net/index.php/cm/article/viewArticle/28/35. March 16, 2015.

Ramirez, Bruno. *Crossing the 49th Parallel: Migration from Canada to the United States, 1900–1930*. Ithaca, N.Y.: Cornell University Press, 2001.

Ramirez, Catherine. *The Woman in the Zoot Suit: Gender, Nationalism, and the Cultural Politics of Memory*. Durham, N.C.: Duke University Press, 2009.

Retzloff, Tim. "Seer or Queer? Postwar Fascination with Detroit's Prophet Jones." *GLQ* 8, no. 3 (2002): 271–96.

Reumann, Miriam G. *American Sexual Character: Sex, Gender, and National Identity in the Kinsey Reports*. Berkeley: University of California Press, 2005.

Rich, Wilbur C. *Coleman Young and Detroit Politics: From Social Activist to Power Broker*. Detroit: Wayne State University Press, 1989.

Ripp-Shucha, Bonnie. "This Naughty, Naughty City: Prostitution in Eau Claire from the Frontier to the Progressive Era." *Wisconsin Magazine of History* 81, no. 1 (1997): 30–54.

Roberts, Barbara. *Whence They Came: Deportation from Canada, 1900–1935*. Ottawa: University of Ottawa Press, 1988.

Roberts, David. *In the Shadow of Detroit: Gordon M. McGregor, Ford of Canada, and Motoropolis*. Detroit: Wayne State University Press, 2006.

Roberts, Mary Louise. *What Soldiers Do: Sex and the American GI in World War II France*. Chicago: University of Chicago Press, 2013.

Rockaway, Robert A. "The Notorious Purple Gang: Detroit's All-Jewish Prohibition Era Mob." *Shofar* 20, no. 1 (October 2001): 113–30.

Rose, Kenneth D. *American Women and the Repeal of Prohibition*. New York: New York University Press, 1996.

Rosen, Ruth. *The Lost Sisterhood: Prostitution in America, 1900–1918*. Baltimore: Johns Hopkins University Press, 1982.

Rosenzweig, Roy. *Eight Hours for What We Will: Workers and Leisure in an Industrial City, 1870–1920*. New York: Cambridge University Press, 1983.

Ross, Becki. *Burlesque West: Showgirls, Sex, and Sin in Postwar Vancouver*. Toronto: University of Toronto Press, 2009.

Rublowsky, John. *The Stoned Age: A History of Drugs in America*. New York: Capricorn Books, 1976.

Rumley, Dennis, and Julian V. Minghi, eds. *The Geography of Border Landscapes*. New York: Routledge, 1991.

Sangster, Joan. *Regulating Girls and Women: Sexuality, Family, and the Law in Ontario 1920–1960*. Toronto: Oxford University Press, 2001.

Schatzberg, Rufus, and Robert J. Kelly. *African American Organized Crime: A Social History*. New York: Garland, 1996.

Schneider, Eric. *Smack: Heroin and the American City*. Philadelphia: University of Pennsylvania Press, 2008.

——. *Vampires, Dragons, and Egyptian Kings: Youth Gangs in Postwar New York*. Princeton, N.J.: Princeton University Press, 1999.

Schneider, Jen. "Queer Wordplay: Language and Laughter in the 'Boys of Boise' Moral Panics." *Journal of Historical Sociology* 21, no. 4 (2008): 466–87.

Schneider, John C. *Detroit and the Problem of Order, 1830–1880*. Lincoln: University of Nebraska Press, 1980.

Schneider, Stephen. *Iced: The Story of Organized Crime in Canada*. Mississauga, Ontario: John Wiley & Sons, 2000.

Sharpe, Tanya Telfair. *Behind the Eight Ball: Sex for Crack Cocaine Exchange and Poor Black Women*. New York: Haworth Press, 2005.

Shogan, Robert. *The Detroit Race Riot: A Study in Violence*. New York: Chilton Books, 1964.

Sides, Josh. "Excavating the Postwar Sex District in San Francisco." *Journal of Urban History* 32, no. 3 (March 2006): 355–79.

Smith, Charleen P. "Boomtown Brothels in the Kootenays, 1895–1905," in *People and Place: Historical Influences on Legal Culture*, edited by Jonathan Swainger and Constance B. Backhouse, 120–52. Vancouver: University of British Columbia Press, 2003.

Smith, Douglas J. *Managing White Citizenship: Race, Politics, and Citizenship in Jim Crow Virginia*. Chapel Hill: University of North Carolina Press, 2002.

Smith, Judith E. *Visions of Belonging: Family Stories, Poplar Culture, and Postwar Democracy, 1940–1960*. New York: Columbia University Press, 2004.

Smith, Marian L. "The Immigration and Naturalization Services (INS) at the US-Canadian Border, 1893–1993: An Overview of Issues and Topics." *Michigan Historical Review* 26, no. 2 (Fall 2000): 127–47.

Smith, Mike, and Thomas Featherstone. *Labor in Detroit: Working in the Motor City*. Chicago: Arcadia, 2001.

Solomon, Robert R., and Melvyn Green. "The First Century: The History of Non-Medical Opiate Use and Control Policies in Canada, 1870-1970." In *Illicit Drugs in Canada: A Risky Business*, edited by Judith C. Blackwell and Patricia G. Erickson, 88–116. Nelson, British Columbia: Scarborough, 1988.

Spigel, Lynn. *Making Room for TV: Television and the Family Ideal in Postwar America*. Chicago: University of Chicago Press, 1992.

Spongberg, Mary. *Feminizing Venereal Disease: The Body of the Prostitute in Nineteenth-Century Medical Discourse*. New York: New York University Press, 1997.

Stamp, Robert M. *Bridging the Border: The Structures of Canadian and American Relations*. Toronto: Dundurn Press, 1992.

Stewart, Robert Earl. "Portrait of a Scandal." *The Times Magazine* (Fall 2005).

Sugrue, Thomas J. *The Origins of the Urban Crisis: Race and Inequality in Postwar Detroit*. Princeton, N.J.: Princeton University Press, 1996.

———. "Reassessing the History of Postwar America." *Prospects* 20 (October 1995): 493–509.

Summers, Martin. *Manliness and Discontents: The Black Middle Class and the Transformation of Masculinity, 1900–1930*. Chapel Hill: University of North Carolina Press, 2004.

Tanner, Julian. *Teenage Troubles: Youth and Deviance in Canada*. Scarborough, Ontario: Nelson Thomson Learning, 2001.

Taylor, Alan. "The Divided Ground: Upper Canada, New York, and the Iroquois Six Nations, 1783-1815." *Journal of the Early Republic* 22, no. 1 (Spring 2002): 55–75.

Teaford, Jon C. *The Metropolitan Revolution: The Rise of Post-Urban America*. New York: Columbia University Press, 2006.

Thomas, June Manning. *Redevelopment and Race: Planning a Finer City in Detroit*. Detroit: Wayne State University Press, 2013.

Thomas, Richard W. *Life for Us Is What We Make It: Building Black Community in Detroit, 1915–1945*. Bloomington: Indiana University Press, 1992.

Thompson, Heather Ann. "Rethinking the Politics of White Flight in the Postwar City: Detroit, 1945-1980." *Journal of Urban History* 25, no. 2 (January 1999): 163–98.

———. *Whose Detroit?: Politics, Labor and Race in a Modern American City*. Ithaca, N.Y.: Cornell University Press, 2004.

Thompson, John Herd, and Stephen J. Randall. *Canada and the United States: Ambivalent Allies*. Athens: University of Georgia Press, 2002.

Tooiday, Steven, and Jonathan Zeitlin, eds. *The Automobile Industry and Its Workers: Between Fordism and Flexibility*. Cambridge: Polity in association with Blackwell, 1986.

Tyner, James. *Oriental Bodies: Discourse and Discipline in US Immigration Policy, 1875–1942*. Lanham, Md.: Lexington Books, 2006.

Valverde, Mariana. *The Age of Light, Soap, and Water: Moral Reform in English Canada, 1885–1925*. Toronto: University of Toronto Press, 2008.

——. "Building Anti-Delinquent Communities: Morality, Gender, and Generation in the City." In *A Diversity of Women: Ontario, 1945–1980*, edited by Joy Parr, 19–45. Toronto: University of Toronto Press, 1995.

Van Houtum, Henk, Olivier Kramsch, and Wolfgang Zierhofer. *B/ordering Space*. New York: Ashgate, 2005.

Van Schendel, Willem, and Itty Abraham. *Illicit Flows and Criminal Things: States, Borders, and the Other Side of Globalization*. Bloomington: Indiana University Press, 2005.

Vick, Dwight, and Elizabeth Rhoades. *Drugs and Alcohol in the 21st Century: Theory, Behavior, and Policy*. Sudbury, Ontario: Jones & Bartlett Learning, 2011.

Vuic, Kara Dixon. "I Have Worn Out Another Pair of Shoes for My Country: Gender Sexuality and World War II." *Reviews in American History* 38, no. 1 (2010): 127–32.

Walker, Barrington. *The History of Immigration and Racism in Canada: Essential Readings*. Toronto: Canadian Scholars' Press, 2008.

Ward, W. Peter. *White Canada Forever: Popular Attitudes and Public Policy towards Orientals in British Columbia*. Montreal: McGill–Queen's University Press, 2002.

Warren, Donald. "Neighborhood Structure and Riot Behavior in Detroit: Some Exploratory Findings." *Social Problems* 16, no. 4 (1969): 464–84.

Weatherford, Doris. *African American Women during World War II: An Encyclopedia*. New York: Routledge, 2010.

Weems, Robert E. *Desegregating the Dollar: African American Consumerism in the Twentieth Century*. New York: New York University Press, 1998.

Welshman, John. *Underclass: A History of the Excluded, 1880–2000*. London: Hambledon Continuum, 2006.

Whitall, Susan. "Woodward: Avenue of Escape: From Jazz Clubs to Dance Halls, Woodward Had It All." *Detroit News*, March 27, 2007.

White, Richard. *The Middle Ground: Indians, Empires, and Republics in the Great Lakes Region, 1650–1815*. Cambridge: Cambridge University Press, 1991.

Wiese, Andrew. *Places of Their Own: African American Suburbanization in the Twentieth Century*. Chicago: University of Chicago Press, 2004.

Wilson, Sunnie, and John Cohasse. *The Toast of the Town: The Life and Times of Sunnie Wilson*. Detroit: Wayne State University Press, 1998.

Wolcott, Victoria. "Recreation and Race in the Postwar City: Buffalo's 1956 Crystal Beach Riot." *Journal of American History* 93, no. 1 (2006): 63–90.

——. *Remaking Respectability: African American Women in Interwar Detroit*. Chapel Hill: University of North Carolina Press, 2001.

Woldoff, Rachel A. *White/Black Flight: The Dynamics of Racial Change in an American Neighborhood*. Ithaca, N.Y.: Cornell University Press 2011.

Woodford, Arthur M. *This Is Detroit, 1701–2001*. Detroit: Wayne State University Press, 2001.

Woodiwiss, Michael. *Organized Crime and American Power: A History*. Toronto: University of Toronto Press, 2001.

Wrynn, V. Denis. *Detroit Goes to War: The American Automobile Industry in World War II*. Osceola, Wisc.: Motorbooks International, 1993.

Zinn, Howard. *Postwar America, 1945–1970*. Cambridge, Mass.: South End Press, 2002.

Zube, Margaret. "Changing Concepts of Morality: 1948–1969." *Social Forces* 50, no. 3 (March 1972): 385–93.

Index

Note: Page numbers in *italics* refer to illustrations.

formalizing control of, 24–25, 41; inspection procedures at, 16–17, 21, 142; postwar tourism and, 47–48; racial tensions and, 150

Borderlands: academic scholarship on, 3–6; asymmetrical relationships in, 12, 141–42, 145, 162 (n. 24); characteristics of, 4–6, 12; citizenship and moral reform in, 10–12, 14, 118–20; drug enforcement in, 121, 140–44; drug investigations on, 121–22, 123–24, 139–40, 173 (n. 4); history of, 17–18; immigration laws and, 20–21; industrial growth and, 26; juvenile delinquency and, 117–18; media on, 121–22, 124; television and films on, 126–28. *See also* Detroit; Windsor

Border Patrol (television show), 127

Border Patrol (U.S.), 21, 37–38, 127

Border Public House, 56

Border spirit, 44–45, 50, 51, 64

Bower, Joseph A., 22

Bowles, Thomas "Dr. Beans," 67

Bridge. *See* Ambassador Bridge

Brothels: establishment of, 26, 42; management of, 55; regulation of, 26, 54, 56, 65; as social entertainment, 8, 44, 68, 152. *See also* Sex trade

Buckley, Jerry, 37

Buffalo, N.Y., 32, 121, 126, 142

Canada: cross-border enforcement, 121–23, 140–44; drug investigations by, 121–24, 129–30, 173 (n. 4), 174 (n. 26); labor unions in, 47; liquor trade regulations in, 28, 31–32; migration to, 19; national holidays in, 48, 51–52, 95–96; nation-building in, 10–12, 50; relationship with U.S., 15, 41, 51–52; sex trade regulations in, 27. *See also* United States

Canada Day holiday, 51

Canadian Agreement (1893), 21

Canadian National railway, 54

Capital flight, 72, 83

Car production. *See* Automotive industry

Cartoons: of border crossing, 21, *22*; of liquor reputations, 29, *30*

Casinos, 158–59, 176 (n. 8)

Casual drug use vs. addiction, 79–80

Chamberlain-Kahn Act (1917), 27

Chicago, Ill., 29, 73, 87, 116, 136, 142, 144

Chicago Defender, 78, 124–25

Chicago Tribune investigative story, 58–59

Children and minors: drug trade and, 78, 115–16, 126, 145; liquor trade and, 34–35; sex trade and, 36. *See also* Juvenile delinquency

China, 124, 125

Chinese Canadian community, 11, 20, 65, 125, 139

Chinese Exclusion Act (1882, U.S.), 20

Chinese Immigration Act (1885, Canada), 20

Chrysler Corporation, 52

Citizens Committee of Detroit, Inc., 37

Citizenship and moral reform, 10–12, 14, 118. *See also* Nation-building

Class divisions: in drug trade, 73, 80–81, 92–93; economic growth and, 7–8, 39, 47, 72, 83, 97; immigration laws and, 21; juvenile delinquency and, 116–19; moral reform and, 99–101, 119–20; scholarship on, 8; in urban renewal projects, 106–7, 110–11; vice economies and, 13, 26, 35, 42, 59, 67. *See also* Gender divisions; Racial divisions

Clerical work, 54, 166 (n. 50)

Clothing and status, 9, 35, 63, 77, 80, *84*, 117–18

Club B & C, 67

Club Zombie, 67

"Clumsy!" (Cromwell), 21, *22*

Cobo, Albert E., 76

Cocaine, 73, 74, 80
Codeine, 73, 74
Cold-turkey treatment, 131
Collins, Herb, 150
Commercial sex. *See* Sex trade
Committee for Community Action for
	Detroit Youth (MCCADY), 113, 114, 117
Communism: borderlands and, 11–12,
	123; Canadian report on threats vs.,
	114; drug trade and, 125, 138;
	tourism and, 52
Commuting, international, 18–19, 41
Consumerism: drug subculture and,
	76–77; in postwar era, 47–48, 51.
	See also Class divisions
Council of Social Agencies, 81
Cresswell, Tim, 98
Crime Investigating Committee of
	the U.S. Senate, 116
Criminal Code (1891), 27
Criminals: families of, 89–91; as villains
	vs. victims, 113–15, 130–36. *See also*
	Organized crime; *specific trades*
Cromwell, Percy, 21, *22*, 29, *30*
Crystal Lounge, 67
Cuba, 28–29
Curb cruisers, 102

Dance halls, 44, 53, 75, 77, 112, 126, 152.
	See also Taxi-dance halls
Davis, Miles, 79
De Bozy, George, 71
Department of Munitions and Supply, 45
Depression era, 38–40. *See also*
	Economic fluctuations and vice
	industries; Unemployment
Detroit, *4, 108*; automotive industry in,
	17–18; commuter culture and, 19;
	drug addict population in, 73–74;
	economic decline of, 158–59, 175
	(n. 1); industrial growth of, 2, 7–8; as
	influencing community, 12, 162
	(n. 24); jazz culture of, 77–78; liquor
	trade in, 29, *30*, 34–35; migrant
	population in, 11, 18–19, 34, 46, 66;

nicknames for, 5, 45; population of,
	46; race riots in, 8, 37–38, 47,
	149–51; racial divide and, 11, 66–67,
	103; reputation of, 33–34, 150, 157;
	sex trade in, 35–39, 56–58; spatial
	transformation of, 58–59, 103–4;
	unemployment rates, 38, 45; urban
	renewal projects, 104–7, 158; vice
	districts in, 27, 81, 169 (n. 46).
	See also Borderlands; Michigan;
	United States; Windsor
Detroit Council for Youth Services, 100
Detroit Edison Company, 85
Detroit Free Press, 122
Detroit Motor Boat Company, 41
"The Detroit Plan: A Program for Blight
	Elimination" (Jefferies), 105, 107
Detroit Police Department, 26, 82, 117
Detroit River, 3, 15–16, 22, 26, 158
Detroit Urban League, 10, 65–66, 103,
	106
Detroit-Windsor Ferry, 19, 31
"Detroit-Windsor Funnel," 5, 29, 42
Detroit-Windsor Tunnel, 5, 22, *25*, 29,
	42, 142
Deviant sexual acts, 60–61. *See also* Sex
	trade
Devlin, Peter, 87
Domestic containment, 8
Dominion Day holiday, 48, 51
Dope peddlers. *See* Drug trade
Drug addict: cures for, 131, 134–37; as
	term, 7, 79–80
Drug trade: arrests in, 82, 121, 125; in
	Canada vs. U.S., 73–74; class
	divisions in, 73, 80–81, 92–93;
	communism and, 125, 139; cross-
	border enforcement of, 121–23,
	140–44; economic benefits of, 72,
	85–86, 90, 92; hierarchy of, 79–81;
	investigations on, 121–24, 129–37,
	173 (n. 4), 174 (n. 26); jazz and,
	78–79; juveniles and, 78, 115–16, 145;
	liquor trade and, 5; media on,
	121–22, 124; networks of, 8, 9, 84–85,

88–91, 125–26; racial divisions in, 9,
81, 89–90, 92–93, 116; regulation of,
27, 73, 138, 145; sex trade and,
135–36; smuggling techniques of, 87,
139–40; street peddlers vs. large-
scale dealers, 87, 91–92; as subculture, 76–77, 79, 92; transnational
culture of, 71–72, 75–76, 87–89. *See
also specific drugs*
Dupree, Fred, 88–89

East Side district (Detroit), 27, 59, 67
East Windsor, Ontario, 18
Eaton Tower, 41
Ebony Bar, 74
Ecological invasion, 103
Economic fluctuations and vice
industries: class divisions, 7–8, 39,
47, 72, 83, 97; Depression era,
38–40; growth, 43–45
Eddington, Virginia, 136
18th Amendment of the United States
Constitution: enactment of, 28;
repeal of, 13, 36. *See also* Prohibition
Elmwood Hotel & Club, 48, *49*
El Sino Club, 78
Emancipation Day riot, 95–96
Essex County Tourist Association, 51
Evangelicalism and Social Service of the
United Church of Canada, 114

Faludi, E. G., 109
Faludi Study, 109–11, 172 (n. 43)
Families and juvenile delinquency,
113–15, 135–36
Farmer, Silas, 26
Federal Bureau of Investigation (FBI),
123
Federal Bureau of Narcotics (FBN), 123,
124, 125, 127, 128, 131
Federal Housing Act (1949), 105
Ferry, 19, 31
Films on vice, 11, 124, 126, 127, 157
Fitzgerald, Ella, 107
Flame Show Bar, 77

Ford Motor Company, 18, 45, 47
Fourth of July holiday, 31, 48, 51
Frank, Charles, 100
Freedom Festival, 51–52
French Connection, 90
French military post on Detroit River, 26
French-style sex, 61, 64
Frost, Leslie M., 143–44

Gambling: investigations on, 124, 128,
143–44; legal, 158–59, 176 (n. 8);
organized crime and, 90, 91;
prohibition and, 26, 33, 35; as social
entertainment, 8; vice economies
and, 5, 6, 42, 59, 100. *See also* Vice
economies
Gangs: in drug trade, 88–91, 126; of
liquor trade, 33, 37, 89; youth,
112–13. *See also* Organized crime
Gender divisions: in African American
families, 113–14; in drug trade, 135,
170 (n. 48); in labor industries, 27,
35, 54–55; mayoral plea and, 54. *See
also* Class divisions; Racial divisions
Georgia, 54
Gillespie, Dizzy, 77–78
Girls' Protective League, 100
Girls' Service Clubs, 100
Girl's Work Council, 100
Globe and Mail, 114–15, 122, 143
Good Will Tour, 20
Gootenberg, Paul, 162 (n. 26)
Gotham Hotel, 91
Goyeau Street (Windsor), 72, 75
Gratiot Project, 105
Great Depression era, 38–40
Great Migration, 18, 34
Green, Fred, 15
Gregory, James, 54

Hale Boggs Act, 138
Hallissey Gang, 33
Hamilton, Ontario, 74, 75, 78, 90, 142,
165 (n. 16)
Hammond, John, 85–86

Licit (category), 6–7
Liquor Control Act (1927), 28, 30
Liquor Control Board of Ontario, 28
Liquor License Board of Ontario, 56, 78
Liquor trade: cartoon on, 29, *30*;
    children's exposure to, 34–35;
    development of, 26; gangs of, 33, 37,
    89; government-controlled, 28–29,
    31–32; regulation of, 5, 16–17, 27–28;
    statistics on, 29; tourist economy
    and, 29–31. *See also* Prohibition
Longo, Julie, 51
Los Angeles, Calif., 73
Luciano, Charles "Lucky," 90

Maclean's (magazine), 71, 73, 110,
    124
Mafia, 89–91, 123–25, 146
Magaddino, Stefano, 90
Mainlining, 74, 79, 80. *See also* Heroin
Mallock, George, 141
Mallock, John, 141
Mann Act (1910), 27
Marijuana, 71, 74, 76, 78, 92, 126, 138.
    See also Drug trade
Marriage, 9, 60, 69, 152
Martin, Paul, 130
Masturbation, 60
Matriarchal families and violence,
    113–15
McClellan, George, 134, 141, 142
McClintic-Marshall Company, 23
McGowan, Helen, 36, 61–63, 80, 90
McKinsey, Laura, 162 (n. 24)
McRae, Charles, 15
Media narratives: on drug trade, 121–22,
    124–25; on race riots, 150–51; racism
    in, 113, 115, 116, 117–18. *See also
    specific newspapers and magazines*
Medical authorities on drug problem,
    130–31, 137, 174 (n. 26)
Meehan, Patrick, 158
Michigan: drug enforcement in, 82;
    liquor regulations in, 28. *See also*
    Detroit; United States

Michigan Chronicle, 59
Michigan Legislative Committee, 85, 86
Middle-class society. *See* Class divisions
Migration: black northern waves, 34;
    economic growth and, 45–46; moral
    reform and, 10–11; for sex trade,
    53–55. *See also* Immigrant
    populations
Minors. *See* Children and minors
Mississippi, 54
Monogamy, 9, 60, 69, 152
Montreal, Quebec: drug trade in, 73, 78,
    90–91; sex trade in, 53–54; wages in,
    165 (n. 16)
Montreal Gazette, 33
Montreal Police Department, 54
Moral reform: citizenship and, 10–12,
    14; class divisions in, 99–101, 119–20;
    juvenile delinquency and, 115–18;
    through medical and legal experts,
    129–35; in postwar urban centers,
    96–97; sexuality and, 60–61, 69,
    98–100; of transient culture, 97–104;
    umbrella effect of, 161 (n. 21)
Morphine, 73, 74, 80
Mosher, Clayton, 81
Motel industry. *See* Hotel/motel
    industry
Motor City Casino, 159
Moyer, Rodger, 79, 83–84, 86
Murders and murder rate, 37. *See also*
    Violence
Music. *See* Jazz culture

Narcotic Control Act (1956), 82, 145
Narcotics. *See* Drug trade; Heroin;
    Marijuana
National Association for the Advance-
    ment of Colored People, 82
National Health and Welfare Depart-
    ment (Canada), 74
National Origins Act (1924), 20
National Prohibition Act (1919), 5
Nation-building, 11, 96–97, 154–56. *See
    also* Citizenship and moral reform

Negro removal, 109
New Migration, 19, 34
Newspaper articles. *See specific newspapers*
New York City, N.Y., 73, 87, 116; drug trade in, 90–91
New York Times, 15, 31, 34, 122
New York Trust Company, 22
Nicholson, Leonard, 131, 132, 139
Niggertown, 27
Numbers running, 53, 91, 110, 128

Ohio, 28
Ontario, 28, 74, 165 (n. 16). *See also* Canada; Windsor
Ontario Temperance Act, 28
Opium, 74, 80, 139, 141
Oral sex, 61
Order 86, U.S. Department of Labor, 41
Organized crime: in drug trade, 88–91; federal investigations on, 121–22, 123–24, 173 (n. 4); in liquor trade, 37; names in, 33, 126. *See also* Gangs
Oriental Café, 56
O'Riordan Gang, 33
Ouellette Avenue (Windsor), 19, *32*, *49*, 72, 75; drug trade in, 75
Outfits, drug, 74

Pagan, Margareta, 100–101
Page Act (1875), 20, 27
Papalia crime family, 90
Paradise Valley (Detroit): drug trade in, 74; liquor trade in, 34, 35; urban decay and renewal in, 67, 103, 107, *108. See also* Hastings Street (Detroit)
Parker, Charlie, 79
Parlor houses, 39
People's Republic of China, 124, 125
Perry, Walter L., 95
Physicians as drug experts, 130–31, 174 (n. 26)
Piggins, Edward, 74, 140
Pimping, 27

Pink-light districts, 58
Pitt Street (Windsor), 75
Plant, James S., 112–13
Pleasure travel. *See* Tourist economy
Police. *See* Detroit Police Department; Royal Canadian Mounted Police; Windsor Police Department
Pop culture and vice, 126–27
Potomac Quarter, 27
Premarital sex, 60
Prohibition: border trade economy and, 16–17, 31–34, 152; enactment of, 28; race and, 34–35; repeal of, 13, 36; supporters of, 36–37; women against, 37. *See also* Liquor trade
Prostitution. *See* Sex trade
Psychiatrists as drug experts, 130–31, 174 (n. 26)
Public housing projects, 105–7
Purple Gang, 33, 91

Race riots: in Detroit, 8, 37–38, 47, 149–51; in Windsor, 95–96, 119
Racial divisions: in cross-border travel, 65–66; in Detroit, 103; in drug trade, 9, 82, 170 (n. 48); family income and, 168 (n. 103); in labor industries, 27, 38, 46; in sex trade, 11, 59, 64, 166 (n. 46), 167 (n. 74). *See also* African American community; Class divisions; Gender divisions
Racism: in crime investigations, 133–34; housing issues and, 46–47; immigration laws and, 20–21; in media coverage, 113, 115, 116, 117–18; northern migration and, 8, 11, 18, 34, 66; in vice districts, 27; in Windsor public life, 65–66. *See also* African American community; Chinese Canadian community
Racketeering, 37, 86, 89–91, 124–25. *See also* Drug trade
Railroad lines, 19, 54
RCMP. *See* Royal Canadian Mounted Police

Real estate, 32, 39, 46, 175 (n. 1)
Reaume, Dan, 99
Redevelopment projects, 104–11, 158
Red-light districts, 55, 58
Reid, Tom, 128, 129
Road building projects, 107, *108*
Roaring twenties mythology, 36
RoboCop (film), 157
Roman Catholic Church, 99
Romney, George, 149
Rooming houses, 54, 72, 74, 88, 89, 92.
    See also Sex trade
Royal Canadian Mounted Police
    (RCMP), 71, 75–76, 82, 131, 142. *See
    also specific commissioners*
Rubenstein Gang, 33
Rum running. *See* Liquor trade
Running numbers, 53, 91, 110, 128

Saloons, 26, 27, 88
Sandwich, Ontario, 18
San Francisco, Calif., 87
Sangster, Joan, 166 (n. 47)
Saskatoon Star-Phoenix, 125
Saturday Night, 50, 64
Schendel, Willem van, 6
Schneider, Eric, 79
Schneider, Stephen, 89
Second Great Migration, 11, 46, 66, 103
Segregation. *See* Racial divisions
Senate Bill No. 144 (Michigan), 82
Senate Committee on Narcotic Drugs,
    75, 76
Seven Mile–Fenelon Improvement
    Association, 46
Sex trade, *40*; arrest statistics, 167
    (nn. 63, 74); autobiography on, 36,
    61–63; children's exposure to, 36;
    defined, 6–7; Depression era and, 39;
    development of, 26; drug trade and,
    135–36; French women and, 64;
    interracial, 11, 35, 66–67, 116;
    investigative story on, 58–59;
    juvenile delinquency and, 115; liquor
    trade and, 5; migration for, 53–55,

166 (nn. 46–47); moral reform and,
    60–61; networks of, 8; racial
    divisions in, 59, 64–65, 166 (n. 46),
    167 (n. 74); regulation of, 27; as social
    disease, 135–36; tourist economy
    and, 9, 44–45; transnational culture
    of, 56–58, 63–64; traveling carnival
    shows and, 100–101; visibility of, 43,
    55–56. *See also* Drug trade; Women
Sexuality: homosexuality, 60, 113, 114,
    137; moral reform of, 60–61, 69,
    98–100, 116
Sexually transmitted diseases, 101, 115
Sicilian Mafia. *See* Mafia
Sing, Lee Won, 141
Siragusa, Charles, 89
Skillman, W. McKay, 134
Slums. *See* Urban community culture
Smuggling rings in drug trade, 88–91
Sobotka, Virginia, 166 (n. 46), 167 (n. 74)
Social Hygiene Association, 61
Sojourner Truth Housing Project, 46, 47
Speakeasies, 33–34, 36, 39, 42. *See also*
    Liquor trade
Special Senate Committee on the Traffic
    in Narcotic Drugs in Canada,
    128–31, 174 (n. 26)
Special Senate Committee to Investigate
    Organized Crime, 124
Spokane Daily Chronicle, 125
Steamship industry, 19
Stewart, Ted, 78
Street peddlers. *See* Drug trade
Streetwalking. *See* Sex trade
Suburbanization, 72, 82–83, 109. *See
    also* Urban community culture
Supply, Priorities, and Allocation Board
    (SPAB), 45
Swing band music, 78

Taxation: of alcohol, 28; evasion of, 91;
    for urban projects, 7, 23, 111
Taxi-dance halls, 58, 59, 74. *See also*
    Dance halls
Taylor, Glen Seymour, 38–39, 61

TBA (television show), 89

Teenagers. *See* Children and minors; Juvenile delinquency

Television shows on vice, 11, 89, 124, 126, 127–28

Temperance campaigns, 28. *See also* Prohibition

Tennessee, 54, 166 (n. 46)

Theaters, 57, 74, 85

Thompson, Leo, 101–2

Tocco, William "Black Bill," 90, 91

Toledo Blade, 150

Toronto, Ontario: crime family in, 90; drug trade in, 74, 75, 76, 78, 87, 89; population of, 142; reputation of, 96; sex trade and, 54; wages in, 165 (n. 16)

Tourist economy: legal gambling and, 158–59, 176 (n. 8); liquor laws and, 29–33; in postwar era, 47–51, 165 (n. 23); public relations strategy of, 20, 44, 50–51; sex trade and, 8, 102

Tramp, 97–98

Transient culture, 97–104

Transnational culture: creation of, 18–19; of drug trade, 71–72, 75–76; in sex trade, 56–58, 63–64

Traveling carnival shows, 100–101

Tree Studios, 58

Trianon Ballroom, 58

Tunnel. *See* Detroit-Windsor Tunnel

Twelfth Street (Detroit): arrests on, 149; drug trade in, 74; reputation of, 103, 106; sex trade in, 59, 67

Twenty Grand, 77

Umbrella effect of moral regulation, 161 (n. 21)

Unbalanced influence zone, 162 (n. 24)

Uncle Tom's Cabin, 74

Underemployment, 27, 34–35, 62, 83–84

Unemployment, 38–39, 45, 54–55, 83. *See also* Depression era

Unions. *See* Labor unions

United Auto Workers, 105

United Church of Canada, 114

United Community Services, 100

United States: cross-border enforcement, 121–23, 140–44; drug investigations by, 121–24, 129–30, 173 (n. 4), 174 (n. 26); liquor regulation in, 5, 13, 16–17; migration to, 11; relationship with Canada, 15, 41, 51–52; sex trade regulation in, 27. *See also* Canada

U.S.-Canada border. *See* Border crossings; Borderlands

U.S. Department of Labor, 41

U.S.-Mexico border, 3, 29, 121, 126, 127, 138–39

Untouchables, The (television show), 127–28

Urban community culture: asymmetrical relationships in, 12, 162 (n. 24); blight in, 95–96, 103–4, 172 (n. 43); opportunities for blacks in, 34–35; renewal programs, 104–11, 158; suburbanization and, 72, 82–83, 109; vice and, 7–10

Vacations. *See* Tourist economy

Vancouver, British Columbia, 53, 73, 125, 127, 128, 165 (n. 16)

Venereal disease, 101

Vice economies: in 17th century, 26; in 1950s, 2, 9; defined, 6–7; economic growth and, 43–44, 53; juvenile delinquency and, 112–19; legalizing, 158–60; moral reform of (*see* Moral reform); representation of, 7, 162 (n. 26); riots and, 150–51; summary of, 1–10, 151–56; transient culture and, 97–104; urban reform and, 96–97, 104–11. *See also* Drug trade; Liquor trade; Sex trade

Villain-hero narrative, 122–27

Villain-victim narrative, 113–15, 130–36

Violence: in drug trade, 90; interracial, 116–17; by juveniles, 112, 117–18;

prohibition and, 37–38; race riots, 8, 37, 47, 95–96, 119, 149–51; against women, 113–14
Volstead Act (1919), 36

Wai, Pon, 125
Walkerville, Ontario, 18
War production and rationing, 45–46
War Production Board (WPB), 45
Washington Post, 121
West Side district (Detroit), 59
West Side Gang, 126
W. G. Wade Carnival, 100
White, George H., 88–89
White community: family income in, 168 (n. 103); housing issues and, 46–47; in sex trade, 59, 64–65, 166 (n. 46), 167 (n. 74); women's work in, 46, 54. *See also* African American community; Racial divisions
White Slave Trade Act (U.S.), 101–2
Windsor, *4, 32, 49, 57*; cartoon on liquor trade of, 29, *30*; commuter culture and, 19; criminal trials of, 1; industrial growth of, 2, 7–8, 45–46; as influenced community, 12, 162 (n. 24); jazz music in, 78, 95–96; migration to, 19; nicknames for, 3, 5, 11, 29, 42; population of, 46, 170 (n. 60); race riots in, 95–96; racial makeup of, 65; reputation of, 1, 5; sex trade in, 43, 53, 55–58, 64, 99; transportation industries in, 18–19; unemployment in, 38–39; urban renewal projects in, 109–11, 158, 172 (n. 43); wages in, 47, 165 (n. 16). *See also* Borderlands; Canada; Detroit; Ontario

Windsor Daily Star: on Detroit beer seekers, 102; on Detroit relationship, 6; on drug trade, 75, 122; on juvenile delinquency, 115; on Peter Devlin, 87; on sex trade, 43, 53, 56, 60, 64, 99; on tourism, 50; on transient women, 98, 101
Windsor Ford Strike (1945), 47
Windsor Police Department, 1, 12–13, 81
Windsor Star: on Belle Isle project, 158; on jazz riot, 95
"Windsor the Wicked," 5, 29, 42
"Windsor Wire Service: Predict U.S. Senate Will Rap Ontario" (*Globe and Mail*), 143
Winters, R. H., 50
Women: in drug investigations, 135–37; as transients, 53–55, 98–100; violence against, 113–14; voting rights of, 37; work segregation for, 46, 54–55. *See also* Sex trade
Women's Local Council of Windsor, 10, 99
Women's Organization for National Prohibition Reform, 37
Woodward Avenue (Detroit), 19, 35, 37, 58, 72
Working-class society. *See* Class divisions
World War II, 44–47

Young, Coleman, 34–35, 82, 157
Young Women's Christian Association, 99
Youth. *See* Children and minors

Zaneia, Joe, 57
Zerilli, Joseph, 91, 124
Zoot suits, *84*, 117–18